Praise for *Abducted*

One of the most basic questions any thoughtful person might ask is, 'Who am I?' A disturbing memory fragment sent Alice Cunningham on a decades-long search for answers, and her story is one of fearless tenacity in the quest for meaning. Join her search with a curiosity about what she—and perhaps you, too—discover.

—Michael D. Yapko, Ph.D. Clinical Psychologist

Childhood trauma is tragic. How is it that some of us find the internal resources to not only sort through the trauma and its effects yet also rise above the haunting memories and dreams? Alice Cunningham faced hers as a researcher on a mission as they gradually seeped into her consciousness. Finding unknown internal strength, courage, and talent, she found resources in herself previously unknown. This account of her quest for answers is a story of how one can face trauma, not be defined by it, and move far beyond. She became a passionate researcher and a gifted writer, careful to support her unbelievable abduction.

—Dianne Bradley, Ph.D. Licensed Marriage and Family Therapist

What an amazing story. Alice Cunningham's thoroughly repressed memory of her abduction finally comes to light primarily because of her nightmares. The extensive recording of her dreams is not only instrumental in recovering the memory of a most sinister experience, they also show the resilience of this tenacious woman who lived a productive and meaningful life in spite of a normally soul-destroying trauma. A powerful message to all of us about suffering and recovery.

—Walter Berry, author of *Drawn into the Dream*

In her book *Abducted,* Alice Cunningham, through fortitude, determination, tenacity and perseverance, strives to discover what happened to her when she was a child. What she endured is tragic, troublesome, and often heartbreaking. The crimes she describes were, and are, very difficult for people to believe.

In 1948, it was the general practice of some therapists to counsel the family and friends to forget and deny what happened. This was believed to be the best therapy for the child so that he or she could resume a normal life. This type of therapy, for the most part, is no longer practiced, as it became apparent that it resulted in more harm than good.

Public awareness and education regarding crimes against children are very important and are the greatest weapons against this horrific type of victimization. There is no doubt in my mind that Alice's book will be beneficial to all who read it. It is my hope that her story will help in the prevention of many of these crimes.

— Roger T. Young, FBI Special Agent, retired

ABDUCTED

ABDUCTED

My Struggle to Remember

ALICE CUNNINGHAM

PRECOCITY PRESS

ISBN: 979-8-9898304-0-4 (Paperback)
ISBN: 979-8-9898304-1-1 (eBook)
Library of Congress Control Number: 2024900142
First edition printed in the United States of America

*This book is dedicated to my mother, who suffered the most,
to my brothers, Arthur and Stephen, who don't remember,
but who nevertheless supported me in my journey,
and to my sister Lynn, who grew up,
unknowingly, in a traumatized family.*

"Traumatic memories are fixed and static. They are imprints (engrams) from past overwhelming experiences, deep impressions carved into the sufferer's brain, body, and psyche. These harsh and frozen imprints do not yield to change, nor do they readily update with current information. The "fixity" of imprints prevents us from forming new strategies and extracting new meaning. There is no fresh, ever-changing now and no real flow in life. In this way, the past lies on in the present; or as William Faulkner wrote in *Requiem for a Nun:* 'The past is never dead. It's not even past.' Rather it lies as a panoply of manifold fears, phobias, physical symptoms, and illnesses."

—Peter A. Levine, PhD, *Trauma and Memory: Brain and Body in a Search for the Living Past*

CONTENTS

PART FOUR
AFTER REMEMBERING

PART FIVE
PUTTING IT ALL TOGETHER

INTRODUCTION

Dreams embody suppressed wishes and fears
but also give expression to inescapable truths which
are not illusions or wild fantasies.

—Carl Jung

TRAUMATIC MEMORY SUPPRESSION AND THE GRADUAL PROCESS that ultimately led to my remembering a horrific trauma—my abduction in 1948 when I was eight years old—is the subject of this book.

I've laid out the months-long ordeal, the brutal treatment I endured as a frightened and innocent girl that included control through drugs, terror, and emotional manipulation. I was forced into child pornography, and became a reluctant drug addict. I developed a venereal disease through forced prostitution that required hospitalization. Eventually, I participated in two legal trials after working closely with the FBI.

Repressed memories protected me from the effects of the intense trauma of those months. I created a life as if nothing had occurred. Without awareness, the ordeal affected my personality and behavior.

Forty years later, the memory suppression began to crumble. On September 9, 1989, I woke up in the middle of the night, terrified, with glimmers breaking through. It was the beginning of a thirty-four-year struggle of painfully piecing the puzzle together to gaining full recall of what I had worked so hard to repress.

THE ELEPHANT IN THE ROOM

The search for corroboration of the abduction mostly ended in frustration. My mother, who died age ninety-one in 2007, flatly denied the kidnapping took place and showed no curiosity about my surfaced memories. She was unwilling to discuss any of it and never showed any interest in supporting me. Unfortunately, my father died before I could ask him about that tragic event.

I grew up with three siblings: two brothers and a sister. Arthur, who is one year younger than I am, would have been old enough to recall my disappearance. However, when I brought up the subject, he said he didn't remember it and ran from the room. It's worth noting that he remembers very little about his own childhood.

My brother Stephen, was six years younger and just two-and-a-half-years old at the time of my abduction. He's the first family member I approached about my recovered memories. His response, in 1989, was much more forthcoming.

"I can believe that," he said. "I can remember Paba [our grandfather] talking about something bad happening to you. When I came into the room, he immediately went silent." I found Stephen's response comforting, and it gave me hope that I wasn't crazy.

Stephen seemed to hold onto this view and, in 1994, he hired an investigator, Barbara L. Wagner, of Denver, Colorado, to look into my case.

At that time, my memory was still sparse, and I couldn't give her much information to help in the search. In any case, she could find nothing, and Stephen dropped his pursuit of the issue. Indeed, when I reminded him in 2021 of what he had told me in 1989, he had no memory of our conversation or that he heard our grandfather talking about it, although he remembered hiring the investigator.

My sister Lynn was born after my kidnapping and has only a peripheral mention in this book. I have not spoken to her. I have seen no reason to distress her with family history that she did not live through.

Other relatives were seldom helpful in providing information about the event. My late Aunt Marianna, my father's younger sister, said she had no memory of it. However, when I asked her daughter, my now deceased cousin Carolyn, who was about Arthur's age, she acknowledged that she had heard Paba talk about a bad man who had used me sexually.

Obviously, I consider my family's disinterest in discussing what surely would have been a family trauma, and showing no concern about what I was currently experiencing, to be peculiar. If the kidnapping was just in my head and not in my reality, why wouldn't they try to find out what was going on with me, and then work to correct my memory?

As a result of speaking with my family, I believe they were in denial. There are several possible reasons: The issue could be too painful for them to face and they believe they are protecting me. In the case of my mother, she had understandable parental guilt associated with the fact that it happened. In addition, what would a mother go through when, for months, there wasn't any word whether her child was dead or alive? I have to believe that the pain, and the not knowing, would have been overwhelming.

At times I fantasize about what went on in the house when I didn't come home. I imagine the police working frantically to find out how I disappeared after school, and perhaps saw my parents as suspects. In a police investigation, I assume my brothers, especially Arthur, would have been interviewed. That could have been so stressful he might have quashed his memories.

I once suggested my kidnapping would have been traumatic for him. "Why would I be traumatized?" he asked. "They just told me you were visiting with Uncle CB," which of course acknowledges that I was, indeed, away for a time.

And, when I initially told friends about my kidnapping, several immediately suspected my father.

These friends came up with all kinds of reasons why he could have been guilty, unable to believe I was, abducted, and suggested there was a conspiracy on the part of my family to cover up the truth.

After my rescue from my kidnappers and subsequent return home, there were police, the FBI, lawyers, trials, and the shame of knowing what had been done to me. Church members close to my family would have provided support for them, but all they could see when they looked at me was a sexualized child.

Today, I still believe memories lurk deep in my brother's unconscious, and that pain is too great to acknowledge. As with many of my family and friends, denial is the answer.

Most psychologists believe denial can have a deleterious effect on the psyche. Experience has taught me that not facing trauma can take a terrible toll on the body and the mind. I repeated unhealthy behaviors and was stuck in a detrimental lifestyle. It wasn't until I faced my past that I understood why I had frightening nightmares, was unable to say "no" — particularly to men — and why I failed to recognize dangerous situations.

WHERE IS THE EVIDENCE?

As writer and humorist Mark Twain once said, "It is wiser to find out than suppose." I have avidly pursued finding evidence. The search hasn't been fruitful. I don't know the exact month I was kidnapped or how long I was gone. My research hasn't found any police reports, or records of what were two trials: a grand jury for my kidnappers, and one for the pedophile/pornographer I was found with when recovered. I haven't been able to find any newspaper reports. It was an exceedingly different time in 1948. Few people had television, there were no computers, and telephones were so expensive people used them judiciously.

Many police departments destroyed their records after a fixed number of years, and my abduction happened more than seventy-five years ago. Even if there are dusty boxes in the basement of the Denver police department, or in the files of the Los Angeles criminal courts, minors' names were expunged from police and court records. Abetting the silence further, newspapers were reluctant to publish criminal behavior for fear of panicking the public. The school from which I was abducted would not want its reputation sullied. All these circumstances have deeply obscured the reality of my abduction.

DREAMS LEAD THE WAY

Deirdre Leigh Barrett, Ph.D. is a dream researcher who lectures at Harvard and is the current president of the International Association for the Study of Dreams. In her book *Trauma and Dreams,* she explains that when dealing with dissociation or amnesia, dreams can be the first clue to help the patient recover repressed memories, especially when they are trauma based.

Dreams have been a powerful tool for me. The first terrifying ones opened the door to my memory recovery and later dreams clearly laid out the past and my deep-seated hidden feelings about those long-ago events. Dr. Barrett also notes the best studies on adult memory she was able locate are on women with documented hospital visits for sexual abuse. For many people, repressed memories often first resurface in dreams.

I have spent many years studying my dreams, and they play an enormous part in my story. Much of what occurred during my abduction is fixed in my dreams. These nighttime journeys have released memories of experiences I intellectually recall. Tucked away in my hippocampus are names of buildings, streets, and people, as well as specific words that have meaning I did not understand until I investigated. Dream descriptions of movie theaters, lakes, mountains, and hotels are vivid reminders of places I have been. Without the dream memories, I would still be back at age eight, dissociating from the shock of what was happening, and remembering nothing of a harrowing past.

I discuss many of my dreams in this book. I included those that import concrete information I would otherwise have no way of knowing about the traumas I experienced. Through my research and from information revealed in my dreams, I have been able to find these places.

When writing down my dreams, I have included the date and calculated the time the dream occurred, before and after the return of my memory. I believe this gives credence to the veracity of the information and will demonstrate my dreams were imparting information well before my memory actually returned, and they continue to do so.

In many ways, dreams are the reason I wrote this book. These nightmares allowed me to remember—in a slow, safe, and disparate way—what happened, while at the same time helping me from feeling crazy. I believe my unconscious wanted me to remember, and kept nudging me to investigate their meaning and help me to face and accept the truth. I also believe my unconscious mind was careful about how it was revealing the truth so as not to overwhelm me or give me more that I could emotionally handle.

STOCKHOLM SYNDROME

Stockholm Syndrome has become quite well known. It's a condition that sometimes occurs when individuals are put in dangerous and stressful conditions, and fear for their lives. Victims survive in part by identifying and joining in with their tormentors.

I believe that I developed Stockholm Syndrome as part of my coping ability to withstand the horrors of life with my abductors, and I exhibited evidence of this in my later life. A striking example has to do with my ongoing attraction, indeed passion, for Italian men, which I now attribute to the encounters I had with the Mafia in Los Angeles. These men oozed power and charisma and, though crazy, somehow made me feel safe. Another side effect of the Syndrome has been my inability to say "no" even to some ridiculous and possibly dangerous requests. I learned to do exactly what I was told. If not, I'd suffer terrible consequences. This behavior that followed me throughout my life has played havoc with my self-esteem.

FINALLY

According to a 1992 FBI report prepared by Kenneth B. Lanning, Supervisory Special Agent at the Behavior Science Unit of the National Center for the Analysis of Violent Crime, "Society's attitude about child sexual abuse and exploitation can be summed up in one word: denial. Most people do not want to hear about it and would prefer to pretend that child sexual victimization just does not occur. Today, however, it is difficult to pretend that it does not happen. Stories and reports about child sexual victimization are a daily occurrence."

I believe too much of what happens to abducted children is still withheld from the public. I hope this book will awaken outrage in the community about the continuing horror of childhood abduction. Law enforcement and government officials need to treat the crime of child prostitution and pornography as so onerous that criminals will be too intimidated to venture into this unspeakable business.

It is my hopes that in sharing my story, outraged voices will be heard, demanding the atrocities of crimes committed against children are given the serious time and attention they demand within society and the justice system.

PROLOGUE

COLORADO, 1948

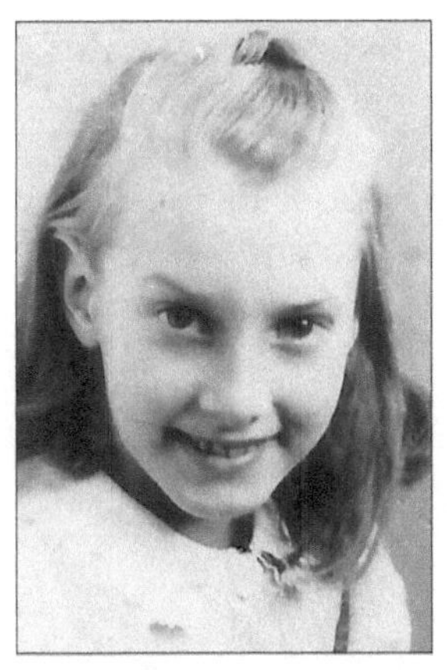

I AM EIGHT YEARS OLD. SCHOOL has ended for the day at Evans K12 school in downtown Denver, where I am in the second grade. Students crowd the walk outside the main door of the three-story brick building. Standing on the front steps down to the sidewalk, I am looking for my brother, Arthur, who is a year younger than I am. We usually walk home together. I look toward the Denver Capitol, a few blocks away, and then strain to look toward our house just one block from the school in the other direction. Not seeing him, I step down to the sidewalk to start my short walk home.

A classmate named Sherrie approaches me. She is in my grade, but in a different class. I know her from the playground. She is blonde, very pretty, and popular. "Alice, my mother wants to meet you," Sherrie says.

We walk over to a beautiful blonde woman. She is wearing a tailored suit and high heels, plus makeup—lipstick and mascara. *She looks like a movie star,* I think.

Sherrie's mother scrutinizes me and then says, "We would like to invite you for a visit at our house. Want to come?"

Front steps of Evans school located at 1115 Acoma Street in Denver,
Colorado. I took this picture in 2010 during one of my trips
to Denver to research my case. The school was closed in 1973
and remained empty until 2001 when it was placed on the
Register of Historic Places. It still stands today.

I am flattered. This pretty and popular classmate wants to be my
friend. "Yes," I say, "but I must ask my mother."

"Oh no, that won't be necessary," Sherrie's mother says. "We live
nearby, and you won't be gone very long."

"Okay," I say.

We walk a few blocks and arrive at a house built on an incline;
we climb steps and more steps before entering the house. The living
room is nearly empty, with only a couch and chair. It's as if no one
lives here. A small kitchen on the left is across from a hallway leading
to what I assume are two bedrooms on the right. The house is cold,
and the lack of color makes the rooms seem bleak. "We just moved
in and haven't gotten settled," Sherrie's mother explains. I stand there
with my hands folded, shy, not knowing what to do.

"Someone would like to meet you," Sherrie's mother says, as she
directs me down the hall.

Curious, I follow her. The wood floor squeaks as I walk to the second bedroom. The door is open, and a lean, dark-haired man sits on the only furniture in the room—a bed.

"I've been looking forward to meeting you," he croons. His eyes are intense and his voice is inviting. "Aren't you pretty? Come over here. I want to show you something." He holds out his hand.

I move closer.

He unzips his pants, pulls something out, and holds it. "Here, come and touch it," he says.

Timidly, I walk over and, at his urging, put my hands on it.

The next thing I remember is walking back to Sherrie who is standing in the kitchen. She points out the window to the narrow space between her house and the next. "If you tell anybody what happened, I will throw you behind the house where the rats will eat you and no one will ever find you."

What Sherrie said terrified me. I always remembered her and what she said to me. It kept my unconscious grounded to the event even while I repressed the reasons for her threats.

I tell neither my mother nor my father—nor anyone else—about any of it.

A few days later, Sherrie and her mother invited me again. To refuse didn't seem nice: you don't say no to adults. Did I remember what happened to me on the previous meeting? I don't know.

I meet the man once more and the events of the previous visit are repeated. Afterwards, I walk back down the hall to Sherrie's mother. She looks at the man, and he nods his head. Sherrie's mother comes at me with a cloth, puts it over my mouth, and holds me tight. I struggle and my arms flail as I try to get away.

Gone.

I wake as the car speeds around a corner, jostling me, but Sherrie's mother, who sits next to me, covers my mouth again.

THE BASEMENT, LATER

I wake up in a basement.
I face a row of floor-to-ceiling metal bars.
Where am I?
A basement.
"Hello?" I cry. "Hello?"
No one answers.
I am numb.
High up there is a small window.
Dusk has arrived.
It is cool.
I curl up.
Night comes.
I am alone in the dark.
Exhausted, I sleep.
Morning comes.
I wait.
A door opens.
There are footsteps.
A boy arrives.
He does not speak.
He hands me crackers and cheese.
He leaves.
I eat.
I wait.

FORTY-ONE YEARS LATER, SAN FRANCISCO, SEPTEMBER 1989

> *It was common for traumatized people to lose all*
> *memories of the event in question, only to regain access*
> *to them in bits and pieces at a much later date.*
> —Bessel Van Der Kolk, *The Body Keeps the Score:*
> *Brain, Mind, and Body in the Healing of Trauma*

I am fifty years old when one night, well past midnight, I wake, gasping. Strange memories float in my mind's eye, and I am filled with a sense of dread. A kind of realization enters my body. There are evil people in the world I haven't remembered and who now have returned to terrify me.

Memory: "I Am Strung Up"

September 9, 1989. The day my memory returned.

I am a child, nude, and hoisted on a metal contraption. My arms and legs are secured, Christ-like.

A woman dressed in shiny black leather stretched tightly over her figure stands before me. Stilettos increase her height. Flaming red hair adds to her diabolical appearance. Her face is distorted in an angry grimace. Pruning shears snap in her hand. She taunts me in a fake German accent, as she grabs each of my toes.

"Dis little piggy looks like a goot von, hee, hee, hee," she mocks, as she puts the blade over a toe.

I struggle.

Two women, dressed like the fiend, trussed by arms and legs, are in a lighted inset in the wall. They are responding to my peril, writhing, and pulling against their bonds, moaning. My terror increases. My scream echoes off the wall.

My offender is encouraged. Her body quivers.

"No, dis von vould be better," she says as she grabs the next toe.

"No, vat about dis one." She moves down the row until she reaches my little toe.

"Maybe vee vill save de toes for another day," she promises as she grabs a whip.

I hear a snapping crack.

I feel something soft and wet drawn across my flesh. I can't breathe. I'm going to die.

It's the middle of the night. My therapist, Barbara Cook, wouldn't be in her office. I call and leave a message with her answering service and hope to hear from her when she arrives at her office in the morning.

Wide-eyed, I lie on my bed.

Barbara calls almost immediately.

"I'm sorry," I say. "I didn't realize I would wake you."

"What's the problem, Alice?" she asks.

"I think I was kidnapped," I say.

"What do you mean?"

"I woke up and remembered I was abducted as a child. Can I see you today?"

"My schedule is completely full, but I can see you tomorrow, Sunday."

"Are you alright?"

"I don't know."

PART ONE

BEGINNINGS

15

CHAPTER ONE

CHILDHOOD

I was born in Pocahontas, Arkansas on June 21, 1939, the first day of summer and the longest day of the year. The Depression had been dragging on for years. My brother Arthur was born in 1940, and a year later, the United States entered World War II. Those were difficult years for many Americans, emotionally and financially, and my family was no exception.

We moved around a lot during those years: Lawrence, Wichita, and Mulvane in Kansas, and Kirksville, in Missouri. My father started his career as a schoolteacher, but soon became a pilot and worked first as a mail carrier, and then for the Civil Air Patrol. When the government closed the air patrol program, United Airlines hired Dad. He had found his profession.

After training in Denver, Colorado, where we lived briefly, Dad was transferred to Seattle, Washington. Because housing was scarce, we moved in with his parents, Momo and Paba, on their farm in Selleck, a rural area near the town of Renton. Paba was a retired American Baptist preacher who substituted frequently at local churches. I still remember hearing his marvelous tenor voice leading the singing at church services.

I began first grade in 1946 in Selleck, and what followed was a series of five school moves in the first two years of my education. Our first move was from my grandparents' farm to Maplewood, a suburb of Renton, where my parents rented their own home. The elementary school there was condemned a few months after I started, and I was transferred to a school in Renton. When the owner of our rented home decided to sell, we moved back to Momo and Paba's farm, where I began second grade. When the war ended, my father transferred back to Denver, a place my parents enjoyed living. Back in Denver, I finished second grade at Evans School.

My brother Stephen was born in 1945, and my mother suffered from postpartum depression, but as nothing was known about the condition at the time, it went undiagnosed. Dad was often away for work, and my mother was overwhelmed by caring for three small children. In the summer of 1947, she had shock treatments, but she continued to suffer from a feeling of worthlessness not being able to cope. She never fully recovered from those feelings.

All these moves and my mother's depression caused havoc in my education, especially in English and arithmetic, and in third grade, in the Fall of 1947, I still couldn't read at age level. I had become an insecure and shy child, and was completely innocent in the "ways of the world."

My abduction took place in the Spring of 1948 toward the end of third grade, as recounted in the prologue. I now skip the details of my kidnapping and put them in the San Francisco section of this book, at the time my memory returned. You will experience my struggle as my memory began returning in September of 1989 when I was fifty years old.

In the Fall of 1948, my mother re-enrolled me at Evans School following an approximately four-month absence from home.

■ ■ ■

The school workers are running around, nervous and tense. They know what happened to me, but not how to deal with it. Shame overwhelms me. I want to hide. I'm put on the student council, with representatives from grades one through twelve. At the first meeting, we are all seated around the large table. My legs swing off the chair, unable to touch the floor. A teacher who is one of the advisors for the group hands me the school prayer book and asks me to open the meeting by reading a prayer. I am humiliated. I can't read. The teacher takes the book away and I am removed from the student council.

■ ■ ■

Nearly fifty years after this experience, and six months after my memories started returning, I had a dream that was related to that experience.

DREAM: "I Meet a Man"
March 4, 1990. 6 months after my memory returned.

I am in school. I go to meet a man in the Evans School auditorium. He is sitting in the back of the room in one of those flip-up wooden seats with metal bases screwed to the floor. Bodyguards are standing around at the back. The man calls me over to him. We have an immediate emotional understanding. There is a strong loving feeling between us. He is gentle. I like sitting next to him and I can tell that he likes sitting next to me. I feel serene and safe. It feels so wonderful; it is hard to explain.

The man takes my hand and opens it. I think that he is going to read my palm, but instead he says that I remind him of someone he used to know. He gently says to me, "Do you remember...."

I can't hear what he says, and don't respond.

"Well, you wouldn't remember that," he says.

I am aware that everyone might think there is something going on between us, which worries me, but it feels so good to be next to him that I put those thoughts aside. At one point, I look up at him and see that he is fat. He has a double chin and a big stomach. He is not physically attractive, but I don't care. I love him anyway.

I put this dream here because this man reappeared later in my life and I now believe he was the court official Max Melville, a Denver District attorney who worked on my case. He is the only nurturing man to be found in all of my dreams. Bodyguards, who are in several dreams, seem to be protecting me.

Within three months of the student council incident, my family moved again. My school records indicate that I was "closed out" at Evans sometime in October (no exact date mentioned) and enrolled in fourth grade at Montclair Elementary School on Monday, November 29, 1948. I had missed at least another month of schooling. Where was I during November? My school records from the time state, "No Trace." It seems that Evans School either did not know where we had gone or had left the information off my school records to protect me and my family.

My father purchased eleven acres of land, including an alfalfa field, that abutted Lowery Air Force Base on the outskirts of Denver. On the property was an old outbuilding we called the "turkey house," and a one-room dwelling where we stayed while waiting for a new house to be built. The dwelling had no electricity, running water, or bathroom, which was located outside. To bathe us, my mom filled a large metal container from the well and carried it into the kitchen. We also swam at the local YMCA where showers were mandatory and where my brother and I began swimming lessons.

Pictures from that time are startling considering that my father was a pilot for a major airline and made a good salary. I was told he bought the property as an investment, hoping that after a few years the price of the land would go up and he would make a profit. My father must have had enormous expenses due to my mother's shock treatments, not to mention my kidnapping, which might have explained the purchase of this inhospitable place. I don't know if United Airlines provided health coverage at that time for such things, but there must have been expenses around my court appearances, hospitalization, and travel as well.

My father immediately began improving our circumstances. In just a few months he tore down the one room dwelling, and converted the "turkey house" into a livable home. Friends and relatives helped. Although it was not an architectural wonder, it was functional. We held a party when it was time to burn the outhouse. The fire department stood by with hoses in hand.

The turkey house and our dwelling without electricity,
running water, or bathroom.

Mercifully, although it was considered, I was not put back a grade at Montclair School. It would have been too humiliating to be in the same grade as my smart brother.

My parents complained to Mr. Thibodeau, my new fourth grade teacher, that I couldn't read.

"Give her easier books," he replied.

Years later, my father commented, "He was a genius."

Mr. Thibodeau is the only teacher I remember from these years.

Mom, a voracious reader, made weekly trips to the library. Soon, I floated in books, and reading became a life-long pleasure. Still, reading out loud in front of people made me fearful until I was well into my fifties.

BRUNO

I finished fourth, fifth, and sixth grades at Montclair, graduating from grade school in 1951, just before my twelfth birthday. That summer we visited Mom's parents, Grandma and Grandpa, on their forty-acre farm in the countryside near Paola, Kansas. Our dog Bruno came with us and enjoyed running freely on the farm.

Bruno looked exactly like Snow White's dog in the Disney movie and that's how he got his name. He was a mutt from the local "pound," as animal shelters were called in those days. His brown chestnut hair was lovely and we adored him. One day, he was chasing the chickens that roamed freely on my grandparents' farm, and he caught one. When I saw the bloody chicken hanging from his mouth, I ran over and smacked his bottom and chided him, "Bad dog, bad dog." Bruno snarled and bared his teeth, naturally protecting his fresh kill. His face contorted. Without warning, he jumped straight up and bit me on the face.

I touched the spot and screamed. Blood stained my hand. Mom and Grandma came running. Mom fainted. I couldn't see the damage, but I felt it. The wound throbbed. Bruno looked at me, his tail wagging. Grandma cleaned my face. There was a big tear on the right side of my mouth. It was late afternoon on a weekend so finding a doctor was difficult, but one agreed to meet us at his office. "I've never done this kind of repair before but will do my best," the doctor said.

He gave me a tetanus shot and something for the pain. Leaning over me, he started to sew. His face, near mine, showed concern.

Cross-eyed, I watched his hand move up and down. He darned me up with twelve stitches.

Back at the farm, Bruno was gone, taken to the pound to be disposed of. I hurt. We always had bad luck with our dogs. Two were hit by cars and suffered horrible deaths, one ran away, and one was shot because he kept attacking passersby—there were no leash laws back then, and dogs ran loose. And now, Bruno. Losing him was worse than being bitten.

CHAPTER TWO

LIFE GOES ON

CHERRY HILLS, COLORADO, 1950s

THE 1950S WAS AN INTERESTING DECADE FOR ME. Life was more settled, but I still felt insecure, had low self-esteem and was self-conscious as a result of my dog bite scar. In 1951, we moved to Cherry Hills, next to Englewood, a community on the outskirts of Denver. Our circumstances had improved.

Previously, in Denver, we attended the First Baptist Church across from the Capitol building. My parents were quite active there and had many friends. After our move, my parents helped establish a new American Baptist Church called Hampton Hills, and it became the center of our family life. We attended services and Sunday School every week, and on Wednesday nights we went to Bible study. Dad became a deacon and built a beautiful altar for the front of the church. I dedicated my life to Christ, thinking I might become a missionary. I became president of our Youth Fellowship and sang in the choir, providing a solo now and then.

Our house was clean and we ate three square meals together every day. Mom made my clothes and taught me to cook, sew, knit, and needlepoint. My father was accomplished on the piano, organ, trumpet, and accordion. He had a natural ear and could play almost anything after hearing it once. He saw to it that we all had piano lessons and played second instruments. I learned the flute; Arthur, the French horn; Stephen, the violin; and Mom, the bass viol. We played at church on Christmas and Easter and other special occasions. I eventually became a part of a flute trio and we performed at school assemblies. Musical training became an important part of my life.

But this stability suffered a shock in February 1952 when my sister Lynn was born. I have a picture of my mother holding Lynn at two-and-a-half months, deep depression showing on her face, and she looks haggard. Lynn is twelve years younger than me, and I'm sure a fourth child was not on my mom and dad's agenda.

A poem my mother wrote sometime in the fifties expresses her despair:

DEPRESSION

You big black giant striding
Across eggshells
You bruise, scar, distort.
Rawness winces as you probe,
Deep you find cowering
Sub-conscious, horrified, I
Recoil
This ugly face cannot be mine.
Climb, climb. Where is the
Light?
It is gone.
It never was.
Embrace me then. Rape my
Spirit
Uproot sanity. Bulldoze the will.
My God, my God.
Save me from myself.

Mom was eventually prescribed medication for depression and anxiety, which she took every day. She became dependent on it, and always made sure she had plenty of pills on hand. Her fear of being without them became obvious on vacations.

■ ■ ■

Something very significant to my story happened shortly after we moved to Cherry Hills. Two cardboard boxes full of my court reports sat on the clothes dryer in the basement. It bothered me. Every time I walked by those boxes I was reminded of my abduction. I complained to my mother. "Do you want us to get rid of them?" she asked. I hesitated for a few seconds, then said yes. I never saw them again.

Today, I regret that decision. Years of wondering whether my memory was true could have been erased. Now, family and friends say they do not remember the abduction. However, it was the absence of those court records that made it possible for me to dissociate from what had happened. I became free to move on with my life. Was the dissociation a good thing? Some would say no. But given the circumstances of my family life, and the lack of support or understanding I needed, would I have been able to heal had my memories remained intact? Once I buried the horrifying memories, I could function well and lead a productive and interesting life.

And, after all the trials and meetings with police and FBI were over, I lived my life without remembering what happened to me. I lived in denial which caused me to experience life in a fog, unable to recognize dangerous situations, or understand my emotional reactions to life's circumstances. The Stockholm Syndrome caused me to be drawn to unconscious experiences that affected my behavior, as you will soon see.

■ ■ ■

I completed grades seven through nine at Cherry Hills Middle School. Before entering Cherry Hills High, the district administration required me to take a psychiatric examination and a Benet Mental Test. No one else, as far as I know, was required to take that test. I was able to obtain a record of it, dated September 8 1954, but the results and pertinent information had all been redacted. The test was paid for by the school district. I remember this experience in part because my father was asked to pay the bill and he refused, believing the test unnecessary. I suppose the school wanted to make sure I was mentally sound before allowing me to enroll.

In 1955, when I was fifteen years of age, Sherrie, who helped facilitate my abduction, reentered my life.

MEMORY: "Incident on the Broadway Bus"

I am on my way home from the dentist's office.

Sherrie and a boy get on the bus.

They hug and kiss.

Sherrie catches sight of me and mocks me.

"I'm glad you're no relative of mine. Ugh."

I shrink into my seat, afraid.

"I'm glad you're no relative of mine," she repeats. "You're ugly."

Frightened, I remain quiet.

Soon, they get off the bus.

At home, I tell my mother, "I saw Sherrie on the bus."

Surprised, she says, "I'll take care of it."

Subsequent to this memory, a man came to visit me at my house. It is likely related to my mother reporting to the authorities that I saw Sherrie on the bus.

MEMORY: "The Mystery Man"

Cherry Hills, circa 1954. I am 15 years old.

My mother tells me a man is coming to visit me.

"Who is it?" I ask.

"Wait and see," she says. "Get dressed up."

He arrives. I walk into our living room and sit adjacent to him on the couch. He is very fat, has a double chin, and struggles to breathe.

"Do you remember me?" he asks.

"No," I say.

He asks again. "You don't remember me?"

"No," I say truthfully. "Who are you?"

He is disturbed and looks disappointed. He gives it one more chance. "Are you sure you don't remember me?"

"Yes, I'm sorry. Should I remember you?"

He doesn't answer and thinks for a moment. "Well, it was a few years ago." He gets up to leave.

I tell him goodbye. I walk into the kitchen where my mother has been listening to our conversation. She appears to be happy. Her mood is light.

"Who was that man?" I ask. "Why did he come to visit me?"

"Never mind, it is not important."

I don't push the issue and return to my bedroom. We never discuss the man again.

At the time of the memory, I didn't know why this man came to our home, but over time I remembered more details that could explain it. When I disappeared from Evans School in 1948, the police interviewed teachers in the schoolyard as students were leaving. One teacher said she had seen me talking with Sherrie and her mother on the sidewalk. The police interviewed the two, and they denied any knowledge of what happened to me. Later, I learned they had disappeared. Without them, the police had no proof of who kidnapped me.

However, when I saw Sherrie on the bus a few years later and told my mother, she called the district attorney. The man who came to visit me could have been the man I met in the auditorium at Evans School. Knowing that Sherrie and her mother had returned to Denver, the man might have hoped he could prove who kidnapped me, if he could get them to talk. Or perhaps it had nothing to do with them. The FBI or DA might have been looking for more information about what happened and wanted me to testify against individuals I met during my abduction. Or perhaps the FBI or DA wanted my help with convicting my kidnappers who lived in Denver and were constantly in trouble with the law—they were being prosecuted at that time for another crime. It remains a mystery to me.

MY DIARIES

In the process of recovering my memory, I started reading my old diaries. 1956, the year I turned seventeen, was extremely eventful.

I quote from my diary:

Up at 6:30 a.m. Had an assembly today about keeping the school clean. Had test in American history. Did experiments in chemistry. In English we had to write down some words that had an emotional effect on us. Mr. Graham asked me to read mine. "God and torture," I say. His startled look indicated my words had unsettled him. He did not ask other students for their words.

Why would I write such a thing? He'd asked for words that had an emotional effect, and that's what immediately came to my mind.

My diary also recorded I obtained a drivers license, had my first voice lesson, and my first date, a blind date with a service man.

Further in the diary, I noted that "John Dilitush [a church member] came over and said Mom was sick with worry because I hadn't come home. I sure felt bad."

After reading this diary entry I remembered I had gone to church that evening and then, instead of going directly home, had driven over to visit friends at my White Castle carhop job. I returned home a couple of hours later than expected. My mother was hysterical and had asked John to come to our house and scold me. My dad was away on a trip and our church pastor was unavailable. I felt terrible, apologized and promised to always tell my mother where I was.

My mother could have spoken to me directly. Why didn't she?

Another entry states that I had had my first date and that my grandfather Paba had talked my parents into the idea that I should skip my senior year in high school and enroll at Colorado Women's College in Denver. I met with the college dean and president, and they agreed to take me. However, when they received a copy of my grades, they changed their minds. Although I was in the upper third of my class, my grades did not reflect my readiness to leave high school behind. When asked, my mom said she didn't know why Paba pushed this crazy idea.

I believe Paba was worried I would become promiscuous due to my sexual experiences during my kidnapping, and because I had had my first date. A women's college would take care of the problem, or so he thought.

ADDITIONAL TRAUMA

I had additional experiences in 1956 that, while not as horrific as my kidnapping, were extremely traumatizing. First, I was molested by my father. I was seventeen years old when it started.

Although nothing was said, I sensed that my parents were having problems. My father seemed vulnerable, unhappy, and depressed.

I didn't recognize what it was at the time, but my dad began "romancing" me. For someone who had not been one for parenting, he suddenly became very fatherly. He expressed new interest in me and offered to teach me to fly. He belonged to a flying club and had access to several planes. I had two lessons. He took me to play tennis once, for which I had neither training nor talent. He began coming to my bedroom in the morning to give me a wakeup massage. He flirted with me in our swimming pool and insisted I swam nude.

One evening, while my mother was at church, he asked me to come to their bedroom. "I think it is time you learn about your body," he said, giving me some books on female anatomy. "Read them and get a mirror and look at yourself down there."

A week or so later, when my mother was again at church, he again called me to their bedroom. I have no recollection of where my siblings were. "When your mother and I got married we knew absolutely nothing about sex," he said. "I don't want this to happen to you. I have decided to show you. I know this is an unorthodox way of doing things, but there are cultures that think differently. I've been fixed so you can't get pregnant. Take off your clothes and get on the bed."

What followed was his attempt to enter me, but my mother arrived back from church before he could achieve it. He scooted me out of the bed and told me to run to my room. Another night, he came to my bedroom and made a second attempt. I complained I needed to go to the bathroom, and that put an end to it. My two brothers were in the next room, separated from mine by a screen. I later learned that both had heard my father in my room. They thought it was strange but didn't comprehend what was going on.

Plagued by anxiety and depression, and worried about my mother, I couldn't concentrate on my schoolwork. What would she do if she knew? What could she do? At this point she had four children, was emotionally impaired, and had undergone a second round of shock treatments. I didn't know what to do, so I did nothing.

When I was ready to graduate from high school, my father announced he was going to take me on a trip to San Francisco as a graduation present. "Won't that be great!" my mother said. Knowing what was coming, I was filled with apprehension.

My father was no longer a co-pilot but had graduated to captain. Because he was now the boss, I was able to ride in the "jump seat" directly behind him in the cockpit for the two-hour flight.

In San Francisco, we checked into a hotel used by United Airlines employees. For dinner, he took me on a cable car ride to the Barbary Coast, a sleazy section of San Francisco. We ended up at "Finocchios," a nightclub where female impersonators performed.

Back at the hotel, my father once more tried to have sex with me, but every time he got on top of me, I complained that I had to go to the bathroom and excused myself. This happened three times before he gave up.

Although my father's attempts to force intercourse on me occurred just four times, the situation was a terrible burden and what to do about it bothered me more and more. I prayed every night for God to help me as I cried myself to sleep. I begged for Him to give me strength to tell my dad to stop.

One morning Dad came to me again. I could hear Mom in the kitchen. I took a big breath and said, "Dad, I've been praying a lot and think you should not be doing this. It feels wrong and I don't think Mom would like it." He shot out of the bed and was gone, never returning.

A few years later, my dad apologized for his behavior, probably because he was worried that I would tell someone. My emotional problems had worsened, and he knew I was seeing a therapist. "For what it's worth, I'm sorry. But I guess it's all water under the bridge," he said.

Years later, while I was living with my mother, she shared one of her own dreams with me.

My Mother's Dream
Told to me circa 1992, El Cajon, California.

"I am standing on a porch and your father walks by. He goes down a path which splits at a fork in the trail. He becomes two people. One person goes left, and one goes right. It was as if he was two different people."

This dream tells me that my mother, at least on some level, understood something was amiss with my father. The following dream is connected, and I love it. It shows I am resilient.

DREAM: "Dad, You Are Running over My Wildflowers"
February 5, 1994. 4 years and 5 months after my memory returned.

Dad has come home. We get in the car to go someplace. Mom and my brother, Stephen, are in the front seat. I am in the back seat. Two other children are in the car.

Wildflowers are growing all over the ground. I tell Dad I have planted them, but for some reason he doesn't care and drives over them. I love one particular wildflower. It is a blue violet. He drives over and demolishes it.

I say, "Dad, you are driving over my wildflowers!" He continues to do it.

We look out and see car tracks all over my flowers. Everyone is sitting quietly in the car. My feeling is they are unhappy that he is killing them, but they say nothing.

At this point I get mad, lash out, and point out his bad behavior. "How could you do that to me? You have absolutely no feelings for me and don't care about me at all." My tirade goes on for quite a while. I am bitter and angry.

Everyone in the car quietly listens. Stephen is looking at me and shaking his head as if to say he totally agrees and is happy I am saying something. At this point, Mom turns around. She is hysterical. She can't deal with my tirade. She doesn't want to hear it. I look at her in amazement. She has become a pathetic person who I know agrees with me but is dealing with it by becoming a mental patient. She can't stand up to Dad.

I shut up, knowing what she is up to and why she is doing it. I am on the verge of telling her I am an incest survivor. It feels to me that Dad is worried I am going to say something. When Mom has her fit, I keep my mouth shut. I turn to Stephen who has moved to the back seat. "See how I always protect her?"

We look out of the window at all my mashed flowers. I notice a bleeding-heart flower. I say to one of the children, "Do you know what a bleeding heart is?" She says she doesn't. I show her one and notice it is not completely developed.

"My flowers will grow back if I water them," I think.

COLLEGE YEARS

Following graduation from high school, I enrolled at William Jewell, a Baptist college in Liberty, Missouri, a small town outside of Kansas City. My grandfather, Paba, and my father and his brother, Uncle C.B., had all gone to Jewell. My brother Arthur followed me a year later and behind him two of our cousins.

Jewell provided a liberal arts degree and gave me the opportunity to continue my education in music. I loved singing lessons and was told I had a better than average voice. I was accepted into the school chorus and performed at school functions and once on television. I also joined the sorority Alpha Gamma Delta and eventually became vice-president.

Aside from my music teachers, I remember none of my professors except for my Spanish teacher. She was an assertive redhead, and she terrified me. It was many years before I realized the significance of Spanish, and of a red-headed woman in my history.

In the meantime, I had begun ushering at the Kansas City Lyric Opera where I saw Puccini's *Madame Butterfly* and *La Boheme*. From then on, I wanted to be an opera singer.

Despite those positive experiences in college, my past came back to haunt me. The movie *Peyton Place* was released in December 1957. When I saw it at the local theater, I was upset by the vivid sex scene in which the stepfather rapes his daughter. The aftermath of this event depicts the town's reaction of alarm and disgust and from it I learned the seriousness of incest. The movie was like a smack in the face and the rape scene preyed on my mind.

During my senior year I had severe emotional problems. I withdrew from friends, couldn't concentrate, cried a lot, and became anxious and depressed. I moved off campus and rented a room from a high school teacher. This proved to be a bad idea, as it severely reduced my social contacts. In addition, the teacher and I ended up not getting along.

In 1961, the year of my graduation, I made an appointment to see the college psychologist. For the first time, and with difficulty, I spoke about my father. The psychologist's body language, voice, and facial expressions indicated he was revolted. The theories of Freud were popular at the time, and I suspect he may have been thinking I seduced my father.

"Do you masturbate?" he asked.

"No," I said.

His smirk indicated he didn't believe me.

"If I could tell you that my father molested me, I think I could tell you if I masturbated," I replied.

He had no more to say on the subject and sent me off to see the official college physician, whom I visited once a week for several months before my graduation. I cried through every session. I had no money for these consultations and my parents were asked to pay the bill when they came to pick me up.

Earlier in the year, I had visited the University of Kansas in Lawrence to audition for their graduate school voice department. They offered me a scholarship. However, after my parents' visit to the college doctor, my dad decided I should move to New York to study voice there. What took place during his meeting with the doctor I do not know. I should have asked. I suspected Dad wanted me as far away from my mother as possible, perhaps fearing I might tell her what he had done.

In June 1961, following graduation, I sang at the wedding of my cousin, Carolyn, in Hutchinson, Kansas, a celebration my family attended. After my mother died in 2007, at the age of 91, I had access to many years of family correspondence. In one letter following the wedding, my grandfather Paba wrote:

We think a lot about Alice and the visit with her in Hutchinson. We think her voice is really wonderful. We also think she is wonderful as a person. We wonder, does the voice carry the person

on the way up or does the person carry the voice on the way up.
She has the qualities of a great personality and in that person is
a great possibility with her voice as well as many other qualities.

I was stunned and moved when I read these words. I think Paba was congratulating my mother for helping me turn out right despite my traumatic past.

After a summer visit to Peru, I moved to New York City to pursue an operatic career. Being on my own put distance between me and the dysfunction in my family and helped me to mature and learn how to take care of myself. I believe the opportunity to sing great music every day in an exciting city saved my life.

PART TWO

NEW YORK

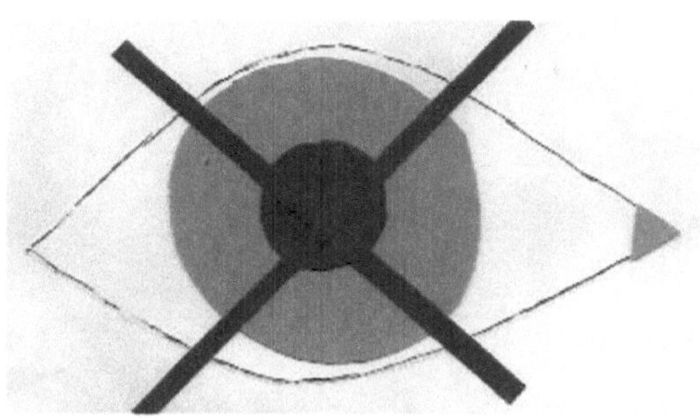

CHAPTER THREE

MANHATTAN

FOLLOWING MY GRADUATION FROM COLLEGE IN JUNE 1961, Dad helped me get a job at United Airlines in New York City so I could continue my singing studies there. I was ecstatic. It was a chance to get away from my parents and start a new life.

At first, New York was a challenge. By this time, I had long repressed my abduction memories and my diaries demonstrate how innocent and undeveloped I was. It was the sixties, and the sexual revolution had begun. My girlfriends' tales of their adventures and overnight escapades shocked me.

My diary entries in 1961 are filled with laments about loneliness, trouble making friends, and confusion over the behavior of women who were sleeping with various men. I felt pressure to conform, but my Christian background dictated I should wait for marriage. I wondered what was wrong with me.

Friends have asked me how my abduction affected my relationships with men. I have thought about this over the years. Insecurity plagued me throughout my dating life and whenever a possible romance appeared on the horizon, I became agitated and nervous. I said "yes" when invited out by any man, whether or not I liked him. Then, after we'd gone on a date, I'd wonder: "Did he like me?

Will he call?" Usually, he didn't, and I viewed it as "to be expected." Although I didn't know it at the time, my eight-year-old experiences programmed me to expect men to use me and then leave me.

As an adult I still had not developed boundaries and I allowed men to walk all over me, causing me untold feelings of worthlessness. I didn't know I could speak up and demand better behavior. I had so little self-esteem that my expectations were very low. As a result, relationships were often brief and unfulfilling.

Trust was always an issue. I never wanted to marry or have children, and I often described matrimony as being "tied to a chair." Given this attitude, I found that some people assumed I was a lesbian.

Once, a co-worker invited himself to my apartment. We didn't set a time, but I assumed it would be at a reasonable hour. He showed up at ten p.m. By the time two a.m. rolled around, he still refused to go home, claiming he had no money for the subway. I let him use a cot across the room from my bed, but when I was settling into sleep, he accosted me, already erect. When I screamed and ran across the room from him, hiding my face in my hands, he promptly went back to the cot and fell asleep. The next morning, I cooked him breakfast, gave him money for the subway, and sent him off to work.

The encounter was traumatizing and caused me a great deal of anguish. I couldn't sleep, felt dirty, became anxious, and couldn't get the image of his "protrusion" out of my head. At work, we didn't speak. Three months passed. I moved through the world in a daze, worried and depressed. Despite the circumstances, I felt a lot of guilt. Finally, I found the courage to approach him, and actually apologized, asking whether it was my fault. Surprised, he laughed. "Alice, it was not your fault. You're a nice girl, and I'm a jerk!"

Just like that, my world changed. I wasn't a bad girl after all. Guilt melted. My smile returned. I slept well for the first time in months.

I believe this experience and my response to it shows how effectively I had detached from my abduction. My denial of the past had caused me to travel through life as an unaware innocent. Why would I scream and hide in the corner upon seeing an erection when I had already been exposed to many? It appears to me that this encounter threatened the dissociation I had embraced to protect myself; it threatened to remind me of the horror I had experienced at age eight.

Once I did become sexually active, I tended to dissociate while having sex, feeling as if I were on the ceiling, looking down on the proceedings. With some men I experienced what I described to therapists as wavy lines, or disturbances in the air. Although I never had any complaints from sexual partners, I didn't really experience intimacy with them. This probably explains why many men didn't stick around.

My entire dating life consisted of men of different ethnicities: an African American, a Russian Orthodox Serbo-Croatian, an Israeli, an Egyptian, a Cuban, and finally Italians. These relationships broadened my sense of the world, but all were short lived, and left me feeling abandoned and unloved.

GROUP THERAPY

Shortly after the experience with my co-worker, I started therapy. I was concerned about my relationships with men and worried I would become promiscuous. I was twenty-three years old.

I had never been in counseling and was uncertain as to how to find a therapist, so I called the Riverside Baptist Church and asked to see a pastor. With great difficulty I told the minister about my father and asked for guidance. He recommended the American Foundation for Psychiatry and Religion, where Norman Vincent Peale, who wrote the popular book *The Power of Positive Thinking*, was the pastor. I called and made an appointment.

I was tested by Dr. Libby Lyons who took me through a Rorschach test and had me organize a series of pictures to make a story, draw a picture of myself, and arrange a series of wood blocks. When discussing the results, Dr. Libby said, "The tests suggest you have had a childhood trauma not related to the incest with your father. We don't know what it is."

I had one-on-one sessions at the clinic for six months. Dr. Lyons and I talked about my family history, father, and dreams for an operatic career. Eventually, she told me she would like me to join a group that met one night a week at her home.

Dr. Lyons lived in a splendid old Victorian House on Manhattan's West Side, somewhere around 23rd Street. She had turned her four-story home into a halfway house for women who had recently been released from a mental facility and needed a supportive place to live. It had a basement kitchen and a large living room on the first floor with beautiful wood floors. A chandelier sparkled from the 15-foot ceiling, lighting up the discussion group below.

Dr. Lyons was easy to love—a six-foot-tall, vivacious woman who was larger than life. Her shoulder-length hair flew around her shoulders as she talked, and she was full of laughter and positive comments. She occupied the master suite and each of the women residents had her own room. There was also a baby, temporarily abandoned by one of the women, and everyone took care of her. Sometimes the two-month-old came to group therapy and sat on Dr. Lyons' lap as we talked.

In the early sixties, group therapy was still in development. Groups were usually comprised of people of similar age, pathology, family, sex, religion, etc. Dr. Lyons, however, followed the model of one of the early founders of the movement, Dr. Irving D. Yalom—a "here-and-now" format where sessions were mixed with individuals from many different walks of life and pathologies.

In Dr. Lyons' group, I was initiated into the lives of people whose lifestyle and difficulties were unfamiliar to me. The group included three gay men, two secretaries with work-related problems, a woman with an abusive husband, a single young woman struggling to take care of her child, a man who had recently become impotent, a scientist with relationship problems, a severely overweight woman, a playwriter struggling to find work, and a girl with suicidal ideation.

Our evenings together were vibrant with emotion as members talked about their problems and received honest—sometimes loud—feedback. For the first time, I learned how others lived. The group chastised me for "playing innocent" and I soon realized I needed to grow up. I went in as a naive young woman and came out with a better understanding of myself and the world. I became, despite my religious background, tolerant and accepting of all kinds of people and empathetic to their problems and different ways of living.

Dr. Lyons retired after I'd been with her for about two years, and the group disbanded. We all went our separate ways.

MY FIRST SERIOUS RELATIONSHIP

I met Ralph Escobar in 1964 at a social club where he was a part-time host. On my second visit, he invited me for a date. He took me to see Maxim Gorky's *The Lower Depth,* a play about society's outcasts. Although the production was excellent, it traumatized me, and I have never forgotten some of the scenes from this grim play in which the characters preyed on each other.

Nevertheless, I enjoyed our time together, and after a few dates, he moved in with me and shared the rent. One evening he announced he had something to tell me. "I'm eighteen years old. I didn't tell you because I was afraid you wouldn't go out with me."

Eighteen! I almost died. I was twenty-four. But I was infatuated, despite the age difference. Ralph was a draftsman at an engineering firm that had hired him right out of high school, which said something about the quality of his education and character. He made twice as much money as I did, had a Thunderbird with bucket seats, treated me well, bought me flowers, and took me to fancy restaurants. And he was enrolled at Columbia University with plans to become a writer.

I soon learned there was prejudice against Puerto Ricans. One friend from work, an older woman, called me to her desk.

"Alice," she said. "I want to have a serious talk with you. You know, Puerto Ricans have lots of black blood in them, and if you have a child, it might come out black. I thought that I should tell you this in case you didn't know." I excused myself post haste.

I met Ralph's mother twice. The first time was in Miami when Ralph took me to meet her. She was only thirty-five years old, but frail, and she complained of constant pain. The doctors couldn't (or wouldn't) tell her what was wrong, and I was disturbed by the lack of clarity about her situation. Within a month she weighed only sixty pounds and was dying of uterine cancer in a hospital in the Bronx.

"Promise me you will marry Ralph and take care of him," she said when I visited. Not knowing what to say, and wanting to comfort her, I said, "I promise," meaning it at the time. She died a few days later.

By October of 1964, Ralph and I were engaged. I called my parents, told my friends, bought a dress, and began to look for a church. Then we went to see the movie, *The Rise and Fall of the Roman Empire*, with Sophia Loren and Alex Guinness. In the middle of the film I began to sob, and it became non-stop. Tears streamed down my face. My emotional outburst had nothing to do with the movie. The wedding date was looming, and I was uneasy with the way my life was going. We left the theater.

At home, I told Ralph I was afraid to get married. Several group therapy friends came to console me. I continued to bawl until I got up the courage to tell Ralph I could not marry him. He didn't take the news easily.

I encouraged Ralph to find another place to live. He eventually found a railroad apartment on the Lower West Side. I cared for Ralph but knew I didn't care for him enough. I encouraged him to go into therapy. I hoped he would be able to let go of me. After his counseling began, I noticed a difference in Ralph's response to me.

"Is anything the matter?" I asked one evening.

"No, I'm just tired."

The next day he called me at my office. "I've met someone, and we are going to be married," he said.

I was stunned. "Who is she? Where did you meet her?"

"I met her at a bar," he said abruptly. "She is thirty-five years old, and I've been going out with her for a month."

"Are you sure this is what you want to do?" I asked. "You only just met her!"

"Yes," he said, and hung up the phone.

Pain grabbed my heart. I was devastated. To stop the hurt, I recited over and over in my mind, "I'm not going to feel anything, I'm not going to feel anything," and before long, it worked. That was the way I dealt with unpleasantness throughout my life. I made every attempt to not acknowledge disappointments, and just go on. This way of thinking may have been efficient in a way, but it did not serve me well. It kept me locked in an unhealthy state of mind, ignorant of lessons I should have learned and unable to protect myself from potentially harmful experiences.

MY GANGSTER

I have always been extremely attracted to Italian men. In fact, any man with an Italian name excites me. While working at United Airlines, I traveled alone to Italy four times. My adventures there were endless. Italian men liked me, and I had many encounters. When my memory returned, I understood this fascination.

I met Lou Borelli in 1962 at the United Airlines ticket counter. He had black curly hair, was my height, slender, and appeared to be in his early forties. He carried a white miniature poodle. We talked as I wrote his ticket to Denver. I mentioned my family lived there and that I planned to go home for Thanksgiving. He asked for my telephone number and said he would call for a date.

He called on Thanksgiving Day. I did not feel I could leave my family and so invited him to spend the day with us. He declined.

An entire year passed before Lou called again and asked to take me to dinner. Surprised, I was happy to accept. He picked me up at my apartment on Charles Street in Greenwich Village. After flagging a cab, he asked the driver to stop at a liquor store where he picked up a couple of bottles of wine, explaining that the restaurant we were headed to had no liquor license.

From there, the cab took us to the Upper East Side where we stopped at a row of lovely brownstones. Beside one, a few steps down, was the entrance to a dimly lit tiny restaurant with five private areas. One other couple was there, an elderly white-haired gentleman with an elegant middle-aged blond woman, her hair teased into a big bouffant. Bedecked with jewels, she looked like a high-class escort or mistress. My homemade blue flower cotton dress made me feel out of place, but Lou didn't seem to notice or care. When I asked him the name of the restaurant, he told me it was a private club.

The young Italian waiter, dressed in a tuxedo, greeted Lou by name. There were only two meal selections, and prices weren't listed. I still remember the meal—a salad and then the main course I'd chosen, veal smothered in a creamy wine sauce with sides of pasta and squash. We had an easy time talking, but he was vague about what he did for a living. When I pressed him, he said he was a businessman who owned about twenty companies.

"What kind of companies?" I asked.

"I provide goods for dime stores," he said. "Things like artificial flowers." Then he quickly changed the subject.

I told him about my career ambitions and my study of Italian. Lou drank most of the wine and was a little tipsy by the time we left. I was new to liquor and stopped after one glass. There was no bill.

A taxi drove us home. As we arrived at my apartment, Lou suddenly became angry at the driver for no reason I could discern. His tone was menacing. I quickly invited him to my apartment for coffee, and his demeanor and attitude toward the cab driver immediately changed.

My apartment was basically one room with a fireplace, a kitchenette, and a bathroom. My couch was a daybed with a thin mattress over springs and two bolsters at the back. How we managed I don't know, but we spent the night closely entwined.

In the morning, Lou said, "I want you to be my girlfriend. I don't care what you do when I am not here, but when I am, I want you to be with me exclusively." I was flattered. I felt safe with him. I was going to be a tycoon's girlfriend, just like in the movies. "We have to do something about this bed," he added, and then asked me to call in sick and spend the day with him.

After I made my excuses to my boss, Lou and I discussed what we would do for the day, and he said he had to "call downtown."

"Uh-huh, yeah, uh-huh, uh-huh, okay, yeah," was the conversation on his end, and when he hung up, he announced he had to go. "Some things have come up," he said. "I'll call you when I can." And just like that, he was gone.

Disappointed, it didn't occur to me to be mad. The whole day was mine. I went back to sleep.

Over the next few weeks, Lou called me from all over the United States. I was impressed. In the Sixties it was not common for people to call long distance because it was so expensive.

One evening, after I had gone to sleep, the telephone rang.

"I'm calling from Cleveland," said the voice on the other end of the line. "Mr. Borelli has asked me to arrange to get you a bed." The voice was gruff and sounded irritated. "What kind of a bed do you want? A round one, a square one, a king size? You tell me, and I'll get it to you."

I knew I should not accept a gift like this from a man I hardly knew. Plus, my apartment was too small to support a big bed. It would take up most of the room.

"Lou didn't say anything about this," I told the caller. "I want to talk with him first. Have him call me. I don't want him to get me a bed."

At group therapy, I discussed the situation. The comments from the concerned group members flew fast and furiously. "Are you crazy, Alice?" "You're so gullible!" "This guy is a gangster. He is a member of the Mafia. You must get rid of him." "No regular man orders his girlfriend a bed, and especially not from Cleveland when you live in New York."

But I liked the guy, and it was exciting to think that he was a little dangerous. Luckily for me, when he called later at my office, I was in the ladies' room. He left a message saying he'd call me back.

I never heard from him again.

I have often wondered who Lou Borelli was and whether, in fact, he was a member of the Mafia. Why was he ordering a bed from a business in Cleveland? Was he associated with the notorious Mafia family headquartered there? Was it an accident I waited on him at the ticket counter, or was there another motive? Over the years I have come to believe my kidnappers kept track of me.

Many years later, in 2019, I learned from a book titled *Mafia, The Government's Secret File on Organized Crime, United States Treasury Department Bureau of Narcotics* (Harper Collins, 2007) that there was a criminal named Frank "the Hawk" Borelli, a member of the Lucchese family who lived on the Upper East Side of Manhattan in the 1960s. He was a wholesale trafficker of heroin to associates in New York, Chicago, Illinois, and Cleveland, and was a trusted member of the Mafia in the East Harlem area. Could he have been a relative of Lou Borelli, and was "My Gangster" working for him? The connection to Cleveland is interesting. Later, I learned that Frank "the Hawk" had been arrested for drug trafficking around the time Lou disappeared from my life.

CHAPTER FOUR

VOICE STUDIES

NEW YORK, 1965–1974

WITHIN A MONTH OF ARRIVING IN NEW YORK, I began looking for a voice teacher. My first teacher kept me working in her studio for four years, refusing to let me practice or sing in outside productions. Finally, I rebelled, left, and began auditioning and performing in opera workshops around the city. My second teacher told me to smile and lift the back of my throat. The third wanted me to drop my jaw. The fourth encouraged me to sing high notes in my head producing a falsetto effect, because I had a beautiful upper range. And on it went. By the time these teachers finished with me, my face and throat were tied in knots.

My last teacher solved the problem. She put a cork in my teeth. This made it impossible to constrict my throat and mouth when I sang. My face relaxed and my voice freed. All I had needed to do was relax my jaw so the sound could flow freely. Yes, you can sing with a cork in your mouth, though not very well!

OTTO

Otto Guth was my first opera coach. Anyone who has ever had a great teacher knows how close a mentor relationship can be. A tiny man in his sixties, Otto became a father figure and a major force in my life. He lived in a studio in a high-rise near Lincoln Center, his grand piano taking up most of the apartment. Enthusiastic about his work, his cheerful energy was infectious, and I loved him from the moment we met.

Otto coached famous singers from the Metropolitan Opera, including Giorgio Tozzi, Martina Arroya, and even Leontyne Price, all of whom I met at lessons. I was honored he took me as a student.

The first opera I learned was the role of the countess in *The Marriage of Figaro,* in English. The opera consists of many arias interspersed with dialogue in the form of recitatives, a way of singing that was new to me. I stood in the curve of the piano facing him. As we worked, he would jump up, come around the piano and write something in my opera score to demonstrate how a musical phrase should be sung.

One day, Otto told me he thought I was ready to be in a workshop and asked me to audition at Mannes School of Music where he was head of the opera program. He would not be there for my audition because during the summer he worked at the Sydney Opera, and in the fall, in California where he headed the San Francisco Opera coaching staff.

I became sick and had to go to the audition with a cold, a problem I encountered throughout my singing career. I suffered from asthma, and the steam-heat system in my apartment didn't help. This was my first audition, and I was terrified. I got lost in the middle of "Dove Sono," a long aria the countess sings, and I fell apart. They did not take me.

I continued to work with Otto and the next year Mannes School of Music took me on scholarship. One of the roles I learned was Margarete from *Faust,* in French. I was to perform the love scene between Faust and Margarete. At the rehearsal, the tenor and I had to kiss. We started to giggle. We tried to stop laughing but were unable to calm down. The stage director stopped the rehearsal and sent us home.

The day of the performance I began to suffer from stage fright. *I can't go on,* I thought, *I'm too nervous and scared.* I went to Otto's apartment. "It's impossible for me to sing tonight," I told him.

"You know you have a better voice than the other students, don't you?" he said. "You must go on and that is all there is to it."

I went on. The tenor and I got through the kissing scene even though I had sat too far over on the bench, and he had to boot me with his rear end to have enough room to sit down.

■ ■ ■

Because I worked at United Airlines, I had flight passes, so could fly to the San Francisco Opera for lessons with Otto when he was there. I could take an early morning flight and arrive around ten a.m., take the lesson, and fly back to New York, all in one day—I did this about six times.

The next year I was also accepted as a student at Hunter College in their opera program. As classes began, it was obvious that the other singers were more advanced. I had little stage experience. When performance time came, once again I had a cold. My allergies continued to plague me. I watched someone else sing Gilda's aria, "Caro Nome," from *Rigoletto*. I was also still attending Mannes. I had classes at Hunter on Monday, Wednesday, and Friday, and at Mannes on Tuesday and Thursday. This was in addition to voice and coaching lessons and private Italian instruction, all while I continued to work at United Airlines. It was a heavy load.

More and more, the stress got to me. I began to cry at lessons with Otto. To be funny, he would make a show of putting a box of tissues on the piano. As he became more and more frustrated with me, he started to push. He wanted me to improve. Instead, I got worse.

At Mannes, I began to work on the role of Mimi in *La Boheme*. The night of the dress rehearsal, Otto, who was playing the piano, kept stopping me and making me repeat the first line of Mimi's aria, "Si Mi Chiamano Mimi" ("Yes, they call me Mimi"). He wouldn't let me get going with the aria. I didn't understand what I was doing wrong. I became unnerved and stomped off the stage, sobbing. Otto followed and cornered me in one of the classrooms where I verbally attacked him. I yelled and cried and asked how he expected me to sing when he kept stopping me. My nose started to drip. Embarrassed, I ran out of the room bawling. Classmates and another coach, Felix Popper stood around with their mouths open watching the drama. The rehearsal was over; everyone went home.

I had planned a cast party at my apartment for the next evening and had invited both Otto and Felix. In the morning, Otto called and said he was upset with our conversation and couldn't sleep the entire night.

"Do you still want me to come to your party?" he asked. "I love you. Do you still love me?"

I was overwhelmed.

"Of course I love you," I said. "Just because I'm mad at you doesn't affect how I feel."

Everyone came to the party. My apartment was crammed with singers. We sat on the floor, ate potato chips and dip, and listed to riotous opera stories offered by Otto and Felix. And the performance went well.

FELIX

At twenty-eight, I met Felix Popper at the Mannes School of Music where he was a coach with Otto. In addition to his work there, he had a powerful position at the New York City Opera. Like Otto, he was in his sixties and Viennese.

When I came out of the bathroom after my fight with Otto, Felix was waiting for me. We left the building together, and seeing how upset I was, he took me to dinner. He had always been friendly and would sometimes make jealous comments about my friendship with Otto.

We went to a quiet pub where we sat in a booth, drank beer, and ordered from a German menu. He told me Otto's story, about how he had lost his family in the Holocaust, and how fortunately, his family had sent him to London early on, where he joined the household of a friend of his mother, Lili Wexburg, a voice teacher. Otto became part of Lili's family and eventually they moved together to the United States.

Felix's family was also killed during the Holocaust. Through the kindness of a train conductor, he was able to escape. After making it to the United States he joined the army, and returned to Germany as a member of the Ritchie Boy's, an elite group of immigrants and refugees who spoke German, knew the culture, and who worked in the espionage section of the service.

Felix also told me about his wife, an accomplished singer. When they met, she was a twenty-two-year-old student at an opera workshop where he taught. They fell in love. At age forty-two he married her and they had a son. After she won a Fulbright Scholarship, she moved to Europe where she became a lead soprano at Munich Opera. She had lived there for ten years. Felix saw her and his son only once a year during his Christmas vacation, but he said he wrote to her every night before going to bed. I wondered how he was able to accept this situation and understood he was lonely. He must have loved her very much to agree to this arrangement.

It was a nurturing evening and it helped me calm down.

It was never the same with Otto after our blow up. I was too emotionally involved, and our teacher/student relationship wasn't good for me. After he left for Australia, I never returned to coach with him.

Years later, in 1974, Otto helped me get a job at San Francisco Opera. I saw him from time to time when he came on his annual trek to head the coaching staff. One year, Otto showed up with a cute wife, a translator at the United Nations. I was happy for him. Then sadly, he developed Parkinson's disease and died in 1979 at age sixty-seven, only a few years after his marriage. I started a memorial fund in his name at the Merola Opera Program, where I was executive director, and as far as I know, to this day a singer receives a scholarship in his name.

After my classes at Mannes ended, I began private coaching with Felix and worked with him in one of the rehearsal rooms at New York City Opera. We became closer. I started to visit him at the theater without an appointment and he always had time for me. I shared my career frustrations, and he reported the events at the evening's opera performance. I recall his saying, "The more things are going wrong, the calmer I get."

Soon, Felix offered me lessons without payment. Although I had very little money, I worried this indicated he wanted a closer relationship. Although I had strong feelings for him, I didn't want to be beholden to him. I also felt that Felix was out of my league and could harm me emotionally if I got too involved.

I joined a workshop run by Patricia Neway, a dramatic soprano who had sung at New York City Opera. She was famous for her role as Magda in Menotti's opera, *The Consul*. Neway liked to work on contemporary operas and selected an aria from the role of Baby Doe Tabor in the opera *Ballad of Baby Doe* for me to perform.

On the night of the performance, Felix showed up then left after I sang. I swelled with pride. I knew he was interested in my vocal progress. The cast was impressed but disappointed he hadn't stayed to hear them sing.

One evening, after I had coached with Felix for two years, he made an announcement. "Alice, my wife is coming back to the United States," he said. "I won't be able to work with you anymore. Since this is the last time I will see you, I want to ask you something. I always thought you wouldn't have an affair with me and that is why I never tried. Would you have had an affair with me?"

Startled, I said, "I don't know. I guess I was afraid."

I walked out of the theater, my head spinning. He was a lovely man and I loved him. But he was at least thirty years older than me and married. I saw him more as a father figure. I wasn't good at saying "no" to men, and I wondered what I would have done if he had made a pass. In any case, my answer to his question was perfect. It did not offend him and at the same time let him know I might have responded in a positive way.

■ ■ ■

After that, I saw Felix now and then. He died in 2000 at age ninety-two. He requested that in lieu of flowers, people send donations to the Parkinson's Disease Foundation, perhaps thinking of his friend, Otto, who died of the disease. Felix is a pleasant memory, and I'm glad he was in my life. He was always there to encourage me when I was depressed about my career and to give me confidence when I performed.

CHAPTER FIVE

NEW YORK ADVENTURES

INCIDENT ON 12TH STREET

Trauma increases the risk of misinterpreting whether
a particular situation is dangerous or safe.
—Bessel Van Der Kolk, M.D.

ONE EVENING IN 1965, I EXITED THE SUBWAY AT TWELFTH Street and Broadway on my way home from work. I was wearing heels which enhanced my already five feet nine-inch height. A man approached me. He looked to be in his fifties and was short with thinning hair. Out of breath, he said, "Can I talk to you?"

"Sure," I replied.

In rapid-fire speech, he declared, "I'm working on my graduate thesis and am conducting an experiment at the nearby New School. I am wondering if you could help me. I would pay you $20."

Some women would have run away fast. I asked, "What kind of experiment?"

"I am conducting scientific research and am in the midst of clinical trials," he said. "I would need you to accompany me to the experimental laboratory at the school." He said his wife would be there and

59

the experiment involved measuring pain thresholds. "For example, a woman in childbirth would rate at fifteen, whereas a bee sting might rate at three," he said. "I will be hooked up to a machine that measures pain. The experiment will consist of you standing, in your high heels, for one minute on my back, and one minute on my chest. My wife will monitor my pain and measure my discomfort."

It was all very unusual. "I don't know," I said. "At the New School?"

"Yes. And remember, my wife will be there, and you will be part of an important research project. It will help me with my thesis, and I will pay you twenty-five dollars."

The pay had just gone up by five dollars.

The man's rushed speech left me confused and I couldn't compute exactly what he was saying. *If it is a clinical trial and his wife will be there, I guess I could help. The money would pay for voice lessons,* I thought. Still, I hesitated.

His voice rose to a squeak as he repeated his request. "Please help me," he pleaded. "I'll pay you thirty dollars."

I didn't question the veracity of his story because I knew the New School had a "New Age" type curriculum and offered courses that wouldn't be on the schedule of other schools.

"My boyfriend is at home waiting for me. Could we perform the experiment on another day?"

"Oh no," he said, now looking disturbed. "My thesis is due soon, and my wife is waiting. We had someone else lined up to help. She cancelled at the last minute. I'm desperate. Please, please help. It won't take very long, I promise."

"Well, okay, if it won't take long."

We walked down the street in the general direction of the school. He started to sweat and became more agitated.

"Thank you, thank you, thank you," he repeated. "I'll be so happy to get my thesis completed. This experiment is the last one. I really appreciate your help."

We approached the door of a hospital with the word "Saint" in the title. He stopped, opened the door, and ushered me in.

This is not the New School, I thought, uneasily. *Maybe I misunderstood where the experiment is to take place. But this is a hospital.*

I continued to follow him as we walked past the front desk. Three nurses watched. We walked around the corner. He opened a door to the stairway.

"The experiment will take place here on the floor," he said pointing at the cement.

Shocked, I suddenly understood. I turned around and ran past the three startled nurses. Their heads swung right as he followed me in hot pursuit.

"I'll let you drive my car and I'll pay you thirty-five dollars," he yelled.

At home, my boyfriend Ralph was furious, and explained that some people received physical pleasure from pain. My therapy group also reminded me to be more astute in my interactions with the world.

■ ■ ■

Years later, I discovered information that convinced me who this 12th Street character was. In 2020, I purchased a newly published book by Stephen Kinzer, called *Poisoner in Chief: Sidney Gottlieb and the CIA Search for Mind Control.* In chapter five, "Abolishing Consciousness," I came across a man named George Hunter White. He had certain personal qualities that made him perfect to head a secret "safe house," where experiments were carried out clandestinely. The group hired prostitutes and lured men to the house where they'd be given drugs like LSD so the "scientists" could study the effects.

White was a drug user and an alcoholic drinker who had a taste for sexual fetishism, especially sadomasochism and high heels and he enjoyed kinky scenes involving leather boots. Not surprisingly, this got my attention. Then I read that he had an apartment on 12th Street in New York and would have used the same subway exit I did.

A simple internet search provided numerous photos of White, whom I recognized as the man who accosted me in 1965. I shudder to think would have happened if I had gotten into his clutches.

This episode provides an example of how my denial worked. Even though an awareness of sadomasochism lurked at the back of my mind, I refused to recognize it. Looking back, I believe if had I acknowledged what was going on, memories of sadomasochistic techniques used to bend my will when I was eight years old may have risen to the surface of my mind. Repressing my knowledge helped me avoid confronting my memories.

ACTING CLASSES

In New York, I often avoided certain experiences without consciously understanding why. In 1967, wanting to improve my acting skills, I signed up for classes at a studio run by Irene Daily, the sister of Dan Dailey, a popular movie actor and dance man of the 1930s and '40s. We performed exercises to help us become comfortable with our bodies and learn how to let go of inhibitions. I hopped around the studio pretending to be a howling monkey and myriad other animals. We sat on the floor in a daisy chain, our legs wrapped around each other, and scooted across the room.

After a few weeks the teacher told us we would start working on dialogue. At this point, without reason, I quit the class. The teacher called and asked why.

"I was uncomfortable with the exercises," I said.

For years I wondered why I did this. It was fun and I was not uncomfortable. It was something about the daisy chain exercise and working on dialogue that bothered me. Unconsciously, I now believe I was worried the class would bring up memories I was not yet ready to receive.

In 1993, more than four years after my memory returned, I had a dream that relates to my experiences of being accosted on 12th Street and leaving the acting class.

DREAM: "The Lizards Are Having Sex"
November 23, 1993. 4 years and 2 months after my memory returned.

A lizard runs up a wall to a group of others. They are sitting on top of each other having sex. It is like a daisy chain. The one on the end switches and another one takes its place. I notice a lizard going up and down on a toy. I am amazed because I didn't think a lizard had the intelligence to figure out you could do that with a toy. I concentrate on who I can report this activity to because it looks scientific.

An aspect of this dream made me think I was being hypnotized. A doctor said we were carrying out a scientific experiment and asked me to help.

SUBWAY CRUSH

In 1969, I was thirty years old and still working at a United Airlines ticket counter. One night I had stayed with my then-boyfriend John at his apartment in the Ansonia Hotel. To get to work, I had to take the subway from 72nd and Broadway to Times Square, where I transferred to the cross-town shuttle. I wore a belted light-weight gray raincoat that came to just above my knees — the style at the time. My hair was opera-diva long and bleached blond. (I wanted to look like Mary Costa, who was a beautiful well-known soprano at the time.) I was carrying a large purse and a briefcase full of opera scores.

It was rush-hour. The subway platform was extremely crowded, and when the express train arrived, there was a push of humanity to get onto it. I was crushed among a mass of commuters, the car so packed that the door could barely close, and I couldn't even see my feet. Suddenly, I felt something rubbing near my upper thigh, which, I assumed, must have been someone's bag. I turned so my briefcase provided a barrier, only for a tickling to begin on the opposite side. I turned a little more. A third rubbing started below my back. I looked at the faces around me. I was surrounded by three late-teenage boys, their faces blank with innocence.

It must be my imagination, I thought. Surely these boys wouldn't be touching me. I began to feel more and more uncomfortable as the rubbing increased in intensity. Because I couldn't see what was happening, I began to panic. *Should I scream? People will think I'm crazy.*

The five-minute ride became an eternity. The rubbing kept getting stronger and I was near hysterical when the train finally came to a jolting stop. The doors opened and the crowd fell away. In one split second, as I looked down, I saw that all three of those boys had their pants unzipped, and their penises out. In a flash they were gone. Stunned, I stumbled out of the car and was in a daze on the shuttle train to Grand Central. The first person I saw when I walked into my office was a male colleague.

"I was just molested on the subway by three men who were rubbing me with their penises," I blurted out.

Embarrassed, he responded, "You know what they always say, just lie back and enjoy it!"

Later, when I told Otto, he didn't give me any understanding or support either. I expected more from my beloved voice coach, but that's the way men dealt with these types of issues in those days—matter of fact, get over it.

I didn't tell anybody else about this incident for many years. When I eventually told a therapist, I learned that what these young men did is called "frottage," meaning "the act of rubbing against the body of another person, as in a crowd, to attain sexual gratification." Back then, no one thought that kind of thing was a big deal—it was just some stupid guys rubbing up against me. But I was troubled by the boys' intent as much as the act itself, as well as the lack of respect behind their actions, and their attempts to obtain sexual gratification from an unwilling participant. They picked me out on the subway platform, plotted their actions, and trapped me where they knew I probably wouldn't defend myself.

Some experiences don't go away. I never got onto a crowded subway car again. As with other disturbing experiences in my life, I just moved on. Nevertheless, the incident threatened my repressed memory, and it wasn't the only one.

THE PERFECT HIGH C

One night in 1969, I was riding the subway in a white chiffon dress and high heels on my way to the Bronx to sing a solo at a church. When I reached my stop, I walked pass the toll booth and entered the long exit tunnel.

I felt a man's breath on my neck. "You're gonna get it, you're gonna get it. You can't go around doing things like that. I'm warning you," he said.

I walked faster.

His voice grew louder. "You're gonna get it, you're gonna get it."

Suddenly, his arm reached over my shoulder and grabbed me tightly across my breasts.

His hand jabbed up between my legs.

"Aaaaaah!" My scream echoed down the subway corridor.

He swung me around. I faced him. His eyes narrowed.

"That's what you get when you go around doing things like that. This is only a warning. Next time it will be worse."

Bewildered, I thought, *what had I done?*

Reason came. I had done nothing.

Courage came. "You better stay away from me!" I said in the meanest voice I could muster.

Surprised, he turned and disappeared down the subway corridor.

Denial came. I ran up the stairs and down the street. *That was a perfect high C,* I thought.

I walked to church, sang my solo, and told no one.

THE BAIL BONDSMAN

One evening, on a Carry Bus to Kennedy International Airport, the man next to me started a conversation. Robert, a bail bondsman, was rugged and muscular, about six feet tall with a craggy pock-marked face. He asked for my telephone number and said he would call for a date.

We went to dinner at a restaurant on the East Side in mid-town Manhattan, and I discovered he had a checkered past. He had just returned from Miami where he had captured a bail jumper. At age sixteen, he and another culprit were caught robbing a safe, and in his attempt to get away, Robert had thrown a wrench at the policeman, hitting his head and scraping his skull. The policeman suffered brain damage and lived in a vegetative state for the rest of his life. Because he was underage, Robert received a ten-year prison sentence, a light term considering the damage he had done.

At this point, I could have become fearful and excused myself. But I didn't feel in danger and I was interested in his story. Besides, I reasoned, it wouldn't be nice to just get up and leave. During his first year in prison, Robert confessed, he had spent two three-month stints in solitary confinement. His first stint in "the hole" was punishment for attacking a guard who had pushed his face in his food. The second time, he'd been violent because another prisoner had tried to rape him at knifepoint. After that, an older prisoner befriended and protected him.

After a few years of good behavior, he was given a job in the prison hospital where corruption was rampant. He stole morphine from the infirmary and disguised the theft by filling the partially empty vials with water—all for some spending money.

"Wasn't that dangerous for the people who were given the left-over morphine?" I asked.

"You bet," he replied. "It hurt like hell for them. But I was expected to do it by the prison gang and would have been in trouble if I hadn't." As he continued his story, he said, "You are easy to talk to."

Robert went on to share that in Detroit, where he had grown up, he knew members of the Mafia. I sat wide-eyed, listening to his story, and wondering if he was telling me the truth. There was nothing in his manner to suggest he was a bad person. Although his English wasn't perfect, he was polite and considerate toward me.

After dinner, he suggested we go for a drink at an upscale bar nearby. We walked a few blocks when he suddenly stopped in front of a third-rate pub.

"I want to go in here for a few minutes," he said. "We'll go to the other place afterwards."

The pub had a seven-seat bar and a pool table in the back. The space was dark, dingy, and I quickly determined I was the only woman there.

Not knowing what to order, I asked Robert to suggest something. He ordered me an Ouzo, which the bartender promptly set on fire.

He seemed to know the bartender and another older man who approached us. After introductions, Robert excused himself and went to the men's room. I was uncomfortable being left alone, but the new man engaged me in conversation.

"You could make a lot of money in Puerto Rico," he said.

"Really," I replied, not knowing how to respond. He obviously thought I was a call girl.

When Robert didn't return, I noticed he was playing pool in the back, so I joined him. Eventually, he excused himself, and said good-bye to everyone.

"Would you mind taking a walk over to the East River?" he asked. "We can sit by the water and talk."

We walked until we got to a gas station by the river.

"I need to use the bathroom," he said.

"Me too," I replied.

When I came out, I heard lots of flushing in the men's room. I moved to the gas pumps and waited for him. Two male attendants watched me. It took Robert at least ten minutes to return.

"Let's go sit by the river," he said.

It was then I noticed he didn't have his jacket.

"Where's your jacket?" I asked.

"Never mind," he replied.

I persisted. "What happened to your jacket?"

"Nothing."

"You left it in the john."

"Be quiet! Don't ask so many questions," he said, looking nervously at the gas-station attendants. I started to protest again, but he raised his hand in a "be quiet" motion.

I didn't mention the jacket again. Robert escorted me to the river, and we sat with our legs dangling over the wood pilings against the water. The gas station was empty, and the lights reflected off the water as our talk resumed. "I have a friend with a yacht," he said. "Would you like to go with me and my friends on a cruise some time?"

"I'll think about it," I replied.

"I'm tired of being with prostitutes," he said with a sigh. "I want to find a nice girl, get married, and have a son. I have ten thousand dollars saved and will leave it in my will to whoever gives me a son. The girl wouldn't even have to love me. We would make a deal—she could have the money and I would have a son."

I had the feeling he was wondering if I would consider being the mother of his child. I kept quiet.

Robert was nervous, always looking over his shoulder.

"My life is rough and dangerous," he said. "I don't think I will live much longer." We walked the two flights of stairs to my apartment. He asked to see me again.

"Frankly, you have just about scared me to death, and I don't think it would be a good idea," I said, and shut the door.

It was much later that I could see and feel the peril I could have been in. Why did he want to stop at that low-life bar? What was the deal with his jacket? Was he a drug or money courier? Why did he think he didn't have long to live? It was another example of the denial that allowed me to take chances I wouldn't have otherwise.

LEDERHOSEN

In 1969, I worked for about a year as a singing hostess at the Alpine Cellar in the McAlpine Hotel on 34th Street and Broadway, a couple of blocks from my apartment on 33rd Street. I worked there several evenings a week to make extra money, and it was my first professional singing gig. I sang opera arias, Broadway musical comedy numbers,

Singing at the Alpine Cellar cir. 1969.

and popular songs. The Cellar, as it was referred to, was in the basement of the hotel. It was a large room with a long bar, cocktail lounge, dance floor, and an enormous dining space. Round tables covered with black and white tablecloths dotted the room, and the dim lighting provided a romantic ambiance. The theme of the restaurant was Bavarian and twenty-minute singing sets alternated with dancing. A grand piano, situated in the middle of the room, was the centerpiece. I was one of three female singers along with a baritone. We all wore lederhosen.

Singing there was fun. In addition to the easy work, free meals, and enjoyable music, we received tips from the patrons. Once, after I sang "When You Wish Upon a Star," a generous patron handed me twenty-five dollars—that was worth two-and-a-half singing lessons.

BICYCLE ROMANCE

A twenty-dollar bicycle was part of my New York life for several years in the late sixties. I rode that bike up and down Manhattan to opera workshops, voice coaching, and Italian and French lessons. To the movies, too. I darted in and out of traffic, passing taxis and slow buses. Late at night, after rehearsals, I sped home down Fifth Avenue. As sweat poured down my face, I carried the bike up three flights of stairs and hung it on a hook in my closet.

On Sundays, my best friend Joan and then boyfriend Kingsley would join me. We would spend the day in Central Park, riding from 59th Street to 110th Street. We enjoyed ice cream at the boathouse and took the ferry to Staten Island to ride to the beach. My bicycle adventures were endless.

Exercise helped me get in touch with my body and eased the stresses of my life. It helped with my low self-esteem, brought balance to my life, and helped me live more fully. When I think of New York now, I don't think about the dangerous moments or difficult situations. I see myself riding through Central Park on a sunny afternoon. It was the happiest time of my life. I was young, looked good, was busy, and was having fun.

Carrying my bike down three floors at my apartment on 33rd Street.

CHAPTER SIX

ITALIAN MEN

NEW YORK, 1970–1972

VINCENT

BY 1970, I HAD LIVED IN NEW YORK FOR NINE YEARS. I had worked with six voice teachers and numerous opera coaches. Italian, French, and German teachers had helped me learn operatic roles. I had participated in five different opera workshops including those at Hunter College and Mannes School of Music. Two well-known coaches had taken me as a student. What I needed now was an opportunity to learn and perform complete operatic roles.

One day while riding my bicycle, I stopped to talk with a singer friend who happened to be walking by. I noticed a man talking to students on the sidewalk in front of Juilliard School of Music.

"Do you know who that man is?" I asked. He was looking at me and I was curious who he might be.

"Sure, that's Vincent La Selva," my friend said. "He's a professor at Juilliard and a conductor. I hear he has launched The New York School of Opera and will teach repertoire. You might consider auditioning."

My heart jumped. I had quit my singing job at the McAlpine Hotel and was looking for something to do. Plus, he was Italian. Although he wasn't handsome, I was attracted to him immediately. A week later, I decided on the spur of the moment to drop in to sing for him. I walked my bicycle into a side entrance and took the elevator. As I exited on the second floor, there, staring at me was Maestro La Selva. He got up from behind his desk and walked toward me, a startled look on his face.

"Hi. I'm Alice Cunningham. I've come to sing for you," I said.

Seemingly charmed, he laughed. "In that case, come on in."

I leaned my bike against the hall wall and entered his office.

"I've been operating for about two months and am just getting organized," he said. "What kind of voice do you have?"

"I'm a lyric soprano."

"Good. I'm about to start a class for *La Boheme*. Would you like to learn Mimi, or Musetta?"

"Both!"

"Let's set a time for you to audition, then," he said. "My pianist isn't here."

A few days later I auditioned with *Madame Butterfly*'s entrance aria hoping to impress him with my high D flat. He liked my voice and accepted me as a student. The class cost $110 for ten weekly rehearsals and a performance.

Thus began the two most exciting years of my life. Vincent, aged forty-two, was masculine, charismatic, and had a strong personality. He had all the characteristics we tend to associate with powerful Italians—forceful, emotional, and expressive. Music came out of his fingertips, and it was exhilarating to be around him.

Vincent gave me a tour of the school. Classes were held in what was once a ballet studio. The room had a cathedral ceiling, and stained-glass windows lined the wall near the top. A grand piano, a couple of chairs, and a music stand were the only furniture in the large space. An anteroom around the corner connected to a large closet for props and was next to a dressing room with mirrors.

Vincent had three volunteers helping him: a set designer named Walter Harper, who was a tenor and a student; a beautiful young woman named Kay Jay who was a costume designer and stage manager; and Janice Yoes, an excellent pianist and dramatic soprano. Before I knew it, I was also a volunteer. For two weeks, along with other students, we painted, built a stage, and installed lighting. Then, we were ready to put on operas.

Kay Jay was Vincent's "number-one girl." One of her jobs was rubbing Vincent's back, which was always sore from waving his arms so much conducting rehearsals and performances. I hung around and took orders, arriving each free evening after work and on weekends.

Rehearsals for *Madame Butterfly* had already begun. In the meantime, I began to learn the part of Musetta for the *La Boheme* performances.

Vincent held a different opera class every night. Students sat in sections according to voice type and we all sang the entire opera together. As classes continued, Vincent taught us the stage directions. Hundreds of singers came and went.

One day, Kay Jay simply disappeared, and I became Vincent's Girl Friday, also in charge of back massage. We became best friends. He gave me the keys to the school so I could come and go whenever I needed. Each morning I couldn't wait to get to the school and spend time with him.

When an opportunity came to cut back my hours at United Airlines, I jumped at the chance. Now I was able to spend four full days a week at the school. I showed up at ten a.m. and left at midnight. My biggest responsibility was scheduling, which I did for all the rehearsals and performances. I also became stage manager. In *Cavalleria Rusticana* I yelled in the most blood curdling cry I could muster, "Hanno amazatto compare Turridu!" ("They have killed friend Turridu!"). Using my sewing skills, I made most of the costumes for *L'Elisir D'Amore* and *Turandot*. Over the two years I was with Vincent I learned and performed eight roles. We produced more than a hundred performances of eleven operas. In one month, I was involved in sixteen performances and two outside professional gigs. At the same time, I planned and organized a school birthday party for Vincent. Two-hundred people attended.

Singing the role of Adina in the opera, *L'Elisir d'Amore*, 1971.

Vincent was very exciting to be around. When we walked down the street together, he would invariably run into someone he knew. We would stop to talk and before long he and the other party would be arguing, Italian curse words reverberating down the street. I could soon repeat these Italian words although I didn't have a clue as to what they meant. Vincent wouldn't tell me.

One evening a soprano had the gall to complain that she wasn't getting enough rehearsal time. Vincent became a raving maniac. He screamed and yelled obscenities and told the girl she was an ingrate. He then picked up a metal chair and threw it at the wall. I had to listen to him complain for two days about how he had taken her out of the gutter.

Another night, a man in the audience booed the tenor. As it turned out, the soprano's friends had come to the performance and displayed their disapproval. Vincent became enraged and decided to track down the culprit. As a group of us walked down the street, we spotted the offender in the corner restaurant. We stood at the window and watched as Vincent ran into the crowded restaurant and in a loud voice yelled curse words, flailed his arms, and made insulting Roman gestures.

When Vincent returned to our group, his furious comment was, "The guy said he had a right to boo because he put money in the basket."

My tenor friend John then suggested, "Give him his money back!"

"Good idea," responded Vincent. He turned and ran back into the restaurant and threw money at the miscreant.

One rainy night, Vincent asked our cab driver to wait while he bought a newspaper at the newsstand. Suddenly, I heard a gunshot and saw a man run across the street and jump the median. Vincent ran back to the cab.

"Someone shot at me," he loudly exclaimed. "A bum asked me for a quarter, and I refused him. I think he's the one who tried to shoot me."

Instead of telling the driver to get the hell out of there, he said, "Drive around. I want to find the guy."

We drove up and down the street but couldn't find the shooter. Vincent learned the next day that the man next to him at the newspaper stand had been shot in the leg.

I stayed with Vincent most evenings until the school closed and then we took a city bus to the Port Authority terminal at Broadway and 34th Street, where I walked him to the bus that took him to New Jersey and his wife and three kids. He would buy grapes at a fruit stand and spit seeds as we ambled along. I waited with him until the bus was ready to leave and then walked home to my apartment on 33rd Street. The bus driver thought I was Vincent's girlfriend. "Where's the blonde?" he would ask when I wasn't there, or so Vincent said.

One lunchtime when we were having our usual pea soup at the local diner, Vincent said, "If I was going to have an affair with anyone at the school it would be you. But you are too nice a girl. I will never leave my wife and I wouldn't want to do that to you."

I was speechless. Though I was crazy about him, I never imagined being intimate with him. While he was only twelve years older than me, I saw him as a father figure. I certainly didn't want to ruin our relationship with an affair.

We never spoke of it again.

■ ■ ■

One night, I didn't go to the school and instead went to an audition. A woman by the name of Virginia Moore was looking for someone to sing the role of Violetta in *La Traviata*. The character was a wildly popular courtesan and I loved her. Over the years I had read many books on famous women who were favorites of kings and for some reason I felt I could do a good job in portraying Violetta.

Moore offered me the role. I would get to perform four or five times with an orchestra. It was a great opportunity and I wanted to do it. When I excitedly told Vincent about the invitation, he blew up.

"I taught you the role," he shouted. "How dare you go to another group and give them the benefit of my time and energy. You are ungrateful. I plan to give you a party and a professional performance of the role at some time in the future."

We argued, I cried, and then I gave up. It wasn't worth losing him as a friend and I didn't know how to stand up to him.

Right then, although I didn't realize it at the time, I gave up my dream. Any singer whose career means everything would not have turned down such an opportunity.

■ ■ ■

One day I ran into Carolyn, a beautiful Italian mezzo friend with long black hair and a gorgeous voice. I suggested she come to sing for Vincent. She followed up and soon became a member of the school. Next thing I knew, while I was cleaning the dressing room, she was in Vincent's office with the door closed, rubbing his back.

Not surprisingly, I became jealous, but tried to control it.

"You are my friend, and I would never do anything to hurt you," Carolyn assured me. She gave me photographs taken during my performances, called me just to chat, helped around the school, and even invited me to her place for dinner.

Whenever I think of Caroline, I think of Betty Davis and Anne Baxter in *All About Eve*. Like Baxter's character, she was all smiles and sweetness while at the same time moving in on Vincent.

I knew that Vincent cared for me, but that he was also attracted to Carolyn. I probably could have put up with the situation for longer than I did because when it came down to it, she had to go home to her husband. Yes, she was married. But the situation had evolved to the point that I was doing all the dirty jobs while she was in Vincent's office with the door closed. My resentment grew to the point that I became an emotional wreck. I told Vincent that he was "putting fire to the flame" regarding Carolyn's marriage. She spent more time at the school than she did with her husband and son. Vincent didn't want to hear it.

Soon I was called back to United Airlines to work fulltime. I was no longer able to volunteer so many hours at the school. However, Vincent decided he wanted to add a performance of Puccini's opera, *Turandot,* with one day's notice, while simultaneously, *Don Carlo* was in production. Both are huge operas and would be performed on the same day.

"I can't do it," I told him. "I'm tired."

He insisted.

I cried and took a walk before the evening performance to calm down. In Central Park I took in big gulps of air and kicked around a few rocks. The voice in my head was clear: *I've got to leave. I've got to leave. I don't like what I've become.* By the end of that walk, I knew what I had to do. Returning to the school, I went into Vincent's office and placed the school keys on his desk. I planned to walk out at the end of the performance. He found the keys, and as singers stood around watching, he tried to give them back to me. I refused and walked out.

Years later, when I was in New York City running auditions for the San Francisco Opera, Vincent and I met for lunch.

"I got into a lot of trouble after you left," he told me. "I started an affair with Carolyn. It was a big mess. She called my wife who gave me an ultimatum. I had to pick. I could never leave my wife," he added with a shrug, and, of course, he didn't.

BENITO

During my time working with Vincent, I met another Italian man who became a fixture in my life for a time. My friend Joannie and I had gone for a bike ride and stopped at a pizza parlor for lunch. At the counter was an Italian waiter who spoke English. Because I had been studying Italian, Joannie encouraged me to practice by speaking with him.

In broken Italian, I told him that I was a singer studying opera.

"That guy over there," he said, pointing at a man on the telephone, "is an Italian, and an opera singer."

We turned and a good-looking man with dark curly hair hung up the receiver and approached us, smiling.

"Sono Benito Cuzzone," he said, extending his hand.

We introduced ourselves and quickly learned that Benito was in the United States on vacation, was a tenor, and sang in the chorus at the Geneva Opera in Switzerland. He spoke some English, and I spoke some Italian, and thus we were able to communicate well enough to invite him to join us for dinner at Margarette and Bianchi's restaurant in Greenwich Village where patrons were invited to sing.

At the restaurant, Benito sang the popular Italian song, "O Sole Mio." He was charming, had an expressive voice, and was well received. Later, as we walked home, Benito serenaded us with various operatic arias.

Benito and I got along well. He ended up spending the night with me. In the morning, because I was enjoying practicing my rudimentary Italian, I invited him to stay with me until he returned to Italy in one month. He enthusiastically accepted.

Benito's olive-toned skin added to his good looks. At only five-feet-nine, he was about my height, and when not singing opera, was a professional stone mason, and had a solid muscular build. Although I liked him, I saw him primarily as a friend and my interest in him was mostly to learn Italian, a skill that would help my career. It wasn't too long before, when singing in Italian, I understood the words as I sang them, which helped with my acting.

We settled in for the month. I kept up my regular schedule and he cooked dinner. I had been in New York for more than ten years at that point and had many contacts in the operatic world, so I could help Benito with his career. I set him up with an operatic coach and sent him to sing for Vincent, who took him on as a student and gave him an acceptance letter to facilitate his return to the States on a student visa.

A month after Benito returned to Italy, he invited me to visit him and meet his family. My airline benefits enabled me to buy a ticket on

Alitalia for $99. Benito met me at the Rome airport and drove me to his parents' home in Venafro, a tiny town located near Naples.

His parents lived in a small two-story, two-bedroom house abutting similar houses on each side. The entry to the house was directly from an unpaved street. Downstairs was a kitchen and living room and upstairs two bedrooms with a water closet in between. His parents occupied one bedroom, and when at home, Benito shared a twin-bedded room with his teenage brother. I was installed in Benito's room with his mother in the other twin bed. Benito slept with his father and the teenage brother slept on the couch in the living room. Although his mother and I struggled to communicate, I was able to discern that she was worried about his pending return to America. I endeavored to assure her he would be okay.

The next day Benito and I visited Naples, took a ferry to Capri for lunch, and returned to visit the U.S. Embassy in Naples, where Benito planned to obtain an educational visa. I waited in the lobby while he talked with the Consul. When Benito emerged from his office he was clearly upset: they would not give him a visa. I asked to speak to the Consul who informed me they were tired of Italian men using American women to get into the U.S. and were not going to allow it.

The fact that he had a letter from the New York School of the Opera made no difference. (In 1980 when I read movie star Shelly Winters' autobiography, *Shelly, also known as Shirley,* I learned that her then Italian movie star boyfriend, and eventual husband, Victorio Gassman, was also refused a visa for the same reason.)

As I walked across the street from the embassy, a man pinched me on my rear end. Later, I mentioned this to Benito, and he berated me for allowing that to happen, stating he would be forced to fight the man and could get killed. This was when I began to understand that Benito had old-fashioned Italian ideas about a woman's place in the world. Men like him thought women potentially dangerous to their honor and therefore best kept under wraps.

On the way home, he pointed to a row of houses on a nearby hill and told me, "Mafia men live there."

"How do you know that?" I asked.

"Non ti preoccupare," he replied. (Never mind.) This was a phrase he subsequently used throughout our relationship when he didn't want to explain something.

Back at the house, his family prepared for dinner as I rested. Benito's brother came into the bedroom to get something and shyly attempted to speak to me. When Benito realized his brother was with me, he kicked him out, and scolded me for allowing him to be there.

"Murders can happen between brothers when a woman gets between them," he informed me.

Shortly thereafter, I heard a loud argument. Angry voices echoed up the stairs. Benito then shouted at me from below.

"Alice, viene qui." Alice, come here.

In trepidation, I walked down the stairs and entered the dining room where I found myself facing a room crowded with expectant family and friends, his two sisters' families having arrived.

"Tu voi sposarme, si or no?" Benito asked in a stern voice. "Do you want to marry me, yes or no?"

Taken aback, I replied, "No voglio parlare di questo qui." I don't want to speak of this here.

Undeterred, he repeated the question again, firmly, "Tu voi sposarme, si or no?"

Understanding I had to answer, I took a breath and replied, "No!"

To my surprise, the room relaxed. I had evidently given the correct response. I later came to understand that the family, like the consul, was concerned about Benito's motives for returning to the United States.

The next morning, Benito and I departed for Geneva. He had decided to introduce me to his voice teacher and wanted to show me where he lived. I would be returning to the U.S. from there.

Benito was short on cash, and we spent a miserable night sleeping in the car in a parking lot at an autostrada way station, with men peeking in the window and jeering. Outside of Milan, we drove the car onto a train that took us into Switzerland. In Geneva, we stayed in Benito's tiny one-room apartment with no kitchen and a bathroom down the hall featuring a hole in the floor. After another horrible night in the apartment, we toured Geneva and met his voice teacher. Benito then announced that we were going to visit a gambling casino in the mountains. This terrified me.

While Benito was off gambling, I sat next to the craps table box man and leaned into him for security. There was something about him that made me feel safe and I thought he would protect me. Over the course of the evening, Benito won thirty dollars, but then, feeling cocky, proceeded to lose it. I refused when he asked to borrow money from me to continue gambling. I was anxious and frightened the entire time we were there.

The next day I flew home and was glad to be back in my own bed.

CHAPTER SEVEN

MY LAST PERFORMANCE

You change your dreams, and then you grow up.
—Emma Stone as Mia in *La La Land*

NEW YORK AND NEWARK, 1972–1974

THE FALLING OUT WITH VINCENT LEFT ME WITH A VOID IN my life. For the most part of two years, I had spent every waking hour with him. I still had a coaching lesson once a week with a woman named Virginia Gerhardt. I was so depressed I began to cry at lessons, and I told her my troubles.

"I don't know what I will do with myself," I admitted. "I've spent so much time with Vincent."

"I know Alfredo Silipigni," she said. He was the artistic director and conductor of Opera Theater of New Jersey. "I can call him and tell him about you. He might like a volunteer."

Another Italian and a conductor, I thought.

Alfredo asked me to meet him at the Russian Tea Room, the iconic restaurant on 57th Street that was a celebrity haunt at the time, and we sat in one of the famous red leather booths that lined the walls. When he learned I could type, he gave me the script dialogue for Johann Strauss's *Die Fledermaus*, which was to be their next production, starring Roberta Peters. The text needed serious cuts and he wanted someone to re-type the dialogue. I enthusiastically attacked my typewriter and a few days later brought the altered wording to the first rehearsal.

This change in my life brought my operatic aspirations into question. I was thirty-two years old and felt my career was going nowhere. I was tired of having no money, and I needed to secure my future. Still working part time at United Airlines, I now spent the entire rest of my day in Newark, or at rehearsals in Manhattan. Alfredo and I got along very well. He was Italian after all.

The "maestro," as I called him, was an excellent pianist and famed for the operalogues he gave for donors before performances. He would discuss the opera, play the musical themes, and provide context about the composer. These evenings were enjoyable and learning opportunities. However, he was also a male chauvinist who freely admitted he would have no problem sleeping with a singer one night and then firing her the next day.

Before long, he suggested I apply for a living-expenses grant from the National Opera Institute while I apprenticed at New Jersey Opera Theater. I promptly filled out the application and used my background as a singer and experience at the New York School of the Opera to give credence to my application.

Virginia Gerhardt gave me a glowing recommendation:

Miss Cunningham has had the experience of scores of performances with Mr. Vincent La Selva, the director of the New York School of the Opera, where she has sung a number of roles, and where she has, to put it succinctly, done everything else there is to do except conduct. She has worked lights, built scenery, made costumes and props, and stage managed the actual performances. I have observed her during these times, and found that she always maintains her poise and is not upset by emergencies. She has that elusive and desirable quality of initiative. She is also responsible and can be depended upon.

Besides such skills and seemingly boundless energy, Miss Cunningham has even more significantly a most pleasing manner of dealing with people. In fact, she told me that this is her prime interest. She is sensitive and perceptive, sympathetic, and yet seems naturally endowed with common sense and a straightforward manner. People like her, and more important, trust her and depend on her.

A few months later I received word that I had been accepted for the grant. The stipend provided $1,500 for six months, not much to live on. But I was happy, and not knowing what the future would bring, retired from United Airlines after eleven years.

OPERA GRANT RENEWED

The National Opera Institute in Washington, D. C. headed by George London has granted Miss Alice Cunningham a six months extension to her grant as an apprentice to the Opera Theatre. She is working in the field of Opera Management.

Miss Cunningham joined Opera Theatre as a a volunteer in June of 1972. At that time she was pursuing a career in opera singing and working part time at United Air Lines. Deciding that singing was not for her and wanting to continue in the field of opera, Maestro Silipigni suggested that she apply for a grant in Opera Management from the National Opera Institute and apprentice to the Opera Theatre. Taking his suggestion, she made application in August and was accepted for her first six months in February of 1973. Miss Cunningham took a leave of absence from United Air Lines at that time, but with the extension of her grant has decided to make opera her life work and has thus resigned from her former job.

Her official title with Opera Theatre is Production Coordinator and Assistant to Maestro Silipigni and in these capacities has been the focal point for bringing all the parts of the production together. Says Miss Cunningham, "The last six months have been the most exciting of my life. Each morning I am anxious to arrive at the office and in the evening I leave exhausted. Working in Opera "feels right" for me and I have developed rather a passion for it."

The job was exciting. As the only fulltime employee besides Alfredo, I was involved in every aspect of creating an opera performance. This included working with singers and their agents.

There was one downside to the job: the opera was always in financial trouble. Although my grant was renewed for a second six-month term, I was always nervous about money and wondered what would become of me if the company went bankrupt. I finally faced facts on the night of a performance of *La Gioconda* starring Richard Tucker and Grace Bumbry in 1974. Earlier in the day, the president of the board had gone on television and announced that the opera was in financial difficulty. If donations were not forthcoming, the opera would have to close.

I called Otto and asked if he would help me get a job at San Francisco Opera. He said he would. Thanks to Otto, they hired me, and I began work there on April Fool's Day, 1974.

THE CAB RIDE

I ran down the stairs of my third-floor apartment and hurried across 33rd Street. I was late for the Thursday night rehearsal. As I crossed Fifth Avenue, I looked up at the Empire State Building, disappearing into the sky. It made me feel good to know I could see this landmark building from my bedroom window. I was living in Manhattan and near the icon that defined the most exciting city in the world.

Tonight, I would meet the legendary Maria Callas, who would be attending the rehearsal in secret. The maestro had told me she was looking for a conductor for her next tour and wanted to see him work. "Don't tell anyone I will be there," she had ordered. "I don't want to be mobbed by fans." I had been sworn to secrecy.

This was a chorus rehearsal night. In addition to dealing with Miss Callas, I oversaw making sure that the stage was set up with props and scenery and the costumes had been delivered and ready for fittings. In addition, I would be at the beck and call of the maestro for any assistance he might need.

I got off the train in Newark and climbed the stairs to the terminal. There were no buses waiting, so I opted to take a taxi. I couldn't afford the fare but didn't want to be late to the rehearsal. I slipped into the back of the only waiting cab, which swung into action and after several turns ended up on Broad Street.

"What's going on at Symphony Hall?" asked the friendly driver.

"A rehearsal for *Madame Butterfly*," I told him, and asked if he liked opera.

"I've never seen one," he said.

"Well, it's an acquired taste," I said. "Two famous sopranos are involved in the production. Dorothy Kirsten is singing, and Licia Albanese is stage directing. It should be a wonderful performance. Opening night is this Saturday."

"Are you a performer?" he asked.

I explained that I was the assistant to Alfredo Silipigni, the conductor and artistic director, and he told me it sounded like an interesting job.

"I'm enjoying it," I said, and then changed the subject. "Broad Street is deserted. There are so many broken down buildings and closed businesses."

"Yeah, Newark is going through a tough time."

"The opera performance will probably sell out so that will mean lots of visitors," I said as I noticed a man beginning to mosey across the street, eating an ice cream cone and in no hurry to make it to the other side. Instead of slowing down, the cab driver sped up. It appeared he planned to run the man down. The jaywalker did a double take and jumped out of the way, just in time, leaping into the air like an elegant basketball player. He flung his cone at the cab, hitting my window with a splat.

"Anyone who jaywalks deserves to be run down, and don't think for a minute I wouldn't have," the driver said in a cool, calm voice.

Speechless, I remained quiet in the back seat. As the cab approached the next stoplight, a car zoomed past and stopped directly in front of us, blocking us at the light. Three men jumped out of their car and began banging on my cab, screaming for the driver to get out and fight.

My heart pounded as adrenaline shot into my veins. I began to hyperventilate. My mind raced. Should I throw the taxi fare over the front seat, jump out of the cab, and run like hell, or should I remain and hope for the best?

While my heart attack continued, the cab driver sat calmly, without emotion, giving no sign he had any concerns. Not getting any response, the three men jumped back into their car and pulled over to the side of the street, which true to its name, is very wide. The cab driver sped up, arriving in seconds at Symphony Hall where he completed a U-turn in front of the entrance. He then turned, pulled out a gun and said in a serene unconcerned voice, "If they had opened the door, I would have shot them dead, and don't think for a minute I wouldn't have."

The taxi incident was traumatic. I have only hyperventilated three times in my life when confronted with a dangerous situation and that was one of them. I suspect it stirred in me hidden memories of men fighting each other with guns.

THE RETURN OF BENITO

I hadn't expected to hear from Benito again, although we had casually discussed more visits. But a few months after I visited him in Europe, I was awakened by a loud pounding on my door in the middle of the night. It was Benito. He had gotten a visitor's visa in Geneva and was back to study opera. He walked in, set his suitcase down and expected to stay.

Over breakfast the next morning, I told Benito he needed to find his own apartment. He agreed to start looking. By then, my life had changed. I had retired from United Airlines and was working full time at Opera Theater of New Jersey, with a grant from the National Opera Institute.

Benito and I settled into a routine. He looked for a job and assured me he was checking out places to live. Soon he came home and announced a pizza parlor near Columbus Circle had hired him. I visited him there and watched him throw dough in the air. Before long, he came home with a Social Security card and said he had obtained it in Brooklyn.

"How could you do that?" I asked, surprised.

"Non ti preoccupare," he said, now a familiar phrase that effectively ended conversations.

I didn't ask him to pay rent because I felt this would give him the sense that he had a right to stay. We shared the food bill and he mostly cooked.

Benito intruded in my life. He showed up at rehearsals unexpectedly, something that irritated Silipigni, who asked me to remove him. He became possessive and jealous and accused me of having an affair with the maestro. One weekend he took me to meet his widowed aunt who lived In Philadelphia. I learned her husband had been murdered, but when I asked for details he said, "Non ti preoccupare."

I kept pressuring him to move and finally gave him an ultimatum. He became furious, raised his hand, and struck me across the face, sending my reading glasses sailing across the room.

Realizing what he had done, he sobbed, "I love you, I love you, and I don't want to leave." He carried me to bed, thinking he could change my mind. Now, I was afraid of him and decided to bide my time.

Benito began rehearsals for *La Boheme* with Vincent and had difficulty hitting the high notes. One evening he came home and announced I had to refuse him sex until after his performance. He needed to save his "essence." I gladly agreed, but every night I lost the battle despite my reminding him of his request. On the night of the opera performance, he missed the "high C."

In October 1972, the Newark Opera Theater performed Giuseppe Verdi's *Attila.* Benito came to the performance and during intermission, uninvited, pushed his way backstage and walked into the Italian tenor's dressing room.

Silipigni was furious. "Get rid of him," he said.

I was mortified. "I'm working on it," I reassured him.

In February 1973, the Opera Theater was presenting *Madame Butterfly.* Two performances were scheduled, one in Trenton. Because of the commute and after-performance party, I didn't arrive home until three a.m.

Benito greeted me at the door. "Where have you been?" he demanded, angry. "Are you having an affair?"

Over breakfast Benito took a fork, slammed the tip of the handle against the table and said, *"Se tu mi fai la corna, io ti ammazzo." If you cuckold me, I will kill you.*

I didn't believe him but decided to do something immediately. Not wanting to call the police, I contacted my old boyfriend Kingsley, explained the situation, and asked if I could stay with him for a few days. He offered his couch. I packed my bag, wrote Benito a letter informing him I was not coming home until he left, and departed. Three days later I called Joannie and she said she had not heard him for several days and she was sure he was gone. I went home, changed the locks and was free . . . but it wasn't to last.

Only weeks later, Benito called and chided me for making it necessary for him to pay for sex with prostitutes. He then asked me to forward his family letters to the Holiday Inn Motor Lodge where he was living, stating he didn't want his parents to know he was no longer with me. How he could afford living in a hotel? I wondered.

Over the next few months, I forwarded him three letters, putting my return address at the top.

A man called and stated he was contacting me on behalf of Benito. "I want to help Benito. He tells me he loves you and wants to get back with you."

"I want nothing to do with him," I stated emphatically.

"I thought perhaps we would meet for lunch to talk it over," he replied.

"Who are you?" I asked.

"I'm like a godfather to him," was the reply.

"Benito never told me anything about you," I said. "I'm going to hang up."

"Don't hang up," he said in a threatening voice.

"I'm not getting back with Benito and don't want to have lunch. I'm hanging up!"

"Don't you hang up," he replied menacingly. By the tone of his voice, I knew not to hang up. I didn't think of it at the time, but I had been trained never to say no to men who sounded just like this man. "Let's meet for lunch." he continued.

I agreed to meet him at the Holiday Inn Motor Lodge restaurant the next day. A waiter escorted me to a table where "the Godfather" and a beautiful teenage blonde were already eating. The man looked like any Mafia type portrayed in movies.

"I've ordered you a salad," he said, as I sat down, and introduced the blonde as his niece. The young girl smiled at me.

"I want to help Benito," he began. "He is very much in love with you and miserable. He wants to be with you. Why are you rejecting him?"

I decided to be forthright. I confessed that I was mainly with Benito to learn Italian, and that when I got to know the language better realized he wasn't very intelligent, and he had become over-bearing and controlling. "When I asked him to move out, he hit me,"

I said. "He became jealous and accused me of unfaithfulness, threatening to kill me. I don't want him in my life anymore."

My explanation seemed to satisfy "the Godfather." He and the "niece" abruptly left, leaving me to finish my salad in the empty restaurant.

I heard from Benito next when he called to inform me that he was going back to Italy. I didn't pay attention to when—it was about a month in the future. Then, one evening, I received a telephone call from a man who said he was with the King Detective Agency located in the Bronx.

"Our agency has a contract with JFK International Airport," the detective said. "We chaperone individuals who are rejected for entry into the United States until they can be put on a plane out of the country." He went on to tell me that while his agent was watching a couple of rejected South American men, he decided to make a telephone call. When he turned around the men were gone, leaving their suitcases. In their suitcases were envelopes addressed to a Benito Cuzzone with my return address.

"I am wondering why they would be in those suitcases, and if these men wanted to hook up with Benito," the detective said. "Do you know where he is? We need to find these men because if we don't, we will be subject to a huge fine. I wonder if you could help us."

"I can tell you about the envelopes, but I have no idea why they would be in those suitcases," I said.

"Okay."

I explained how Benito and I had lived together for a time, and then when he moved out asked me to forward his family letters. "He called me a month ago and said he was returning to Italy," I said. "I don't remember the date, but come to think of it, it might be today. Do I need to be afraid? Might these people show up at my house?"

"Oh no. You don't need to worry about that," he assured me. "Thank you for talking with me."

I hung up and looked in the telephone book. The King Detective Agency located in the Bronx was listed.

I wondered for many years about this conversation until one day I read an article in a magazine written by a detective. He discussed techniques used to find out information from interviewees. One way was to make up a story which included the person being interviewed and which would cause the unsuspecting person to divulge information they otherwise might not.

I suspect Benito left the hotel without paying his bill, perhaps having thrown the forwarded envelopes into the wastebasket. But would a hotel hire a detective to chase down an unpaid bill?

Approximately seven years later, I received a telephone call from Benito when I was living in San Francisco. He was in New York and returning to Italy the next day. His call made me a nervous wreck. Subsequently, I wrote him a letter stating in no uncertain terms I wanted nothing to do with him and he was not to contact me ever again.

Before I began to write this book, I wrote a screenplay about our relationship and wondered if Benito was still alive. In 2016, on an impulse, I searched for him on YouTube. To my surprise his name came up. There he was, singing a couple of Italian songs somewhere in Italy, in what appeared to be a talent competition at a local Italian television station. He would have been seventy-three years old.

Why did "the Godfather" feel any responsibility for Benito? I have pondered this question for years. In 1973 it's entirely possible Benito was connected to the Mafia in some way.

In the outstanding book *Octopus*, Claire Sterling writes about the drug connection between the Sicilian and New York Mafia. In a chapter entitled "From the Pipeline to the Pizza Parlor," I learned about "The Pizza Connection."

From 1963 onward, nearly all Cosa Nostra troops in America
got into the pizza business, sheltered behind it, washed their

drug money through it, skimmed the cash take, worked it to extort payoffs by arson, acid, bombing, and murder, pulled a thousand scams on its customers, and passed dope on from one of its kitchen doors to another. Two decades passed before the FBI discovered that Sicilian Mafiosi were running 'a sizable portion of the heroin importation business to the United States' through these pizza parlors.

Finding the proof that would stand up in court took five years, and every step was like walking under water. From two agents watching a couple of "zips" [curriers], the case progressed to a hundred agents watching a nearly unending procession of them. Men whose faces meant nothing to New York cops moved in and out of a bakery in Queens, a pizzeria near Columbus Circle in Manhattan, a cheese store in Brooklyn, a restaurant in New Jersey, a car cemetery, a garage, a shopping center parking lot . . . Knickerbocker Avenue in the Bushwick section of Brooklyn, was the Bonanno Family's territory.

I remembered that Benito had gotten his Social Security card in Brooklyn. And, of course, I'd met Benito in a pizza parlor and later he had worked in one near Columbus Circle. Truth is stranger than fiction.

■ ■ ■

I had been working at the Opera Theatre of New Jersey for nearly two years on the National Opera Institute grant when the company's financial difficulties became serious. I was thirty-four and tired of being poor. My young hopes were dashed; it was time to leave singing behind. My final performance was as the lead in Donizetti's *Lucia di Lammermoor*, performed at the New York School of the Opera with Vincent La Selva.

Bow for *Lucia di Lammermoor*, May 1972.

Over the past years, however, I had gained experience in opera management, and I liked the work. I asked Otto Guth for help. He was head of the San Francisco Opera coaching staff, and he sent my resume and a recommendation to the appropriate people there.

One evening that Spring, the telephone rang.

"Hello, this is Richard Rodzinski, Kurt Herbert Adler's assistant," the voice said. "He would like to speak with you."

Maestro Adler was the Artistic Director and conductor of the San Francisco Opera.

"Can you meet Maestro Adler at Carnegie Hall tomorrow?" he asked. "He will be there judging the annual New York area San Francisco Opera Auditions."

When I arrived at Carnegie Hall the next day, auditions were in progress. During a break I met Maestro Adler. The heat wasn't on, and the hall was cold; Adler had a bright blue scarf wrapped around his neck.

"Your eyes match your scarf," I offered impulsively.

Startled, he blinked his eyes a few times, but then seemed pleased. "Can you begin work on May 1st?" he asked.

A mad scramble ensued. I had one month to close my affairs and make new living arrangements.

PART THREE

SAN FRANCISCO

CHAPTER EIGHT

MEROLA OPERA PROGRAM

SAN FRANCISCO, 1974–1990

ADJUSTING TO LIFE IN SAN FRANCISCO PROVED TO BE difficult. I was used to being out and about, but now I was tied to a desk in a suffocating office space. Everyone worked exhaustive hours, six days a week, and on Sundays during opera season, usually late into the night. I was at the office six days a week except during the summer months when the work was seven days a week.

After years of this demanding schedule, one day I said to myself, *I'm not going to do it anymore.* I abruptly stopped working on Saturdays. No one said a word.

Although General Director of the Opera, Kurt Herbert Adler was the force behind everything, including Merola, a separate entity under the San Francisco Opera's umbrella. Merola—pronounced *MEH-roh-la,* named after the Opera's founder—had its own board of directors, headed by James Schwabacher, whom I'd met in New York. He was a musician—a tenor—but also my direct supervisor, and made all the artistic decisions for Merola. That was a disappointment, as it was a part of the job I'd hoped to do. Instead, I was responsible for fundraising and for overseeing everything having to do with the singers, and summer staff.

On arrival, I hit the ground running. My first task included getting twenty singers and a staff of coaches, conductors, teachers, and production assistants to San Francisco for the ten-week summer program.

The singers, already selected, arrived in San Francisco in mid-June. For many, this was their first time away from home. At that time, singers were required to provide their own transportation and housing. I decided that each artist should begin Merola with as little stress as possible and resolved to make it easier for them. Over time, I was able to provide orientation materials, banking services, housing, airfare, and even a weekly stipend.

My strategy was to involve as many small donors as possible in a personal way and marketed the idea to opera lovers with slogans like "Share in the Magic" and "Keep Merola Singing." We offered each donor the opportunity to support an assigned artist, advertising the idea with a brochure reading: "We're reaching for the stars." It worked. Eventually, each singer was sponsored by four donors with whom they became acquainted. The donors enjoyed seeing their young artists perform throughout the summer, and later when many of them had become internationally known opera stars.

I also established a thirty-member group called "The Amici." These "friends" provided services throughout the summer including picking up the artists at the airport and delivering them to their housing. They also volunteered in the office, providing lunches for donors who were invited to "A Day at Merola."

It was a busy schedule. During the year I had one fulltime staff member, but in the summer, we added two more, not including all the coaches, stage directors, scenic designers, and schedulers. I also began photographing the Merola activities and my pictures were used extensively in fund-raising materials, and opera programs.

The *piece de resistance* each year was the Grand Finals, a voice competition (the prizes were monetary) held on the last day of the summer program with a full orchestra on the stage of the opera house. The event was free, but at the end of the evening we passed baskets among the 3,000-odd attendees. I was tasked with delivering a speech to encourage their generosity.

Every year, we raised more money, the sum eventually reaching $7,000, although donations were mainly only one to five dollars. Despite my success, that speech became stressful for me. The minute I finished, I began to worry about the next year and whether I'd continue to meet my fundraising goals.

Speaking from the stage of the San Francisco Opera at the Grand Finals, 1986. I am forty-seven years old.

Over time, my title transitioned from Coordinator to Executive Director, and my fundraising success did not go unnoticed. I received respect and support from colleagues. However, after fourteen years I decided it was time to move on. In October 1988, I walked out the door and never returned.

WILDERNESS

Though I learned to drive at sixteen, I had no need for a car until 1975. At age thirty-five, I became the proud owner of a standard-shift brown Civic Honda. I gave the car a name—Jasper—and Jasper became part of my life.

My first new discovery with Jasper was the countryside. As I drove on backroads, California began to speak to me. In the spring, vibrant fields of wildflowers brushed the hillsides yellow, orange, and blue. I was dazzled by cream cups, baby blue eyes, tidy tips, and fields of California poppies, lupine, and mustard.

Photography became a serious hobby, and California, Oregon, and Washington my studio. On weekends, my tent tossed in Jasper's backseat, I traveled many miles a day to find the perfect pictures in the wild. I crawled around hillsides and photographed to my heart's content. I joined a photography club and won many awards at monthly meetings, even eventually entering a local photography competition. All my images were chosen for display, and several won first place in their category. I was also invited to show my photographs at exhibits around the Bay Area.

One day, Jeremy, the set designer for our production of *Madame Butterfly,* entered my office. He admired my wildflower photographs and suggested I sell them. Thus, my extracurricular activity was born. Mass producing my best images, I mounted them on cards and offered them to friends and board members for $1.25 each. A commercial printer bought many of my negatives and reproduced them on cards to be sold around the country. He called them the "Alice Cunningham Collection."

Some of the happiest days of my life were spent photographing nature. Along with my singing, being in the wild helped bring balance to my life, enabling me to overcome my childhood trauma.

One of the many fields of wild flowers I encountered on my photographing adventures in the Sierra Madra Mountains.

In the mid-eighties my vacation took me south to Big Sur. In that magnificent area, I camped and roamed state and county parks along the ocean and in the Redwoods. Late one Saturday afternoon, I noticed fog rolling in on a panoramic vista. A chain link fence with an open gate and dirt road winding up the hill enticed me to enter. There didn't appear to be a no-trespassing sign.

I pulled in a short distance and stopped on the side of the narrow dirt road. As I prepared to set up my camera, two pickup trucks appeared. Each one was crammed with workmen sitting in the open backs of the trucks. I was startled, but I kept my head down as they approached. The first truck slowed down as they were passing. I turned my head to see a man glaring at me from his driver's seat.

His face wore a snarl so angry it made me think of the devil. I was relieved when the two trucks continued past me.

As I set up my tripod, I could hear whispering sounds floating through the air from around the corner where the trucks had gone. After taking several photographs, I packed up and returned to the gate. To my alarm, the men had locked me in.

Panicked, my heart went crazy, and I began hyperventilating. Overcome with fear, I drove up the hill and hoped to find someone to help me. I throttled the car and bounced over the ruts of the driveway up the steep incline. At the top, two large house trailers, surrounded by trees with no obvious purpose, greeted me, as several guard dogs barked at me. No one was there.

I backed out and raced down the hill to face my jailer—the locked chain-link fence. With difficulty and still gasping for air, I focused on how to get out.

Remembering I had a pair of pruning-shears in the glove compartment I retrieved them wondering if they would be strong enough to cut the metal. Using every bit of strength I could muster, I squeezed the shears. It took a while, but I was eventually able to cut through.

My anxiety continued as I sped along the highway, wondering what those men had in mind.

This incident has plagued me since it happened in 1985. There I was, confronted by two pickups filled with hostile men. At the time I didn't understand it, but in retrospect I am sure it was an unconscious reminder of the men I was surrounded by during my abduction who had complete control over me. Not knowing what those men were up to and what would have happened if I had not escaped added to the burden. I've since realized I'd probably run into a drug operation; they were likely growing marijuana somewhere on the hillside long before it was legal to do so.

What remains from erasure is the likely existence of unknown
triggers to unconscious procedural memories,
which stay intransigently lodged in the client's body psyche,
causing ongoing distress and mercurial trauma symptoms.
—Peter A. Levine, PhD, *Trauma and Memory*

THE PHOTOGRAPHER

In 1983, I met a professional photographer at a party and engaged him in conversation. He was easy to talk to and we hit it off.

"Do you give private lessons?" I asked.

"Sure," he said. "Come to my studio and I'll see how I can help you."

He lived in the Castro District of San Francisco and his sunny photography studio was located on the lower level of his house. Mounted on the wall in the stairwell was a series of artistic photographs of nude same sex couples, embracing. I sat at a large table and displayed my photos taken at the opera. He talked about cropping and commented that I had a good eye.

"How much do you charge?" I asked.

"Rather than asking for payment, I like to exchange services," he said. "For example, I might ask for a massage in exchange for a portrait session." He brought out photographs of couples and a man dressed in bondage garb. The man had on a head mask, neck collar, chains, high heels, and glossy black leather pants that exposed his buttocks. He watched me closely.

Completely oblivious to what others would surmise, I reminded myself he was an artist and lived on a different plain than others.

At the end of our session when I insisted on paying him, he said, "Take me out to dinner."

A few days later I called and invited him to a popular restaurant. We talked well into the evening. His life history was unusual and his stories interested me. Then he shared more.

"I belong to a bi-sexual sex club," he said. He told me that the club met regularly at the home of a married couple and that he'd had a long-term affair with both the man and the woman. "My relationship with the man has been the most satisfying liaison of my life," he said, and added, "I'm also into bondage. A psychiatrist helps with my masochistic feelings."

Sitting quietly, I was pleased he trusted me enough to share his feelings. Life and group therapy in New York had taught me to be non-judgmental about people's lifestyles. At the same time, I was disturbed and wondered what had happened in his life to cause him to enjoy being abused.

Near midnight, I drove him home.

"Would you like to come in and see my whips and other paraphernalia?" he asked.

Shocked, I declined with a shake of my head, and started home. Now, feelings came to the surface. My mind reeled. *Why had the various clues gone unseen? What was there about me that refused to see what was going on? Why was he so forthright with his lifestyle? Why would he think I would participate?*

Deep depression descended upon me. Empathy for this sad man was mixed with distress over what had transpired. *Why hadn't I picked up on his proclivities when he showed me the S and M pictures?* My mind was in turmoil.

At four a.m., when sleep would not come, I called him and said, "I feel bad."

"Don't worry about it. I'm okay," he replied, ending the conversation. I never saw him again.

SELF-DEFENSE

When I moved to San Francisco in 1974, the Bay Area was reeling from news about the self-proclaimed Zodiac serial killer. He had murdered five people and was thought to have killed over twenty more. He had communicated with local newspapers, confessed his crimes, and challenged the police to find him. The news coverage caused fear and anxiety and traumatized Bay Area residents. As a result, several programs were developed to help individuals, especially women, learn to defend themselves. I signed up for the class in 1977 after I experienced a terrifying incident at my apartment.

I lived in a studio apartment at the back of a historic Victorian house on California Street. It was charming. I decorated with many plants, and it was altogether a magical place to live. It was also a goldfish bowl. Several floor to ceiling French windows lined one side of the room, and a large window at the back framed the deck.

One night I was startled out of sleep by an eerie sound of two voices moaning in perfect harmony, ascending and descending the musical scale in thirds. It was coming from under my deck. Terror overtook me and I gasped for air; Charles Manson and a satanic cult came to mind. I wondered, were there people outside under the deck, taunting me?

I called 911. Because I was struggling to breathe, it was difficult for me to speak. The dispatcher said, "Stay on the line." Shortly, a policewoman arrived running down the side of the house, gun ready. Still shaking, I was mortified to learn that two cats were the cause of the weird noises. I had heard cats courting before, but this noise was otherworldly. I felt like a fool and apologized to the officer.

"Don't worry," she said. "Another woman also called, as frightened as you were by the noise."

At the time, I thought it odd that howling made me think of a satanic cult.

This incident caused me to take a course in self-defense. A friend told me about a class called "Model Mugging," offered by the police department. I signed up.

The class met in a high school gym, and I joined another ten women in the bleachers. The teacher, a muscular and authoritarian policewoman, said, "Contrary to what you have probably been told, if you are accosted by a perpetrator, you should not comply. Statistics show he is probably not going to let you go, even though you do exactly what he says. Your best bet, at the outset, is to fight."

At this point, a tall man entered the room dressed from head to toe with heavy padding. He had on a football helmet and a codpiece.

"I'm going to have each of you come down and face Tony," the police instructor continued. "He is a policeman and has offered to be the bad guy. He will attack you. I want each of you to fight back as hard as you can. Use your arms as little as possible. Men's arms are longer than women's, and if he can get ahold of yours, you will be in big trouble. Use your legs. Kick! Kick as hard as you can. Stomp on his feet. Make noise! Holler as loud as you can and scream 911 over and over again."

Each class member confronted Tony and tried to get away from him. It was tough going, and most of the women had trouble screaming 911. It was not a problem for me. My opera background kicked in and I was not afraid to make my voice heard.

From behind his mask and after each confrontation, Tony apologized to the women. He was worried he might have a traumatizing effect. For me, the class was cathartic. I came out feeling that, if necessary, I could attempt to defend myself, and my vocal 911 might make the perpetrator think twice.

Unfortunately, the class was cancelled. It was Tony who was traumatized. He didn't feel right attacking women, even for a good cause.

Next, I signed up for a police-sponsored class on the use of mace. The room was packed with women and police officers who gave us four-inch-long brown canisters with chains. We were informed of the laws governing mace. Basically, it was only to be used for self-defense. Any other application was illegal. After the lecture, each of us took a test. I carried the mace around my wrist and kept it in the glove compartment when I traveled. Fortunately, I never had to use it.

MEADOWLARK

Illness is a tremendous opportunity.
Our bodies are telling us something.
—Evarts Loomis, M.D., Founder and
Executive Director of Meadowlark

In 1980, I had been working at San Francisco Opera for five-and-a-half years. Maestro Adler continued scowling and intimidating me. My self-esteem was at a low point and I wanted to do something to bring balance to my life. I heard about a wellness center called Meadowlark, in Hemet, California. The center offered a fasting program as well as yoga, art expression, journaling, body awareness, and nutrition classes. I decided it would be a good place to help me lose weight.

While there, I took the Taylor-Johnson Temperament Analysis Profile, which provides a personality sketch using nine areas of personal development. The results were eye-opening and indicated that my life was seriously out of balance. The chart indicated that I was "nervous," "depressive," "inhibited," and "subjective," yet also "acceptably tolerant," "self-disciplined," and "sympathetic."

But I was shocked to learn that I was "totally submissive." I knew I found it hard to say "no," but to find out that I could almost *never* say "no" was mind blowing. That is a dangerous trait. Memory of my abduction had not yet surfaced, and I did not yet know I had been programmed to do what I was told.

The saving grace of my personality was my "active-social" behavior, which rated high on the chart. Later, I realized I had learned to be outgoing and friendly during my abduction. I believe it's what kept me alive: I made sure people liked me.

CHAPTER NINE

EVENTS STIMULATE MY MEMORY

*It was common for traumatized people to lose
all memories of the event in question, only to regain access
to them in bits and pieces at a much later date.*
—Bessel Van Der Kolk, *The Body Keeps the Score:
Brain, Mind, and Body in The Healing of Trauma*

AS MY LIFE MARCHED TOWARD THE RECOVERY OF MY MEMORY, a series of events occurred which, although I didn't know it at the time, stimulated the process.

In 1987 I met Robert Lytle, a Buddhist monk at a fundraising seminar. As a result of our friendship, and hoping to lower my stress level, I left my two-bedroom apartment on Fulton Street across from Golden Gate Park, got rid of most of my furniture, and moved into a small room on the second floor of the Zen center not far from downtown San Francisco. I slept on a trundle bed and lived out of a suitcase in a room brightened by corner windows.

My duties at the Center included work in the vegetarian kitchen once a week, attending the wonderful Zen Garden located in the open-air center of the building, and watering the flower and vegetable garden on the roof of the building once a month.

Meditation started at four-thirty a.m. with a forty-minute sit, followed by a twenty-minute break and another forty-minute session at five-thirty a.m. I bought a zafu—meditation cushion—and sat cross-legged with my hands entwined across my belly. This gave me a chance to think. But instead of clearing my mind, which I was supposed to do, I sat there for each forty-minute session concentrating on "why." I contemplated my life and tried to zero in on what was making me so unhappy.

One day, we had a special ceremonial tea presided over by a monk. Each of us in turn, moved to sit in front of him, bow, and asked a question. Dialogue was not the purpose. The idea was to challenge the monk to respond with a short answer that illuminated Buddhist theories. The answer was meant to challenge one's thinking. When my turn came, I was surprised to hear myself say, "Why?"

The monk's answer was, "Why 'why'?"

Befuddled, I returned to my zafu. The monk had turned the question back on me and I was annoyed with his response. No help.

I lived in that room at the Zen Center for about a year and then moved into a studio apartment in a building next door owned by the Center. The schedule had proven too rigorous when added to my heavy workload at the opera, and the menu, crammed with milk products, did not agree with my stomach. Although I had planned to continue my meditation, I never again attended any activities there.

In December 1987, I wrote these lines which were published in the Zen Center newsletter:

> Be still oh busy mind
> Empty thy thoughts
> And rest.

But my mind did not still, and I did not rest. Two years were to pass before I began to understand "Why."

In February 1989, I attended a healing seminar at the Marin Center in Mill Valley. A friend had invited me to a program where two Buddhist teachers would speak. Jack Kornfield and Robert Hall, members of the American Theravada Buddhism movement, were both well-known, highly respected teachers.

In addition to listening to a talk by Jack Kornfeld, the assembly watched a video Robert Hall presented—a personal look into his life and his relationship with Buddhism. He then revealed a traumatic event that shaped his life. While in the middle of a massage, he experienced a flashback. He saw himself tied up, and abandoned in a shed. Not understanding the meaning of this, he called his mother and asked, "Did I have a trauma when I was a child?"

He was shocked to hear her answer. She told him he was kidnapped as a child and taken to a shed where he was tied up, sodomized, and abandoned. The police found him three days later, nearly dead. "Not knowing how to handle the ordeal, we decided never to speak of it."

This revelation unlocked Robert Hall's whole being. He began to understand how this repressed experience had formed his behaviors and understanding of life.

His story moved me, and I marveled at how he had managed to survive and give meaning to his existence. How was it possible to forget such a dramatic and traumatic life experience?

At home, excited, I decided to record the events of the evening and Hall's revelation, exhausted as I wrote. A few years later, I searched my diaries for the recounting of Hall's story. To my surprise I found

I had written about the entire evening except for Hall's repression of his childhood trauma. Why had I left that out? The answer was yet to be discovered.

■ ■ ■

On February 6, 1989, I applied to the San Francisco Peace Corps office, and within a few days, I was called for an interview. San Francisco Opera board members, pillars of the community, wrote letters of recommendation. After several interviews, the staff indicated I would probably be accepted if I passed the health test. They suggested I might be posted in Micronesia. I immediately purchased and read books about the area. When it looked like South America would be my destination, I signed up for Spanish class.

When a letter of rejection arrived, I was devastated. Why hadn't they taken me? What happened? Was I too old? Did they think I couldn't live a rugged life? What was wrong with me?

Without reason, it came to me that there was information about me in the records of the FBI that had caused my rejections. I perused my life and wondered what could have happened to cause the FBI to be involved. Nothing came to mind, but the idea persisted.

■ ■ ■

In May 1989, I was shopping at the Zen grocery store for millet for the birds at my windowsill, and a man approached me.

"I like your red dress," he said.

I thanked him, and after we exchanged a few words, I departed. He followed me out on to the street and invited me for coffee. He was in his early thirties, and I was fifty. When I brought up the age difference, he acted offended, but repeated his offer.

Over coffee, he told me his name was Frank. Not conventionally handsome, he was slender. He said he gained taut muscles from walking everywhere. New in San Francisco, he was looking for a job as a baker. The conversation was pleasant and before I knew it, he had invited himself to dinner at my house, where he would cook. He spent the night.

Frank was basically an uneducated street person. Although I wasn't attracted to him, I slept with him, and then let him stay so that he didn't have to go to a homeless shelter. At the time, I wasn't sure why but I felt sorry for him and didn't want to hurt his feelings. It took me three months to work up enough courage to tell him to leave.

I'd been seeing my therapist Barbara Cook for several years and she was troubled by my behavior. This kind of thing wasn't normal for the person I'd become. Why had I gotten involved with this guy? She and I had discussed my lack of boundaries many times, but this situation was over the top.

From the time I met Frank, his name began to appear in my dreams, thirteen in all and continued over a span of more than twenty years.

DREAM: "The Hanging Child"
August 6, 1989. 1 month before my memory returned.

Frank and I go down into the basement. A blond child is hanging from the ceiling. This makes Frank happy. He laughs as she kicks at him. Startled, because she looked dead, he says, "So you still have some oomph, you little booger." He takes her arm and sticks it with a needle. She shrivels down into something. Supernatural scenes appear. Animals switch around or become something else. The blond child becomes a burn or brown smeer on the ceiling.

This dream made no sense to me. But one month later, it became clear.

JURY DUTY

In June 1989, I had the privilege of serving on a jury—and it was a doozy. The trial concerned six-year-old Brendan O'Rourke, who had acquired AIDS from a blood transfusion at the time of his premature birth in 1982. His birth weight had been a meager one pound, thirteen ounces. His parents were suing the Irwin Memorial Blood Bank.

It's hard to express the enthusiasm I felt over this chance to serve. To be on a jury sounded exciting while I struggled to figure out the next phase of my life.

I was picked to serve on the jury and placed in the seat directly below the witness stand. I sat for the six-week trial and looked directly up into the eyes of each witness.

At the end of the trial, to reduce the number of jury members to twelve, my number was called and I was dismissed. Devastated, I became depressed. Why did the trial mean so much to me? What I didn't know at the time was that the court process had stirred my memory and challenged my unconscious to reveal an event that took place forty-one years earlier, when I was nine, in a witness box, and looking down at a woman in jury seat number one.

The jury fell on the side of the blood bank. I felt sorry for Brendan. AIDS was not yet known to be caused by infected blood. He died at age seven.

CHAPTER TEN

MY MEMORY ACTIVATES

*Nightmares and recurring dreams are among
the most common symptoms of PTSD.*
—Deirdre Barrett, editor of *Trauma and Dreams*

SAN FRANCISCO, 1987–89

BY 1987, I HAD WORKED AT SAN FRANCISCO OPERA FOR thirteen years. I had long forgotten my abduction and all the surrounding events and had spent nearly forty years in complete ignorance of my childhood trauma. But I had been plagued by nightmares for many years.

■ ■ ■

I have been recording my dreams for decades, partly because they were so strange, and also because something compelled me to do so. In 1989, my dream activity increased substantially. I recorded 136 dreams that year, almost all of which were nightmares. Night after night I jerked out of my sleep, heart pounding. I wanted to know why. I began to read books about dreams, including Freud and Jung, and several contemporary writers who had theories about how to interpret nighttime messages.

DREAM: "The Spider-Crab"
July 16, 1989. 2 months before my memory returned.

All of a sudden, I think lying in the dirt in a gully is not a good idea. I am on top of some animals. I see a drain nearby that goes under the road. There is a screen across it and two black widow spiders are on it. I look down and see a plant like spider-crab with long pincers. It is coming out of the ground and is snapping at my feet. I wake up in fright.

When I had this nightmare, two months before my memory returned, its meaning was completely obscure. I now know that it foreshadowed the return of my memory. My unconscious was preparing me for what was to come.

This is how I eventually interpreted this dream. Lying in the dirt on top of animals is a metaphor for being involved with pornographers and pedophiles. The spider-crab with long pincers is the woman in leather, recounted at the beginning of this book, speaking in a fake German accent and threatening to cut off my toes. The two spiders on the wire are the two women inserted in the wall. The drain under the road represents the underground activities of the porn ring.

■ ■ ■

Later, I researched sado-masochistic behavior and found in a college textbook, *Human Sexuality* by Carole Wade and Sarah Cirese, that "Play-like SM scenarios often involve elaborately staged fantasies and expensive props, sets, and costumes. The essential elements seem to be the illusion of violence and the ritualization of dominance and submission."

I perused newspapers and found a dream group run by Naomi Epel, author of *Writers Dreaming* and *The Observation Deck: A Tool Kit for Writers*. We met at her Berkeley home. The all-woman group sat around a table and worked on analyzing one another's dream adventures by using a prompt and completing it: *If it was my dream, it might mean . . .*

In August of 1989, Naomi organized a weekend at the Asilomar Retreat Center in Monterey, California. She brought piles of magazines and newspapers, and each of us spent an afternoon creating a collage to honor our dreams. My artwork would prove to be prophetic:

To Sleep, Perchance to Dream, Seeing the Answer, Knowing,
Are You Watching, Healing, Discover the Truth in the Dark, Finally Free.
Collage from Naomi Epel dream workshop at Asilomar Retreat Center.

After the seminar, I decided to peruse all my dream journals to see if there were any clues that might suggest what my unconscious was trying to tell me. Reading through them revealed disturbing images and themes that repeated night after night. This led me to suppose that by cross referencing the dreams, I might find answers. Each morning, I typed the dream and gave it a title and date.

To help identify similar themes easily, I designed simple icons to paste on the typed pages. One particularly repetitious theme had me floundering around: I can't see, I'm lopsided, and I am trying to get to a telephone booth.

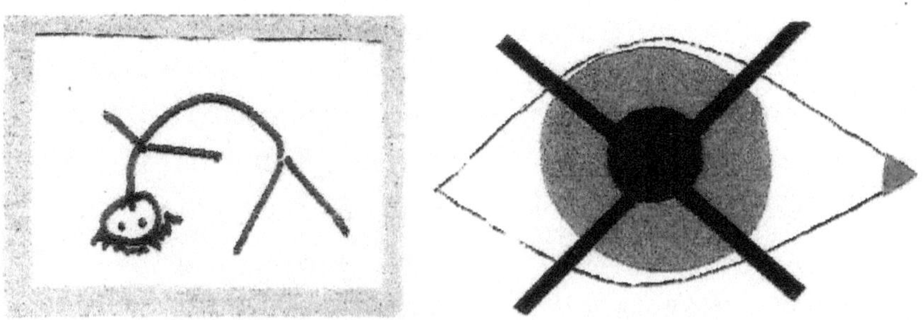

Icons for the themes "I'm lopsided" and "I can't see."

Eventually, I had fifty-four icons representing repeated dream themes, and many were unsettling. Repeated themes included the mafia, family gatherings, secret agents, guns, police, bathrooms, movie cameras, sex acts, drugs, and screaming. In most of the dreams I was a child. I found that attaching a visual image to a nightmare, over repeated dreams, helped me understand what it was about.

Here are some of the icons I created:

Two people, dangerous man, gun, policeman, screaming, toilet, movie camera, pounding heart.

All things one has forgotten scream for help in dreams.
—Elias Canett, Holocaust survivor and
Nobel prize winning novelist

Twelve days after this seminar, my memory activated, and long repressed events began to emerge. This changed the course of my life forever. Please notice the countdown of dream days as my memory prepares to return: Nine day, seven days, six days, and five days, until the night of September 9, 1989 when I woke up in terror, remembering I'd been abducted.

DREAM: "The Spider with a Message"
September 1, 1989. 9 days before my memory returned.

I stand up just as a giant spider is sliding at me along the wires of a telephone pole. The spider has pincers. I wake up in fright.

This dream is a precursor to what is going to happen in a few days: my memory will grab hold of me, and there will be no more avoiding it. The artwork clarifies the dream and illustrates where my unconscious is about to take me.

DREAM: "Mr. Go Calls"

September 2, 1989. 7 days before my memory returned.

A man named Mr. Go calls. He asks to speak to my mother.

I say, "She is not available. Can I take a message?"

He seems to think I should get her. "She is swimming. I'll have her call you."

He replies, "You will have her call me? I don't have to call her again?"

"Yes," I reply. "I will tell her."

This dream seems to suggest that my unconscious is letting me know it is ready to "go" and wants to make sure I am ready to receive. I agree to have her call Mr. Go.

DREAM: "The Wounded Butterfly"

September 3, 1989. 5 days before my memory returned.

I am a child and stand on the porch of my grandparents' home in Paola, Kansas. It is night.

Family members are talking about me in the living room. Something unpleasant is happening. I am stressed and feel humiliated. I hear my grandmother exclaim in a loud voice, "What?" I hold my hands over my mouth.

I notice a big white butterfly sitting in the grass at the edge of the porch. The light from the house shines on it, and it glows. I try to capture it, but it flies behind an old-fashioned car parked near the house.

I then notice four pastel-colored butterflies sitting together in two rows in one of the trees. I shake the branch and three fly away. I grab the fourth one and hold it between my hands. It is beautiful. I don't mean to hurt it, but knock off some of its scales. I want to take it inside but realize it might die. I say, "I should let it go free," and I do, but feel I have damaged it.

I then notice a brown bird in one of the trees pecking a limb. It breaks one of the small branches.

My grandparent's farm house in Paola, Kansas, taken in the 1950s.

This dream is full of symbolism, while also identifying a specific time and place: my grandparents' house. The white butterfly, a symbol of purity, is me; its flying away represents the loss of my innocence. The pastel butterflies represent me and my three siblings. The captured pastel butterfly, no longer white, causes me to wonder, "Will I be able to survive?" The bird breaking the limb suggests an assault.

DREAM: "The Magnificent Great Wall"
Monday, September 4, 1989. 4 days before my memory returned.

A huge map of China is lying before me as I stand on the Sea of China. I hear a voice say, "I thought I had seen all of the Great Wall." A line appears and draws itself—dot, dot, dot—across the map, as if a new section of the Great Wall is being created. This extension travels from the northern part of China to the Sea.

"Isn't that a magnificent Great Wall?" I think.

This dream illustrates the progression of memory repression. It symbolizes the process of denial that took place in my conscious mind. I cut off my memories by creating a "Magnificent Great Wall." The Wall is about to come down.

CHAPTER ELEVEN

SUFFERING FROM MEMORIES

I think this man is suffering from memories.
—Sigmund Freud

THE MAGNIFICENT GREAT WALL CAME DOWN IN THE EARLY morning hours of September 9, 1989, and my meeting with my therapist, Barbara Cook took place the next day as described at the beginning of this book. In Barbara Cook's office, I recounted the "I Am Strung Up" memory. "It feels true," I said, explaining it was a real memory of something that happened to me.

Over the day-and-a half I had waited to see Barbara, new memories emerged. As I sat in her office, I shared many things that after our session, I once again erased from my mind. In 1995, six years after my memory returned, when I was no longer living in San Francisco, I wrote Barbara to ask her for copies of her therapy notes. In her record of our September 10, 1989 meeting, she mentioned I told her I believed I was filmed for child pornography and forced to participate in satanic rituals, and that after I was found, I testified in court. I had forgotten I had told her any of this information, and it would be years before I was able to put it all together.

In her office I was caught between conviction and doubt. *How could this be true? Who was this woman? Why would she be threatening to cut off my toes? Satanic rituals? Child pornography?*

"Do I have to worry whether you are going to hurt yourself?" Barbara asked.

"No," I replied, "I don't want to kill myself. I want to find out what happened."

"I can count on that?" she continued.

I told her she could. It was the truth.

■ ■ ■

The minute I remembered my abduction I knew I was in trouble. Although I wasn't suicidal, I was falling apart. I needed stability. Aside from temporary work for a few months, I hadn't worked in nearly a year and had slipped into a major depressive episode. I needed to do something to occupy my time, and fast.

I called Ione Gille, a friend and member of the Merola Board, and asked if she had a job available. She and her husband owned an import company that dealt in wholesale crafts for hobby and party stores. Goods came in from Europe and Asia. She hired me immediately, and I went to work in their warehouse filling orders and organizing stock. The salary was less than half of what I used to earn at the opera, but I was glad for the job.

I pretended to be happy. Everything was great in my life! I was friendly, outgoing, personable, and upbeat! "You are always happy," marveled one of my co-workers.

Ione offered me a promotion. I declined. It would not be right. My life was moving in a different direction and I did not plan to stay there.

■ ■ ■

Although I had the following dream in March, six months before my memory returned, I am putting it here because it wasn't until December, three months after my memory returned, that I understood the dream and experienced mental trauma from the memory.

DREAM: "The Jail/Bouncing 'John'"
March 25, 1989. 6 months before my memory returned.

I'm in jail having been arrested for something I don't remember. There are people watching. I am on a mat in the middle of the floor. A tough female guard wearing sado-masochistic garb enters carrying a bamboo stick. We argue and she smacks me across the face with the stick.

"If you don't behave, I'll beat you. Go to the john," she says.

I leave the jail and go to the john.

I'm embarrassed, but I get on the john and bounce up and down.

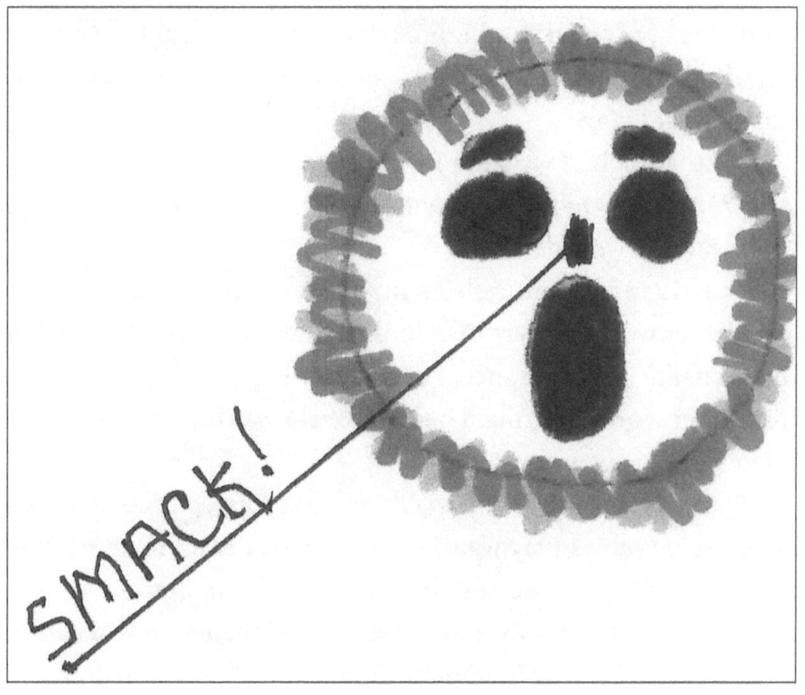

This dream recounts being abused by a woman who is forcing me to have sex with a pedophile, a "John," the word prostitutes use to describe a customer. Because people are watching, I believe there is an element of pornography in this dream, like the scene is being filmed.

In December 1989, three months after I recovered my memory, I decide to look in the mirror and see if there was a scar. There was a tiny scar and it corresponded to the dream.

In my next session, I told Barbara about the correlation.

"Do you have any other scars?" she asked, not referring to the dog bite scar on the right side of my mouth.

"No," I answered.

However, at home I wondered, *Could there be other scars?*

I sat down at my mirror to look and discovered an "n" shaped scar on the right side of my chin. I thought about it all afternoon and then looked in the mirror again. I found the whole side of my face had scars. I had no idea how I got them. It made me anxious. I felt I should look at my back, and I did. I wrote these thoughts in my journal, adding: *There are scars there. I can't see very well. I'll ask Barbara to look on Thursday.*

Later that night, I wrote in my journal: *I just now discovered scars on the front of my right leg and one on my chest. I looked right at them like I knew they were there.*

This written account reflects my mental state at the time. I was convinced I saw these scars. As I looked into the mirror, I moved into a sort of hallucinatory trance. I seemed to leave my body and move into another world, floating. I began to feel I was losing myself. *What is happening? Am I crazy?*

I placed a large mirror on the floor and propped it up by my bed. I could see myself as I lay waiting for the next dream to come. It was comforting. If I could see myself, I knew I was still there.

When I saw Barbara the next time, she said there were no scars. It is hard to understand why I temporarily convinced myself that my body was covered with scars. But could they have been emotional scars, the unconscious memory of parts of my body that had been violated?

Periodically, I have asked friends if they could see the scar, and they never could. But now that I am past eighty years old, and my face has relaxed, the scar is very evident, and it has been confirmed by a dermatologist.

JESSE SCOTT

I had begun individual counseling in the late 1970s with a psychiatrist I will call "Jesse Scott." He was an avid opera lover and knew many employees at San Francisco Opera. Because I wanted help dealing with my job and my father's molestation, I thought he would be a good choice for therapy.

DREAM: "Jesse Owen"
October 28, 1989. 1 month after my memory returned.
As I wake up, I am thinking about Jesse Owens and the year 1948.

I knew Jesse Owens was a famous Olympic athlete who won four gold medals at the 1936 German games. When trying to analyze this one-line dream, I couldn't imagine why I was thinking about him and what he could possibly have to do with 1948, the year I had not yet identified as the year I was abducted. It was shortly after this dream that, while sitting in my apartment in a semi-hypnotic state, I heard a soft voice in my ear which said, *call me when you are ready.*

I had always been interested in hypnosis, and Dr. Scott had hypnotized me. After I heard this voice, I realized that three of the numbers in his home address were in the number 1948. Grasping at straws, I decided the dream was telling me to call Dr. Scott. I made an appointment and met with him in November.

The session began pleasantly enough. I then related details of the return of my memory and asked if under hypnosis in 1980 I had told him about my abduction.

Dr. Scott became outraged. "How could your father have done that to you if you were kidnapped?!" he said, referring to the incest. Then he added, "You're crazy."

He then described what happened during our hypnosis session. "You were acting strange, and I asked what you were doing."

I'm flying around the ceiling and getting big and little, I had said.

Why are you doing that? he had asked.

I don't know, I just thought I would, I had answered.

"You then began to gobble like a turkey, I couldn't make heads or tails of it and decided to bring you out of your trance."

I left our meeting in a daze and drove immediately to Barbara Cook's office to catch her between therapy sessions with other patients.

"Dr. Scott says I'm crazy," I told her. "He wants to talk to you."

Barbara agreed to call him.

I went home, my mind reeling. I also had a hard time understanding why my dad had taken me to bed knowing I had been kidnapped.

Was I crazy?

■ ■ ■

As I pieced these few months back together much later, therapy notes Barbara kindly shared with me came in handy.

November 9, 1989: [Alice] showed up last night. Upset re [Dr. Scott's] visit as he told her he didn't believe her, and she felt he thought she was crazy. Feels she's right about what she remembers and not crazy.

November 12, 1989: Call to [Dr. Scott]. Very arrogant and pushy—wants us to meet to "confront" Alice. He feels she's schizo-affective with brief psychotic episodes—angry that she has less now than she had three years ago—very blaming and directing.

Barbara left it up to me as to whether we should meet with Dr. Scott. I refused. I did not think a three-way therapy session would be helpful, and I was happy with my work with Barbara. I also felt she would think I was not pleased with her—she was supporting me and staying neutral on the question of my abduction. Dr. Scott, on the other hand, wanted me to take medication, which I did not want to do. I felt that medication could mask what was going on with me and I wanted to be present through the process as I endeavored to unravel my past. That was the end of my relationship with Dr. Scott.

I remained confused. The extent and context of my continuing nightmares reinforced the idea that something traumatic had happened, and more memories of my abduction kept coming to light, but I continued to question the veracity of my recollection. *Am I making this stuff up?* I wondered. *Could I be diverting my attention from another traumatic event, like the molestation by my father?*

Later, I remembered that I did tell "Dr. Scott" under hypnosis that I was kidnapped. Right after I went under, and before I began flying around the ceiling growing large and small (and gobbling like a turkey!), I mumbled under my breath, "I was kidnapped, I was kidnapped," in a fast clip.

Apparently, Dr. Scott was so excited by the fact he was able to hypnotize me that he missed what I said.

MARY CIOFALO, MFT

From the time my memory returned, the desire to be hypnotized plagued me despite the fiasco with Dr. Scott. I thought that through hypnosis the truth would be revealed. I asked Barbara for help, and she arranged for me to meet with Mary Ciofalo, MFT. I showed up at her office with a long list of questions. After our session she gave me the tape of our visit. We had talked about Dr. Scott.

Mary: Is he someone in your dreams?

Alice: Yes. He is a therapist who hypnotized me in the early 1980s. One day I was sitting in my apartment and suddenly I heard a voice in my ear. The voice said, "Call me when you are ready." I assumed it was Dr. Scott telling me, under hypnosis, to call him, so I did.

Mary: And this information came back last year?

Alice: Yes, in my ear. I told a hypnotist about my kidnapping, and he said, "Do you want to remember it?" I said, "I don't know," and he said, "Well, let's leave it that you will remember it when you are ready, and you will call me."

Mary: Did you call him?

Alice: I called him and he said I was "crazy." He had no recollection of my telling him I was kidnapped, said it never happened, and that I made it all up. He wanted to put me on medication.

Mary: Oh, God.

Alice: So, I don't know if it happened or not.

Mary: You don't?

Alice: I don't know how I could have heard a voice in my ear. I was sitting and all of a sudden . . . unless I made it up . . . I mean there are a lot of screwy things going on here.

Mary: And a lot of things you can't explain to yourself. That's the way it works. Memories unveil as you take this journey. A lot of stuff just doesn't hang together until some other point down the road. I've watched this so many times. A lot of pieces come in their own time and when they do, things behind them begin to make sense.

Alice: He said that I was up flying around the ceiling and getting small and large. He couldn't make heads or tails of what was going on. I then remembered that I did something like this . . . *(I wiggle my tongue and make a noise like a turkey gobble)*. He said, "What are you doing?" I said, "I'm getting small." Barbara Cook suggested that my behavior had to do with evading or not wanting to divulge something, or it might have been a diversionary tactic.

Mary: Unusual behavior is a normal trance response for children who have been abused. They find ways to transcend. If you are being hurt and can't physically leave, the only recourse is to be there and leave at the same time, to be there and not feel the pain. They make themselves go into a crack in the floor or make themselves fly away. They just get out of there. I have come across this again and again. It's an intelligent response to a difficult situation. This is replicated when people go into a trance.

Listening to the tape of my conversation with Mary I realized I had completely forgotten about that voice in my ear. It was not Dr. Scott's voice I had heard. It was the voice of a man who had hypnotized me soon after I'd been found as a child. This man asked me to call when I was ready, and forty-one years later I was, but had called the wrong person, and one who was not very helpful.

PART FOUR

AFTER REMEMBERING

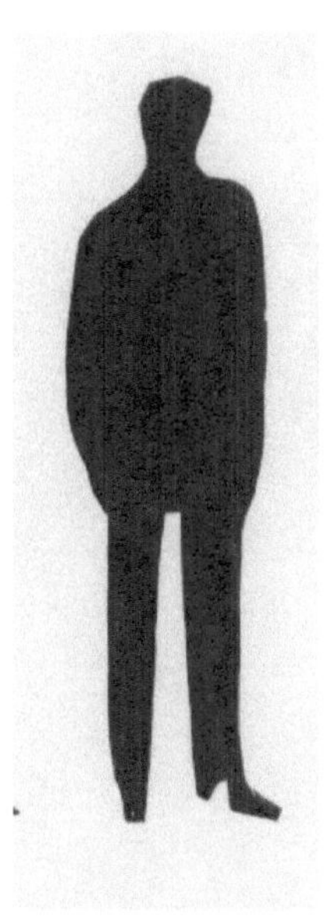

CHAPTER TWELVE

RETURNING HOME

EL CAJON, CALIFORNIA, 1990s

As a United Airlines pilot, my father was required to retire at sixty. He wasn't the kind of man who liked to sit around, and he immediately became busy with a variety of projects. One was building an airplane. He built a two-seater Sonerai II in a year-and-a-half. He then decided to build a four-seater. He sold the Sonerai and began working on a Prescott Pusher, an airplane design with the motor in back. The idea was to design an engine that was less expensive than the usual $10,000 amount.

Without fail, Dad got up each morning and headed for his shop. He worked daily for two-and-a-half years and then decided to unveil his creation at the annual air show in Wisconsin. He would "fly-in."

First, the plane had to be qualified. He towed it down to Brown Field outside of San Diego. After several weeks of preliminary testing and revving of the engine, he received approval to take off.

The minute he left the ground he ran into trouble. As the plane lost altitude, it fell below the level of the airfield into one of the surrounding canyons. Then, in the calm voice of the trained airline captain he was, he said, "I'm not going to make it," and plowed into a canyon wall. He died instantly. He was seventy-five years old.

143

My father with the airplane he built, a Prescott Pusher.

I took leave from work and visited my mother in El Cajon. She was overwhelmed with grief and cried nonstop until I offered to move home with her. My life was a mess, and I thought we could help each other and heal together. I'd support her as she grieved, and she would help me deal with my past. We would ride off into the sunset together.

I went back to San Francisco to pack and my mother flew up to help. Now, it seemed like a good time to discuss my kidnapping at a therapy session with Barbara, who would provide a safe environment. I thought Mom would validate my memory and we would work together.

Here are Barbara's notes from the meeting.

Mother in. Relates her history rather flat. Denies 'kidnapping' and any of this … interesting! Related story of baby-sitter in Denver who 'slapped around [Alice and brother Art].' Told of her own nightmare from age six on. Can't see. Scared frozen. Alice, almost fearful, handling this OK. Needs continued work. What does this mean?

I learned that my mother had "can't see" dreams, just like I did. Unlike me, however, she had no desire to find out what she "couldn't see." I had told her I remembered I was kidnapped, and instead of questioning my revelation, related discovering the babysitter mistreating my brother and me, and fired her.

I had my last therapy session with Barbara the next day. Her notes read, "Terminated. Handling disappointment well, hard to say goodbye."

It *was* hard to say goodbye. I had bonded with Barbara and loved working with her. She was kind and generous and a great support throughout our three years together. She didn't take sides on the kidnapping issue but took care of me as I struggled to figure out what was going on.

On the other hand, my mother's denial of my abduction devastated me. Was I daft, thinking we'd help one another heal? She showed no interest in my revelation, didn't ask questions, and never brought up the subject again.

■ ■ ■

In the 1970s, my mother and father had built a 3000-square-foot home in El Cajon, California, a forty-five-minute drive from San Diego. Following my father's cremation, we held a memorial service at that home. About 125 people attended, including relatives from across the United States. A few days later, the family gathered, and we sprinkled his ashes along the creek behind the house.

I did not miss my father and have never shed a tear over his death. Although he worked hard all his life and took care of the physical needs of our family, he wasn't good at expressing appropriate affection or offering emotional support. He never seemed interested in my life or voiced pride over my accomplishments. I mourn the fact that we didn't have a kind and loving relationship, and that we missed out on an appropriate father-daughter bond.

When I started therapy with Barbara Cook, she reported him to the authorities, as was the law. Nothing ever came of it, probably because the statute of limitations had passed. I was relieved. I didn't want my father to go to jail. It would have ruined my family.

■ ■ ■

After the memorial service, it was time for me to get a job. I eventually ended up at a Japanese firm, where I worked for several years as a secretary.

■ ■ ■

Once settled with my mother, it felt like a good time to start working on recovering more memories, or at least validating what I had remembered. I decided to visit my siblings and tell them about my abduction memories, and how our father had molested me. In 1992, I met with brother Arthur and his wife Sharon. Arthur, who is one year younger than I am, would certainly have memory of my abduction. Or so I thought.

"I don't remember it," he said.

Not remembering it is different from, "It did not happen," but nevertheless he was no help. I loaned him all my dream books to read. He returned them a month later with post-it note comments stuck on many pages. He handed the books back without comment and never mentioned them again. In fact, when in 2017 I brought up the subject of my dreams, he had no memory of reading them or of his post-it remarks.

I asked my mother for my school records. She gave me copies of everything she had, beginning at the end of second grade at Evans school and continuing at Montclair for fourth through sixth grades. The information consisted of a one-page record of teacher's comments at the end of each semester from 1947 through 1951. I found it hard to follow and made a timeline to organize the teachers' comments according to my age and grade.

The teachers' comments said I was insecure in my work but able to keep up with my class. They also said I had an interest in music and I was reliable and generous.

In 2018 my brother Arthur gave me copies of his report cards which our mother had saved for him. She kept all his records, but not mine, aside from the one-page teacher's comments. I was missing report cards from third grade through sixth grade (1948–1951.) The missing report cards would have recorded days absent from school as well as my grades. Involvement with the court system from 1948 through 1951 would have taken me out of school on several occasions. I believe my mother destroyed those records to protect me.

I subsequently wrote twice to the Denver Public School, and even drove to Denver to visit the district offices in an attempt to get my complete records. Except for the one-page comments, there were none until I entered High School.

My mom did supply my fifth-grade report card which recorded vacation absences and showed I needed to improve work habits, self-direction, leadership, reading, and arithmetic. Why, when I had already missed so many days of school, would my parents consider taking a vacation during the school year? My father probably had no choice as to vacation dates due to his then low seniority, but why not vacation at home so there were no more disturbances in my schooling?

■ ■ ■

Stephen's back and forth on what he remembered was confusing and disappointing. Stephen was nearly three when I was kidnapped. Although he initially said he remembered Paba saying that, a few years later he had no recollection of telling me that. I don't know when Stephen might have heard Paba's comment, but it could have been later than 1948, when he was older.

Peter A. Levine, PhD, in his book *Trauma and Memory,* writes that our earliest episodic memories start at the age of three-and-a-half, because that is when the hippocampus becomes significantly functional. He adds that there is also evidence they can reach back to earlier ages, and as Stephen was amid family trauma during my kidnapping, it's possible he retained more from that time. Memories seem to come and go, sometimes surfacing at random times and then retreating into the distant reaches of his memory.

In January 1994, I was still plagued by nightmares and memories. Stephen offered to help me. He hired Denver researcher Barbara L. Wagner, a consulting technical librarian. I had few concrete memories to help her investigation. What were the names of my kidnappers? When was I abducted? Where did the trial take place? In fact, I wasn't even sure my memory was correct. I still wondered if I was making it all up.

Wagner's research included checking indexes at the Denver Post Library that were not open to the public, as well as at the Colorado Historical Society, the Denver Police Department, Evans School, and old telephone books. She found nothing. I was devastated and continued to wonder if I was crazy.

At that point, Stephen pointed out that his memory was probably just faulty. "I think something traumatic happened to you, but we don't know what," he said. That wrapped it up for him.

As an aside, both brothers did say that they remembered hearing Dad in my bedroom, and, although puzzled, didn't think anything more about it.

My sister Lynn hadn't yet been born when I was kidnapped, but I told her about our dad and asked if he had molested her. She had no memory of it but recounted a dream: *"A big spider is dipping down into me. I wake up terrified."*

One evening my mother recounted something that happened with Lynn.

"I was sleeping in my bedroom when I heard Lynn screaming," she said. "I ran and tried to get into her room, but the door was locked. I banged and banged and finally she opened it. She was asleep and had no idea she was screaming."

I asked Lynn about it, but she had no recollection of it.

■ ■ ■

I was working to put my memory back together, but I was also trying to build a future. I needed a master's degree if I wanted to improve my circumstances, but my low self-esteem stood in the way. Evening courses at Grossmont Junior College in El Cajon seemed like a good place to start. I signed up for math, reading comprehension, psychology, English, and sex education.

The sex education class was interesting and informative. In November, the class was assigned a critical thinking exercise in which we had to write pros and cons about whether teenagers should tell their parents if they are pregnant. A law was currently being considered which would require parental consent for an abortion.

I asked my mom what her thoughts were on the subject.

"Well, for one thing," she said, "if a child is pregnant as a result of incest, she wouldn't want to tell her parents."

"Why wouldn't she want to tell her parents?" I asked.

"Well, she could get her face bashed in!" she replied forcefully.

There was nothing in my question that suggested incest, which made her vehement response especially puzzling. I now began to wonder if her father, my grandfather, had molested her and her mother had not believed her.

■ ■ ■

I experienced something odd—a memory breaking through—in the summer of 1991. On June 19th, I wrote in my journal:

Several weeks ago, I called to make an appointment with my mother's eye doctor who I had seen for the first time a year ago. As I drove to the appointment, I became unsure of the doctor's name and the exact address of his office. After some thought, I recalled the name Dr. Spector. However, when I stopped the car to look in my address book, I discovered his name was not listed. Fortunately, I then recalled his office location and proceeded to the parking lot.

In the building, I perused the directory. Dr. Spector's third floor practice was listed. Upstairs, I attempted to check in, and was startled to learn that Dr. Spector was a gynecologist, and not the eye doctor I was looking for. Puzzled, I returned to the lobby. It was then I realized that, when I visited the eye doctor (Dr. Rhein) a year ago, also located on the third floor, I must have noticed Dr. Spector's name on the building directory and for some reason stored his name in my memory.

I found this journal entry ten years later and decided to do an internet search for Dr. Spector's name. To my surprise, I found there was a gynecologist with his name practicing in Denver in 1948. I believe I did have an appointment with Dr. Spector when I was nine years old and home after my abduction.

It is amazing to realize that after a chance glance at this name on a building directory, I would recall his name after sixty-two years without knowing why.

Now that I had a regular paycheck, I was able to continue therapy. I arrived at the office of Dr. Michael Yapko after I read his book, *Trancework.*

At our first meeting I told him of my kidnapping memories and that my family had denied it had happened. I asked him to hypnotize me to help me recover memories. Dr. Yapko refused, stating that hypnosis was known to cause false memories. "But I can help you improve your life," he said.

I told him of my wish to attend graduate school and obtain a master's degree, the problem being that I had test anxiety.

"You don't have to be tested," he said. "Go to National University."

Within the month I was enrolled in a two-year course, attending classes two nights a week and all-day Saturday. For my five hundred hours of required practicum, I worked a suicide hot line and counseled teenagers at a group home. At age fifty-five, I graduated with straight As and a master's degree in counseling psychology.

Meanwhile, Dr. Yapko used hypnosis in our sessions a few times to help with test anxieties and to reduce insecurities. Once I began therapy with him, I started to have many dreams about hypnosis.

My fascination with hypnosis didn't come from nowhere. In 1989, soon after my memory resurgence, I had a random memory about being hypnotized when I was so young my feet didn't reach the floor:

MEMORY: "I Am Hypnotized"
November 11, 1989. 2 months after my memory returned.

I walk into an office.

The lights are dimmed. It feels safe.

Books line the walls.
A tall thin man greets me.
His voice is calm, quiet, and gentle.
I sit in a chair with butterfly wing arm rests.
My legs swing off the floor.
He sits in front of me, a watch in hand.
"Follow it with your eyes," he says.
My mind shifts. It expands. I puff up.
I tell him things I don't remember.

In 1989 I remembered what that doctor said to me.

1. Stay away from drugs.
2. Stay away from bad men.
3. When you are ready, call me.

I have never tried any recreational drugs of any kind although I have had the opportunity. But, I have a recurring fantasy that if someone tried to make me take drugs, I would put up a fierce fight, kicking and screaming. No one is going to make me take drugs.

■ ■ ■

During the time I was exploring hypnotism with Dr. Yapko, I had the following dream:

DREAM: "The Doctor Hypnotizes Me"
August 4, 1993. 3 years and 11 months after my memory returned.

I have been to see the hypnotist. I lie back on the couch. The doctor is in my peripheral vision. He does something like snap his fingers. I immediately go into a hypnotic state in layered shifts.

My awareness increases and it feels like how I imagine an atomic bomb would look. My whole being expands, stretches out in sections and jerks: expand . . . stop . . . expand . . . stop. Very fast. When the expansion stops, I am totally aware, or alive. It is a real feeling, and it wakes me up. My heart is pounding.

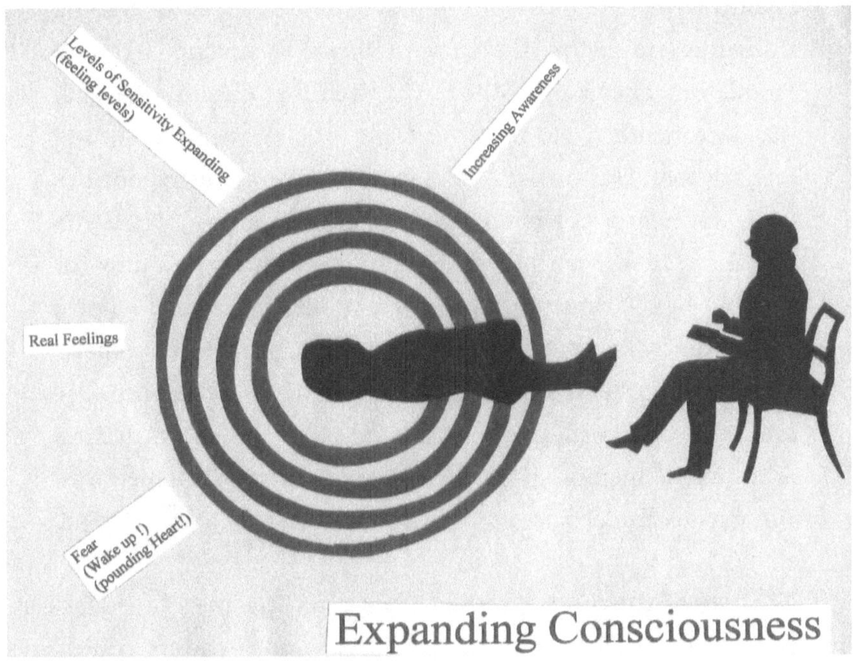

Increasing awareness, levels of sensitivity expanding (feeling levels), real feelings, fear (waking up with heart pounding).

DREAM: "Communication with the outside World"
June 30, 2010. 21 years after my memory returned.

A telephone technician is working on my phones. He says to me, "I want to make sure your communication with the outside world remains intact while we are working on the inside world."

In this dream the telephone technician is a hypnotist. He is telling me he wants to make sure he does no harm while I am under hypnosis.

In his 2014 book *The Body Keeps the Score,* Bessel Van Der Kolk states:

> Hypnosis was the most widely practiced treatment for trauma from the late 1800's, the time of Pierre Janet and Sigmund Freud, until after World War II. On YouTube you can still watch the documentary, *Let there Be Light,* by the great Hollywood director John Huston which shows men undergoing hypnosis to treat 'war neurosis.' Hypnosis fell out of favor in the early 1990's and there have been no recent studies of its effectiveness for treating PTSD. However, hypnosis can induce a state of relative calm from which patients can observe their traumatic experiences without being overwhelmed by them. Since that capacity to quietly observe oneself is a critical factor in the integration of traumatic memories, it is likely that hypnosis, in some form, will make a comeback.

Because of the large number of dreams I wanted to include in my book, I decided to add an appendix where readers could find more dreams on related subjects. Additional dreams associated with hypnosis: (page 271) *Would You Mind Getting Rid of the Cigarette?, Who Are You?*

FALSE MEMORY SYNDROME

Through all my academic and my personal memory work, I continued to ask myself, *Am I suffering from false memory?* I researched the subject, wrote papers, read books, attended lectures, watched documentaries and other films, and discussed the topic with therapists. In graduate school, planning on becoming a counselor, I didn't want to cause my eventual clients to conjure up false memories. Still, I could not give up my own memories.

WAVY LINES

After I had been meeting with Dr. Yapko for a few months, I told him about a curious phenomenon I was experiencing and described noticing that around certain men I experienced what I described as "wavy lines," or "disturbances in the air." These men were all a certain physical type: late twenties, slender, and all-American.

As I talked to these men, I would become extremely uneasy, unable to concentrate on the conversation. I felt I was picking up feelings indicating they were uncomfortable with me and decided to ask if this was true. Puzzled, they all replied in the negative. Now, I understood that I was the one who was uncomfortable. The wavy line experience was similar to some characteristics of a hypnotic state; it was as if my unconscious was warning me about these men. Once I discovered this possible connection, I never experienced wavy lines again.

LOPSIDED CAN'T SEE

I first began seriously studying my dreams in 1988. At that time I noticed a recurring theme: I am floundering around, can't see, and am lopsided. There is action in the dream, but I can't see what it is. Beginning in 1981 and through 1983, I recorded thirteen of these dreams. They were disturbing and stressful and I wanted to know what they meant. Over time, more content crept in. It was as if my unconscious was gradually giving me clues as to their meaning. Here are a couple of examples:

DREAM: "Barbara Helps Me"

September 1988. 1 year before my memory returns.

I enter a room. I am lopsided and can't see. Barbara Cook appears. She holds me up and helps.

DREAM: "The Giant Penis"

June 1989. 4 months before my memory returned.

As I start to walk through double doors the dream becomes technicolor and is lucid. I am in the dream and controlling it. Two men pass me. The men are slender and lean. I decide to follow them. The men transform into nude men and are in full erection. I look at them and am angry at their exposing themselves to me in this way. I say to myself, "I'm not going to let them get away with this, I'm going to ridicule them. If I laugh and make fun of them, their penises will deflate fast enough!"

I start to approach them. They immediately disappear and become one giant penis laying on the hillside in the distance. The penis is huge—like the size of an elephant. I can't see who the penis is attached to, but decide to go over and have a look. Within my lucid dream I become lopsided and can't see.

I have had many dreams with these two men in them. I believe they are pedophiles who abused me frequently. Because the dream is in technicolor, I believe I have been drugged. I don't have lopsided, can't see dreams anymore.

CHAPTER THIRTEEN

MOM'S DENIAL

After I had been seeing Dr. Yapko for a few months, I took my mother to meet him. She was seventy-seven years old. Mom talked about her childhood on a Kansas farm and mentioned she was the first person in her family to go to college, the University of Kansas.

Dr. Yapko recorded our sessions and always gave me the cassette. Here is a partial transcription of the recording from the meeting with Mom.

Yapko: Are there any experiences that stand out in your awareness as being particularly powerful in Alice's life . . . major events that happened or unusual things?

Mom: No. Seems like we went along pretty smoothly. Every time the kids got sick my husband was away. Any kind of emergency (laughs) . . . but we enjoyed our home in Cherry Hills.

Yapko: Were you aware of any unusual things happening with Alice? Did she tell you anything that was unusual in school or with her friends or friend's houses, anything that stands out in your memory?

Mom: No.

Yapko: Did Alice ever run away from home?

Mom: Oh no. (laughs)

Yapko: Did she ever leave home for any reason for any period of time?

Mom: No.

[Here, Mom described vacations Arthur and I took with Momo and Paba.]

Yapko: She was never gone for days at a time, or weeks at a time under any other circumstances?

Mom: No, no.

Yapko: What would you say was the best experience that Alice ever had growing up?

[Here, Mom talked about my singing and a voice recital at William Jewell College.]

Yapko: Let's do the flip side of that question. What would you say was the worst experience Alice ever had growing up?

[Here, Mom recounted the dog bite and the scar that resulted from it.]

Yapko: Were there ever any kinds of family struggles that involved lawsuits or any legal proceeding that you recall?

Mom: No. I was on a jury once and I think that was the first time I had been in a courtroom.

Yapko: Has Alice ever described memories she seems to have had or experiences that you have no idea where she would have got that idea?

Mom: Oh no, I don't think so.

Yapko: Did she ever come up with stories that you are wondering where they came from?

Mom: (laughs) I don't think so. (laughs)

Yapko: Does she seem to have a pretty good memory for things that have happened?

Mom: Oh sure, I suppose, just as good as anybody.

Yapko: Are there any other significant things you can think of that have been part of her background that you think might influence the work I do with her in getting her ready for the next phase of her life?

Mom: How do you know what would influence people?

Yapko: So, to the best of your knowledge she has never been traumatized nor has she ever been through any nasty episodes. I'm talking about through childhood from the time she was living with you. As far as you know she hasn't been through any weird or unusual experiences.

Mom: I can't think of anything. Maybe I could think of some things with the other children.

[Here, Mom talked about a man who tried to pick Stephen up on a bus by offering him candy. Mom didn't discuss being hospitalized for her depression or that she went through a series of shock treatments. Since she didn't mention it, I brought it up myself.]

Yapko: Was that for postpartum depression?

Mom: No, it was for nausea of pregnancy. I was so nauseated the doctor said, "You are going to lose the child . . . we think you should have shock treatments."

Yapko: For nausea?

Mom: Yes.

Yapko: That is a new one on me.

Mom: I spoke to a doctor here in El Cajon and he said he never heard of it either. At the time, in Denver, there was a psychiatrist who used shock treatments for a lot of things. He had more patients than he knew what to do with. The days he was giving shock treatments we would be lined up in wheelchairs outside waiting for our turn.

Yapko: How many treatments did you have?

Mom: I think I had ten or twelve treatments every other day and on the off day they would give me insulin shock.

Yapko: Wow. . . . This was not for any psychological reason that anyone knew anything about, just physical because you were pregnant?

Mom: Yes.

Alice: What was the name of the doctor?

Mom: Bradford Murphy. He talked to me some. It was very unsat-
isfactory because he was very popular. He lectured around at
places. Everybody knew his name. The phone would ring and my
whole hour would be taken up with him talking on the phone.
And I didn't know of any problems I had. I just described the way
we were living . . . after this first shock treatment I couldn't move
the next morning, and they thought they had broken bones. They
X-rayed me and decided it was just muscular. But when I got
home from that, I couldn't get my arms over my head . . . I think
I still suffer from weakness in my arms. (laughs)

Yapko: Did there appear to be any impact on your memory?

Mom: Oh yes, the day I got home, I couldn't remember anything.
Everybody was teasing me. I had to stay with some friends the
first night because my husband was not at home. But there were
things I should have remembered because we were moving into
our nicer house. I didn't remember some of those things.

Yapko: So, soon after the shock treatments were over, was your memory pretty much . . . ?

Mom: Oh yes, but it did help the nausea.

Yapko: Could things have happened after the shock treatments that
you couldn't remember?

Mom: Maybe a day or two . . . . The second set of treatments were
maybe five years later. I started having hysterics when we were on
vacation . . . . [The doctors] said I had acute anemia and recommended shock treatments. I said, "Why can't I just have a blood
transfusion?" They said, "Well, those only last three or four days.
We've got to give you liver shots and B12 shots and other things
so that your blood builds up by itself, but in the meantime, we
can help your depression by the shock treatments." I complained
bitterly about how they had hurt me the first time, and they said,
"We've learned a lot about shock treatments since then and we
don't use such strong methods." I don't remember how many I

had then, but not as many as the first time and by the time my
family got back from their vacation I was back home.

Alice: Mom, this was a horrible experience. I never heard what they
did to you.

Mom: Well, they sedated you. I remember dreading going into the
treatment, but you don't know anything about it. You wake up in
this wonderfully cool room totally relaxed and you don't have anything to do the rest of the day except lie in bed and eat and read.

It is interesting that my mother said the first shock treatments
were for nausea from pregnancy and the second for acute anemia.
By the end of the conversation, she used the word "depression" but
couldn't think of any problems she might have had. She seemed to
be unaware her thinking was distorted. Later in her life she started
taking anti-anxiety medication. I can't remember the name of the
medication, but we knew she was dependent on them.

I CONFRONT MY MOM

Two years later, I decided to confront my mom about my memories
and struggles with nightmares—she still hadn't acknowledged my
childhood trauma. Her behavior didn't seem like a normal reaction
to what was going on with me.

Over breakfast one morning in June, I placed a cassette recorder
in the center of the table and told her I was recording. This is a partial
transcription of our conversation:

Alice: I just want to let you know that the question of my kidnapping is not a dead issue. I haven't asked you about it for a while
because it seemed to upset you and because you would not
talk about it. So, have you ever thought about why I am the
way I am? Why I don't have good relationships with men, or

why I have horrible nightmares night after night? And why the dreams are of an extreme sexual nature. Have you ever wondered about that?

Mom: Well, I wondered about that, but it's not anything I can help you with or...

Alice: Why couldn't you help with it?

Mom: Because I don't know anything about... well, this is the first time I've heard about it for one thing, and in the second place it seems like it needs a psychiatrist or something.

Alice: Why, when we were in Dr. Yapko's office and he asked if I ever told you about anything bad happening to me, or any abuse, didn't you say 'yes'?

Mom: (pause) I don't remember him asking me that.

Alice: I have it on tape so I can prove that he asked you, and you said "No," knowing full well that I had told you I thought I was kidnapped during our meeting with Barbara Cook.

Mom: Well, I thought he meant prior to the present... when you were a kid you never told me anything like this.

Alice: But he said, "Has she ever told you?" That was really a blow to me, Mom. It was like you were lying, that you were covering up something. You never once wanted to look at my dreams, you never wanted to discuss anything with me.

Mom: But dreams are personal. I wouldn't want anybody...

Alice: But I showed them to you, and you didn't want...

Mom: When did you show them to me?

Alice: When I got my memory back. I got my book out and I went through and showed you all the artwork... you were like... err... *I don't want to look at it* or... you never asked me any questions and you never asked to see them, you never asked... I just thought it was very peculiar.

Mom: I don't think it's peculiar, Alice, because it just didn't happen and, if you think so, there isn't any way I can deal with it.

Alice: Well, don't you think I'm sick in the head?

Mom: Well . . .

Alice: I mean, wouldn't you say there is something wrong?

Mom: Yes, but I thought you were trying to deal with that with your psychiatrist.

Alice: I get the impression you don't think I should be there. There is this sort of attitude I pick up . . .

Mom: You're right. This is upsetting me. I don't know why you are digging up all kinds of . . .

Alice: Because I'm having nightmares and they are not going away after four years and after being with a therapist for a whole year . . .

Mom: Well, how it is helping?

Alice: It's helping. I'm trying to find out why I am the way I am. Putting it aside and not dealing with it is what prolongs the agony and the dysfunction.

Mom: So, dealing with it is dragging it around behind you all the time.

Alice: I'm having nightmares night after night. I wake up. They are sexual nightmares. Would you like to see [my descriptions of] some?

Mom: I've had sexual nightmares.

Alice: Let me show you some [of my dream journal entries]. There are some really bad ones.

Mom: Well, is it going to help you?

Alice: It would help me if I felt that you were concerned and interested and involved in this process, as my mother.

Mom: You want me to admit that all this stuff happened.

Alice: No, I want you to be supportive, be curious about it, offer memories, work with me, talk about it, and ask questions.

Mom: When we talk about it, it seems to end up with you accusing me all the time of things that I don't think are true.

Alice: I get combative because of your lack of interest in the topic.

Mom: It's not lack of interest, it's just not knowing anything to do about it.

Alice: To me, a mother whose daughter came and said this stuff to them would say "WHAT?! Let me see those dreams. What are you talking about? Tell me more." That's the reaction of somebody who is concerned and supportive.

Mom: I'm sorry I'm not getting your idea of a mother, but maybe that is just my personality. I don't know how you could think that if these things happened to you and I knew about it that I could forget it.

Alice: That's a normal human thing that happens to people.

Mom: Well, maybe that's your body taking care of you. I just can't believe. (long pause)

Alice: Okay. I believe that you can't believe . . . . Why didn't you tell Dr. Yapko that I had mentioned it?

Mom: Well, I must not have been fully conscious when I was there. Why would I deny it?

Alice: Yes, why would you? I'll get the tape and prove it to you.

Mom: He already knew that we talked about it?

Alice: Yes, what do you think he thought? (very long pause)

[At this point I decided to stop. The conversation was distressing my mother too much and we weren't getting anywhere.]

Alice: I guess we can end the conversation. I just wanted to bring you up to date.

[However, the conversation continues before I turn off the tape recorder.]

Alice (looking out the window): That bird looks like it got fatter. I was going to say Thrush . . .

Mom: The Rufus Crowned Sparrow.

Alice: It has spindly legs.

Mom: Oh no, we haven't had one of those for months. Maybe we will get to see one on our trip. The program I was listening to about the rain forest on Vancouver Island showed some of the birds and I thought maybe we will see some of those ... the Glaucous Winged Dove ... (reads off a list) ... what else ... the eagles of course ...

Alice: The travel agent has the ferry schedule. We could tour the islands if you want to.

Mom: If we have time. If we cover the land, we will be doing good.

Alice: Okay.

My mother never brought up the subject again.

■ ■ ■

In the eighties, before I moved to El Cajon, my mom was called for jury duty. After the jury pool was called into the courtroom, she wrote a note to the judge to tell him she should not serve because she was "mentally ill." She was dismissed. My mother was so disturbed about serving on a jury that despite her inability to admit she had been depressed, she described herself to a judge as "mentally ill."

I had to wonder if she watched me sitting in the witness box during one of my trials, or if she herself had to testify, thus causing her such anxiety that she was willing to debase herself to the judge in order to get out of having to serve.

SAND PLAY THERAPY

*A primary aim of Jungian analysis and sand play therapy is
"to relativize the ego"—that is, for the ego to relinquish its
illusory dominance and to reestablish a connection and continuing
relationship between consciousness and the unconscious.*
— Estelle L. Weinrib, *Images of the Self*

While living in San Francisco, working with my therapist Barbara, I discovered sand play therapy. Barbara had used this technique in her counseling sessions, and I had found the experience both nurturing and calming. Sand-tray therapy provides an avenue for expressing emotions in a non-threatening way. It gives insight into the inner struggles and conflicts of the user, and the choice of toys and where they are placed have metaphorical and symbolic meaning.

In El Cajon, I began collecting objects from garage sales and flea markets to use in a newly purchased sand tray of my own. I added materials from nature, such as seashells, pinecones, along with colorful buttons, rocks, children's toys, animals, woodblocks, and houses.

I began working in the sand, creating scenes using my collection of objects. When finished, I would write a story about my creation and then photograph it. When my nieces, nephews, and friends visited me, we had fun playing in the sand. I took pictures of their arrangements and they told me their stories.

Although my memory was continuing to return, I found these sand pictures hinted at experiences I had not yet recalled, or I was not yet ready to allow into my consciousness. In August 1991, I described one of my sand tray creations like this:

Description
A large house sits in a forest of trees on a hill in the upper third of the tray. Sticks jut from a tube behind the house. A row of people are entering the house. A serpent is hiding beneath the sand in

the lower right quadrant of the tray. A child sits among rocks in
the lower left side of the tray.

Interpretation

The house represents me and places I have lived. People are
entering my house. Sticks protrude from a tube at the back of the
tray and symbolize uncontrollable emotions. A serpent, hiding
in the lower right of the tray is hiding his evil intentions. A child,
not easily seen in the picture, sits among the rocks, and watches
the scene. She is me.

People are entering my house.

The sand tray was a part of my life until I moved to live on my
own and had limited storage space.

■ ■ ■

Despite my disappointment that my mother couldn't or wouldn't help
me with my memories, we had a relatively easy time living together.

After I graduated, my mother sold her house and moved to Leisure
World, a community in Orange County. Although I had a master's
degree in counseling psychology, I did not feel I had a future as a therapist. However, my degree also qualified me to be a social worker. At

age fifty-five, I was hired by California's Riverside County Social Services, where I worked with foster children for eight years until I retired in 2004. I started with a caseload of seventy-five children. Learning the job and getting control of the workload took an emotional toll. I gained thirty pounds and returned home each night exhausted. Making friends was difficult as I had no energy for extracurricular activities. But I wanted to do well, and I took pride in completing all court reports on time and doing my best to help the children.

Each foster child had to be seen once a month. There were visits to schools, therapists, foster parents, lawyers, grandparents, and parents, who were sometimes in prison. I might drive as much as two hundred miles to see one child.

One of my stressors was the constant necessity to relocate the children. It was not uncommon to move a child three times or more. Finding a new home was always challenging, as many of the children had behavior problems. As I tried to help, I found myself wondering if we were actually hurting them more than we were helping them. The many moves and disruption of their education took a toll on their self-esteem. I know of no child in my caseload who attended college directly after high school. When they turned eighteen, we turned them out into the world, unprepared. Many returned to their parents.

One high point of those years was buying my own home.

My first home at age 62, in Moreno Valley, California.

CHAPTER FOURTEEN

RETIREMENT

NORTHWEST ARKANSAS, 2004

AFTER EIGHT YEARS AS A SOCIAL WORKER, I WAS GLAD TO retire.

My entire family and longtime New York friend, Joannie, gathered to help me move. In a few hours we were in a caravan on our way to Bella Vista in Northwest Arkansas. My brother Arthur had purchased a house in Bentonville a few years earlier and, after several visits, I decided it would be a good place for me to retire. It would be less expensive than California, and I would have family nearby.

Once settled into my brother's house, I began looking for my own place to live. The profit from the California house made it possible for me to pay cash for a brand new three-bedroom house on a winding road nestled in the woods in Bella Vista. Deer, raccoons, opossums, skunks, groundhogs, and a multitude of birds were regular visitors to my backyard.

Now, I turned my attention to designing a garden. The house had no landscaping, which meant I was able to be creative. I fashioned a park-like backyard. Soon my near-acre lot was vibrant with iris, day lilies, rhododendrons, azaleas, hundreds of daffodils, and several species of blooming trees. In a few years it was so beautiful I was invited to participate in the bi-annual Bella Vista Garden Club tour.

My Bella Vista, Arkansas, home. I designed and created the gardens.

I also joined several book clubs, plus quilting, writing, and photography clubs. I became a Master Gardener eventually serving as vice-present. My interest in daylilies led me to join the Ozark Hill Daylily Club where I became president for a couple of years. I also organized my own movie group. Bella Vista had an active crime watch group. I volunteered and eventually became an area director.

In 2006, I went to California to bring my mother back to Arkansas, and while there spoke on the telephone with my mom's best friend.

"I'm glad you are taking her home with you," she said. "She should not be driving." After a short pause, she added, "Your mother is the strongest woman I have ever met."

This comment surprised me as I saw my mother as quite the opposite. Later, I considered calling this woman to ask her what she meant by that remark, but I decided it might not be appropriate. I wish I had.

I know I have been hard on my mother. I don't know all her demons, but I do know some. She loved my father, but he was a self-centered philanderer who caused her great pain. At one point he left her and moved in with a stewardess, the mother of a teenager, only to return to my mother after a few months. Dad often wasn't home when she needed him. He didn't even take time off from work to be with her when she had shock treatments. I also believe she was an incest survivor, and that trauma, along with my father's infidelity and my abduction, must have taken a terrible toll on her ability to acknowledge her emotions.

My mother was intelligent. Early in her life, she wanted to be a writer, but couldn't find the time to sit down and express herself. She loved classical music, was a voracious reader, loved to paint, and was great at working cross word puzzles. I mourn the fact that her life was not fulfilling, and that my abduction was the cause of much of her suffering.

Mom eventually was placed into a nursing home and died on February 12, 2007.

My three siblings and I received a sizable inheritance and I was able to purchase a 30-foot RV with a living room which could be expanded, and two televisions. In 2006, I had purchased a three-month old Chihuahua whom I named Button. She became my constant companion. Over a four-year period, we traveled 40,000 miles together, visiting many of the Southern and Western States.

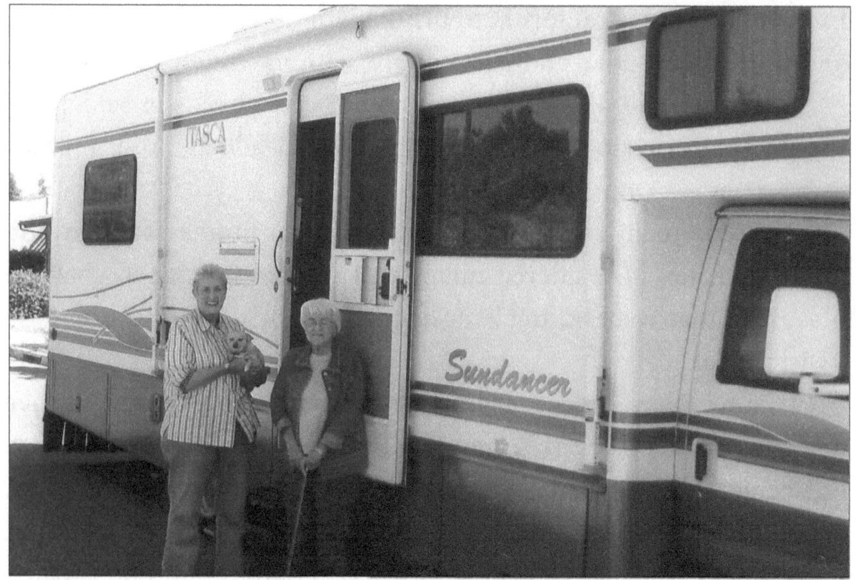

Alice with Button and beloved Aunt Marianna.

I was thriving in so many ways and having wonderful adventures, but throughout it all, I continued to have nightmares and to record them. In 2010, I began counseling with Virginia Krauft, Ed. D. She was a senior analytic licensed psychologist and used the theories of Carl Jung in her practice. For two years, we analyzed my dreams.

■ ■ ■

Dream: "The Strange Word"
June 15, 1992. 2 years and 9 months after my memory returned.

I wake up and the word epogency comes to mind. I spell it out. E P O G E N C Y.

In the middle of a therapy session with Virginia, I wondered out loud if it could be a foreign word. She went to the computer and typed the mystery word. Stunned, I learned it was the name of a care manual for Yamaha Pianos.

Three days after that session, I remembered that when I was thirteen, my father took me with him to a local Yamaha dealer. My dad was a musician and wanted to buy a piano. While he talked to the salesman I was left on my own. I opened a piano bench and found a pamphlet with the word written across the top: EPOGENY.

At the time, I was trying to expand my vocabulary. I concentrated, repeating the word over and over again to help me remember. When my father and I drove away I was disappointed with myself. I could not remember the word.

The experience of this dream made it clear that there are many memories stored in the unconscious. Milton Erickson, the founder of the American Society for Clinical Hypnosis, taught that the unconscious knows more than the conscious. I now absolutely knew what I always believed. My unconscious had memories to give me, and my dreams were an important means by which I could access them.

■ ■ ■

By 2015, intrusive thoughts and nightmares continued to plague me. My brothers still did not support my memory. "There is no way that if this happened to you, we would not remember it," was their reasoning. My history of incest caused many to believe that this was the real problem, and I was using my "made-up" abduction to take attention from the trauma of incest.

Back in 2003, Dr. Yapko had asked me why it was so important for me to validate my memory.

"I want to know that I am not crazy," I told him. I wanted to honor my eight-year-old self. I wanted everyone to know that I did pretty well in my life, despite what happened to me. I wanted people to know what happens to kidnapped victims in explicit terms and about the cruelty involved in child pornography. It would explain so much about my life and my lack of self-esteem, and it would free me from my obsession.

"Alice," Dr. Yapko said, "I worked in a mental hospital for three years, and it is full of people who knew the truth.'"

He gave me something to think about. I had gone through a period of major depression for several years after my memory returned, and I worried I was losing my sanity. But I was always able to take care of myself and to continue functioning. I have never been discouraged from seeking the truth, whatever it was.

In February 2016 I experienced something called a "cognitive shift." I recorded the details in my journal.

DIARY ENTRY: "Cognitive Shift"
February 28, 2016.

Today, while sitting at my desk, I experienced what is called a "cognitive shift." My mind moved like a zoom lens. Reality sharpened. The top of my head seemed to lift off. It felt like I was moving into a hypnotic trance. My ego seemed to remove a blockage and a light bulb went on.

What came to me at this moment was: *HE WAS A PEDOPHILE AND A PORNOGRAPHER.*

This revelation removed for me, once and for all, any doubt that I was abducted. Somehow, I suddenly knew for sure that my memory was correct. I just didn't have all the particulars and I didn't know how to prove it. I decided to write a book—the preliminary title being, "The Other Me."

In the Fall of 2016, I contacted Dr. Yapko who suggested I see a student of his, Dr. Dianne Bradley. I had my first meeting with her in October. She lived in Franklin, Tennessee, a 650-mile drive from Bella Vista. At our first meeting, with Button snoozing quietly at my feet, I told her about my kidnapping and asked her to hypnotize me. No surprise, she declined, and talked about the ethical issues around hypnosis and how easy it was to produce false memories. Exactly what Dr. Yapko had said to me in 1994.

"But I can empower you," she said. "Think creatively, use the internet to research. But you don't need to have proof to write your book."

And she said, "I believe you." *Finally.*

■ ■ ■

I joined Newspapers.com and began perusing old issues of *The Los Angeles Times* and other newspapers, and began using the internet extensively to research related subjects. Frustrated by the lack of specific information regarding the underworld, I sought out books on the subject. My library is full of books on organized crime, dream research, and post-traumatic stress.

I began having dreams again. I also re-read my entire collection of recorded dreams and was surprised to find clues I hadn't noticed before: names, places, dialogue, images, and actions. Over the years, options for research had changed dramatically. Now, Google Earth provided a way to research places named in my dreams, and online bookstores made it possible for me to easily find books about the Mafia and the history of Los Angeles.

I found an interview by retired FBI special agent, Roger Young, in which he discussed his undercover work in the area of child pornography, prostitution, and obscenity from 1977 until his retirement, in 2001. During his time in the FBI, Young worked on three national obscenity cases, code named: MIPORN, (investigation involving fifty-four major pornographers), BLUE DARCY (case against Reuben Sturman, who ran a massive pornographic syndicate), and WOODWORM (targeting major pornographers in the San Fernando Valley in Los Angeles).

In the interview, Roger talked about his father, who had been an FBI agent from 1950 until 1972. He'd been stationed in the Los Angeles office from 1955 to 1972 where he worked to find and convict pornographers. In 1968, Roger's father was declared the national coordinator for all pornography cases nationwide.

In May 2017, I wrote Roger a letter. To my surprise, he answered. We planned to meet in Reno on June 21, 2017, the day of my seventy-eighth birthday.

I arrived for our interview with a list of questions and, with his permission, recorded the conversation. Later, I transcribed the conversation and sent it to Roger for approval. From our conversation I learned that in the 1940s, child pornography fell into the same category as adult obscenity. There were no specific child pornography or child prostitution laws, although there were sentencing differences for cases in which a minor was taken across state lines "for immoral purposes." In those cases, sentencing was more severe than in cases of transporting adult prostitutes.

In an interview with the Catholic News Agency, Roger stated:

When I began working child pornography cases early in 1977, we used obscenity laws to prosecute child pornographers. In 1978, Congress enacted a law that specifically addressed the production of child porn. Proof of obscenity did not apply. The law was limited to material produced for pecuniary profit. It wasn't until after 1982, when the Supreme Court held that child porn could be prosecuted without the need to prove that the production of it was for pecuniary profit. The laws passed involved the noncommercial production and distribution of child pornography.

I learned that a child's name would have been removed from the permanent record in pornography cases, and that I would need the name of the perpetrator to find a record of the trial. To complicate matters, some pornographers were involved in Satanic Cults and used aliases.

Roger was an enormous help. Some of the many takeaways from our interview include:

- Persons of every segment of society, every race, every religion have been involved in crimes against children.
- Olvera Street, in Los Angeles, was a place where pornographers rented space for filming.
- Porn groups often rented houses or estates for filming.
- Children's photographs were published in magazines, and in sets, for pedophiles.
- Child sex offenders will often show children photographs, movies, or actual acts, to normalize the behavior and so that the child knows what to do.
- Children were told/taught how to perform for particular pornographic films.
- Children were filmed in sexual situations with animals.
- During a trial it is common practice to show the jury pornographic films and/or photographs as evidence of crimes committed.
- Juries can be shown photographs and movies of specific child pornography if necessary for conviction.

Following my visit with Roger, I traveled to Lake Tahoe looking for familiar places, but once again, I found nothing concrete to verify my memory.

I then began organizing family photographs and school records on large foam boards. I placed my brother Arthur's records next to mine for comparison. It soon became apparent that I was eight years old when kidnapped. Also, when looking at a map of California,

I remembered there were two large lakes in the San Bernardino Mountains, outside of Los Angeles. These lakes provided vacation opportunities with surrounding forests, mountains, luxury hotels, and conference centers. This scenario dovetailed exactly with my dreams. I realized my dreams weren't about Lake Tahoe, but instead Lake Arrowhead and Big Bear Lake.

I was ready to center my research there.

PART FIVE

PUTTING IT ALL TOGETHER

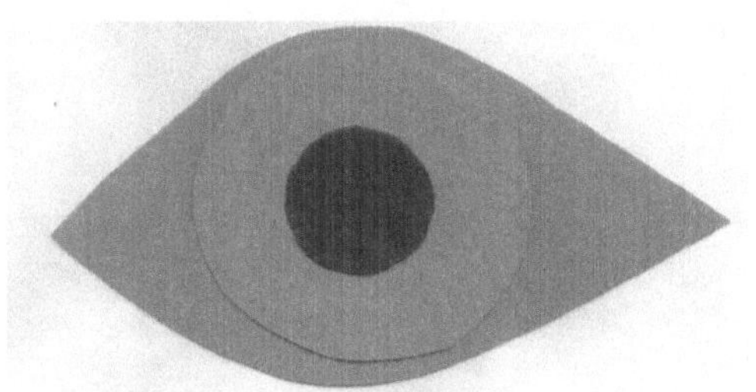

CHAPTER FIFTEEN

DREAMS ABOUT LOS ANGELES

Find joy in the journey.
—Thomas S. Monson

MOVIE THEATERS

WHEN PERUSING MY DREAMS ONCE AGAIN I FOUND references to buildings, streets, and movie theaters, and wondered if they were located in Los Angeles. If I could find them, I could prove once and for all that I had been there. The following two dreams led me to research the *Rialto Theater*. (Trigger warning: these dream sequences include explicit sex.)

Dream: "Looks Like We Are Going to Be Needing You Today"
June 10, 1991. 2 years and 9 months after my memory returned.

There is a movie theater and I now recall that I have been in this theater many times in my dreams. There is a woman, and she is sticking her finger up the anus of a girl child. The woman goes over and puts soap on her hand and washes. I'm sitting on a chair on the side watching this.

181

There is a man there and he is a director. My impression is that this is being filmed, but it also feels like an audition. In another scene, I go into a theater with a man and his wife. We get there early. I am dressed up in a nice dress and shoes, and sit in a chair.

A man sees me and says, "Looks like we are going to be needing you today."

DREAM: "The Rialto"
October 16, 1993. 3 years and 9 months after my memory returned.

I am in a movie theater I have been in before. It is on a cobblestone or brick street. There is an old-fashioned barbershop. It is the Rialto Theater. I have been in there with another girl, who is a teenager. She is bending over the back of a chair and a man is entering her.

Through my research, I discovered a picture of the Rialto Theater located in South Pasadena, and it corresponded to my dream. I lost my breath for just a second when I saw the street appeared to be cobblestone and there was barbershop in the picture. My heart pounded. It appeared I was on the right track and this encouraged me to research many other clues found in my dreams.

This Rialto Theater was opened in 1925 and had a Wurlitzer organ. But most striking, I found it was possible something called the Ordo Templi Orientis (OTO) had held rituals in the theater. This quasi-religious group allegedly worships semen and the penis. I found myself wondering if it had something to do with the Satanic cult about which I had memories; maybe the cult had rented the theater for ritual ceremonies.

A few days later, I began serious work on my dreams. I retyped every dream I'd had since 1962, pasting icons where a word that caused an emotional reaction was repeated in other dreams. I then put these corresponding dreams together in files and began to get a clear idea what the dreams were trying to tell me.

A diary entry from that time reads:

Today I worked on [the Rialto] dream. I became dizzy, my mind felt as if it was moving back and forth as it does under hypnosis. It occurs to me that there was a separate section in the theater where live sex performances took place, or perhaps it was a place where people auditioned to be in the sex industry.

The front of the Rialto Theater taken in 1933 corresponds to my dream.

In the summer of 2018, I visited my brother Stephen, who lived in Southern California. He agreed to take time off from work and drive me around to some of the locations recorded in my dreams. His wife Mary Anne joined us. The Rialto was closed, but when we looked in the front window, we saw a small lobby with stairs left and right, ascending to the theater. I was reminded of a dream in which I walked up stairs on the lefthand side of a small lobby that led to the auditorium. I knew this was the theater from my dreams.

I recalled another dream I'd had several years prior.

DREAM: "I Am in a Porn Theater"
December 4, 1989. 3 months after my memory returned.

My boss has called me on the telephone and invited me to go to the Empire movie theater where I am to work. This is a porn theater, and I am working in the back room. Normally, the movies are shown in the front, but there is also a little theater in the back where I am. The owner of the theater comes into the room. He says he needs to use the space for a few minutes because some people are going to audition. A couple of people perform, but I can't remember what they did.

Things change into a combination movie and open audition. People are coming and going. I am seated in the little amphitheater observing.

There is a movie going on and a group of homosexual men are in a row on the stage and one of them is putting his fist up the anus of the man next to him.

While this is going on I am giving a hand job to another homosexual man who is sitting in front of me. At one point he shows me how to do it and I continue and get my hand full of semen.

The movie stops and the lights come on. The man says to those around him, "How does one keep from being frustrated when this happens?"

A woman responds, "You have her continue on and go down on you."

Some people come in and go up into the projection booth at the back. My impression is they can see everything that is going on in the theater and they are having their own sex scenes.

A young girl comes in. She is around sixteen years old. She takes her clothes off.

There is a long wait, and I am embarrassed. Everyone is very relaxed and natural and seem to feel it is okay for me to be there.

I decide to get up my nerve and walk across the front of the theater and leave. I walk out the front of the building and remember I have left my purse. I turn around to go back and run into a group of women who are coming out. One of the women says to me, "How can you be so impersonal?" referring to the fact that I had given the man a hand job.

I say, "That's what this is, isn't it?"

My research revealed that there was an Empire movie theater in Los Angeles at 2131 W. Pico Blvd. It dated back to the 1930s and ran adult films, but live sex shows were also performed there. I had these two theaters in my dreams within three years of my memory returning—many years before I remembered I had been in Los Angeles, and well before I began my research.

Stephen drove me by the Empire Theater, too. It was closed and in rundown condition, which was disappointing. But this theater was located near where I eventually learned I had lived for a time.

Empire Theater, 1962. *The World's Greatest Sinner,* starring Timothy Carey, is showing.

BUILDINGS

DREAM: "I'm Helping a Sick Child"
April 22, 2003. 13 years and 7 months after my memory returned.

I am with people in a brushy area. Someone brings out a little girl. I say, "She needs to go to the hospital."

She doesn't want to go. She is frightened and doesn't want to be taken away from her family. They give her to me to carry.

We go to the hospital, and I meet a woman named Clarice. We run into a doctor in the lobby. He is Dr. Anderson. He has been helping someone earlier in the dream.

He says, "Oh yes, this is the little girl that has such and such a disease." He gets out his chart and says, "Oh, she also has this other disease. Take her to the room upstairs and I will be right up."

Clarice and I get on the elevator. It is a two-person elevator, and we stand close to each other. I am uncomfortable because it goes up so high. I wonder if I am going to have trouble coming back down. Clarice says we are in one of the tallest buildings in the area. I imagine riding in an airplane and looking out of the window.

Now I am taking Clarice over to my house. We call the little girl's parents and tell them that she needs an inoculation, and we will bring her home after she gets the shot. We must take her because she doesn't want to go.

The parents say they are not going to be home. They will be at the Colorado Park.

I am now going up the side of the building and looking in the windows. There is a movie star with blue eyes. I can't think of the movie he was in. He is embracing his girlfriend. It is apparent they are making up. He has tried, on a number of occasions, to get back with her and this time it has worked. The other people in the room seem disappointed.

This dream is loaded with clues: one of the tallest buildings in the area; Colorado Park; Clarice; man with blue eyes; Dr. Anderson; and the comment, "she has this other disease, too."

I found that from 1928 until 1964 Los Angeles City Hall was by far the tallest building in the city. The Federal Courthouse building located next door was also tall. The dream suggests I was in these buildings with someone named Clarice, which is the FBI name of Jodi Foster's character in *Silence of the Lambs,* a 1991 film I had watched several times. I deduced I was in the Federal Courthouse with an FBI agent, probably a woman, where the trial at which I had to testify was held. The two-person elevator suggests I am a witness being taken to the courtroom by the back entrance for safety purposes.

Los Angeles City Hall and Federal Courthouse (on the left) circa 1948.

The dream suggests it takes place after the police raid that resulted in my being discovered. The agents performing the raid saw I was sick and took me to the hospital. I didn't want to go. I was frightened to be away from my "family," with whom I completely identified by then, and I didn't understand what was happening.

I visited both buildings with my brother and sister-in-law. They are no longer the tallest, but City Hall is still an impressive height. We had to transfer to three different elevators to get to the top where the panoramic view of the city was amazing.

The next clue, Colorado Park, at first misled me since the name suggested it could be near Denver. However, I discovered there is a Colorado Park near the Santa Monica Pier which in 1948 would have been close to the subway line that then existed. I have a memory of being in a subway and visiting an underground open-air shop.

I was hospitalized after I was found and diagnosed with chlamydia in addition to having a drug dependency—both common among sex-trafficked children. Maybe "Anderson" was the name of the physician who took care of me. I have had several dreams that mention doctors I do not remember.

Lastly, the movie star with blue eyes could have been Frank Sinatra, who was in the news at the time because of his contentious on and off relationship with Ava Gardner. He was often seen in the presence of the Mafia, and one of his nicknames was "Old Blue Eyes." One of my dreams also includes another celebrity from the time. In the dream, a woman says, "Don't you want to stay so you can meet Sammy Davis, Jr.?" when I want to leave a party.

DREAM: "The Building"
September 7, 1990. 1 year after my memory returned.

I am in an old building. The lobby is massive like the inside of Radio City Music Hall in New York. The building has the feeling of being Art Deco or of that period.

As part of my research, I purchased *L.A. Landmarks, Lost and Almost Lost,* a book about iconic Los Angeles buildings and was surprised to find that this building was the NBC Radio City Hollywood Building. It met the description in my dream which convinced me I had indeed been there in person.

NBC Radio City Hollywood.

NBC Radio City Hollywood exemplified the heyday of Hollywood as a broadcasting hub. Renowned architect John C. Austin designed the sprawling Streamline Modern complex, which contained eight studios and three office buildings. The main lobby rose three stories and embodied the power of radio, from a soaring mural by Edward Turnbull (who also painted the lobby ceiling of the Chrysler Building), to zigzag sound waves coursing through the terrazzo floor. This building was torn down in 1964.

STREETS

I also had vivid dreams about streets that turned out to be in Los Angeles.

DREAM: "Spanish Day"
February 16, 1993. 3 years and 5 months after my memory returned.

A movie star takes my hand, and we go into town where I live on the fourth floor of a tenement building. It is Spanish Day and as we go up the stairway there are people sitting in their windows looking out and waiting for the parade to begin.

Olvera Street is where the Spanish Cinco de Mayo parade takes place annually. According to retired FBI agent, Roger Young, Olvera Street was an area where pornographic movies were made during the forties.

DREAM: "Henry Street"
December 20, 2017. 28 years after my memory returned.

I am thinking the words Henry Street as I wake up.

I often woke up with a few words in my memory. Over time, I learned that important information was imparted in this way.

N. Henry Street, I learned on Google Earth, is within the East Lake Juvenile Court and drug rehabilitation complex. The street is in a parking lot next to a building that looks like a social service receiving center for children when first removed from parents.

There is a swimming pool and a cement walkway to the court-house. It seems logical that I would have been placed in a receiving home while the court decided what to do with me.

Henry Street and East Lake Juvenile Court complex,
as shown on Google Earth.

DREAM: "I Keep Getting Robbed"
October 26, 1989. 1½ months after my memory returned.

I remember I am on "Cold Water Canyon Road." I yell at the police so they can start on their way while I find the exact address.

Just a month after my memory returned, Cold Water Canyon Road appeared in a dream. Cold Water Canyon is a road that leads up from Hollywood to the San Fernando Valley where pornographic movies were made.

In 2018, my brother Stephen drove me up this street. In the 1940s, Virginia Hill and actor George Raft had homes there. The madam Brenda Allen had a "house of pleasure" nearby, as did Mickey Cohen in 1948. These underground characters appear later in my book.

DREAM: "Connecticut Court and Connecticut Street"

October 13, 1993. 4 years and 1 month after my memory returned.

I wake up dreaming the words Connecticut Court and Connecticut Street.

Connecticut Street in Los Angeles is a one-block street where there is an old apartment building with a center courtyard. Stephen took me to this Connecticut street where we found the building pictured below. The building corresponds to my dream, "The Dinner Party."

DREAM EXCERPT: From "The Dinner Party"

October 4, 1990. 1 year and 1 month after my memory returned.

The apartment building is rectangular and has an inner courtyard with a balcony you can walk around on the inside.

Google Earth photograph of the Connecticut Court
apartment building on Connecticut Street, Lost Angeles.

The Connecticut Street apartment house was remodeled in 1962 and part of the courtyard was covered over. I feel certain I lived in this building at one time.

SATANIC CULT

At my first meeting with therapist Barbara Cook, after my memory began to return, she wrote that I had said I was involved with a Satanic cult. I had forgotten I said that and was surprised when I received her therapy notes. Upon organizing and reviewing materials to write this book, I realized I'd had many dreams related to a satanic cult. I found six dreams I had previously not understood, two of which I had before my memory returned.

DREAM: "The Strip of Fire"

July 23, 1989. 1 month before my memory returned.

I am in a room and a man is incanting sacred words in a tongue that might be Greek or Latin. He is wearing a robe. A strip of fire shoots at me and then he gets on a table with me. I wake up in fright.

DREAM: "Being Initiated into a Satanic Cult"
September 6, 1991. 3 years after my memory returned.

I am taken to meet the head wizard. Someone is playing an organ. I say, "Hail, oh great Wizard," or something like that. I am worried about what is going to happen to me. A man tells me to "Suck up to the grand wizard" and his wife.

I wake up and am uneasy.

MEMORY: "Satanic Cult"
February 11, 1994. 4 years and 5 months after my memory returned.

I am with a group of children.
   We are wearing robes and walking down a hall.
   We carry lighted candles.
   I am lying on a table in the front of a room.
   A man in a black robe is standing over me.
   A torch is in his hand.
   He waves it over me.

Additional dreams associated with the Satanic cult: (page 273) *The Girl in the Black Robe, I Light the Candles, Cartagena, The Man With the Black Cape Massages my Bottom.*

SATAN'S CASTLE

In 2017, I researched the Big Bear Lake, Lake Arrowhead, and Crestline areas. I wanted to visit The Tudor House and Bracken Fern Manor which had been owned by the mobster Benjamin "Bugsy" Siegel, one of the men responsible for developing the Las Vegas strip. The Tudor House and Bracken Fern Manor, built in the 1920s, were part of an exclusive members-only resort offering, above all, privacy. The Tudor House was a gambling establishment, connected by a secret underground tunnel to the Bracken Fern Manor, a brothel on the Manor's top floor that was also known as "The Crib."

I believe I was in the bracken Fern Manor as part of an extortion plan as related in the Brenda Allen section of this book.

"Satan's Castle" was in Crestline. I'd learned that all but the tower of the building had burned down, allegedly by neighbors who didn't want this building in their area. In 2017, a video on YouTube showed the partially destroyed castle as a young man walked around the grounds discussing the site. He showed a pentagon carved in the cement at the side of the building. When I watched this video again in 2022, the part that showed the pentagon had been removed.

Satan's Castle, Crestline, California.

I drove around a small community, where I noticed a street. I thought, *It could be up there*, but continued on. Back on Highway 18, in a few miles I approached a house on the right side of the road. Startled, I said to myself, *That's the white house.* I turned my head to look cross the street from the house and there were cement stairs leading up from the road to a path that wound up the hill. At the top was a burned down house with two stone piling sticking up. *That's*

Satan's Castle, I thought. But, too exhausted to investigate further, I drove on to Big Bear. The next day, I began the 1500-mile trip back to Arkansas, telling myself I would return another time.

A Google Earth photo of what I thought was
the burned down Satan's Castle and the surrounding area.

In October 2022 my brother Stephen visited me in Arkansas, and we looked for Satan's Castle on Google Earth. Stephen was able to pull up a picture of the ruins which showed the location of a church about a block away. But this was not the same location I had identified as Satan's Castle, back in 2018. Why was I remembering the white house, steps, path, and house at the top of the hill? Although not the correct location of Satana's Castle, I believe I was there, and for some reason find myself thinking it was a party house.

Subsequently, I found an article about Satan's Castle on HiddenCA.com that stated there were said to be underground tunnels linking to other places on the mountain used mainly during

Prohibition, both for smuggling and "for darker purposes" and that one of the tunnels "is rumored to connect a . . . church to Satan's Castle."

The author shares that the home was built in the 19th century by a newspaper tycoon but later sold to a Dr. Russell Atkinson, who "rubbed shoulders with some of the most powerful figures in the area." Atkinson held "elaborate parties" there and it was known as a "space for social affairs of importance." It was rumored that the home was used for "dark, ritualistic practices which included both human and animal sacrifices along with other dark ceremonies."

CHAPTER SIXTEEN

MY ABDUCTORS

DREAM: "Checkers"

May 5, 2017. 27 years and 8 months after my memory returned.

I wake up thinking the word "Checkers." Weird. I have no idea what it means.

LUCKILY, I RECORDED THIS ONE-WORD DREAM WHICH TURNED out to be prophetic.

In 2018, it occurred to me I might have been abducted by someone involved in organized crime. In the nearly thirty years since my memory had returned, I never once thought there might be gangsters in Denver, Colorado. However, a quick internet search led me to the book *Smaldone: The Untold Story of an American Crime Family,* by Dick Kreck. Kreck was a retired reporter who had written for *The San Francisco Examiner* and *The Denver Post.* In his book, I recognized a photograph of Eugene "Checkers" Smaldone.

The Smaldone brothers, Clyde George and "Checkers" gained criminal control of the Denver area in 1933. For forty years they were heavily involved in gambling, bookmaking, loansharking, and slots.

In September 2018, I contacted the author and arranged to meet him in Denver, Colorado.

I told Mr. Kreck about my struggle, as well as my new belief that "Checkers" was one of my kidnappers. He said he knew nothing about any kidnappings, but offered to help me.

▪ ▪ ▪

Another book, *Mafia*, published by the U.S. Treasury Department Bureau of Narcotics in 2007 gives "name, aliases, description, localities frequented, family background, criminal associates, criminal history, businesses, modus operandi, and a picture" for known criminals.

This eight hundred and forty-two-page book is divided into states in which the criminals operated. The Colorado section included among others, Clyde George Smaldone, Eugene "Checkers" Smaldone, and James Spinelli. It is through this book that I discovered that the Smaldone brothers and James Spinelli had connections with organized crime individuals in Los Angeles.

Clyde and Checkers Smaldone and James Spinelli were business associates of Los Angeles criminal Joseph Sica, who had a record of an arrest under the Mann Act, a federal law also known as the "White Slave Act," that criminalized the transportation across state lines of any woman or girl for the purpose of prostitution or other uses in the sex trade. Sica, who was a partner with Los Angeles gangster Mickey Cohen, ran, among many other illegal activities, an extortion racket using prostitutes to trap unsuspecting men by surreptitiously filming their sexual activities. Cohen was also involved in prostitution, pornography, and drug rackets.

During World War II, according to Kreck, Clyde Smaldone was friends with a man named Frank Curley, who oversaw stamp rationing for the United States Government over seven states. Curley, as a gesture of friendship, gave gasoline stamps to Clyde, who then passed them on to friends in the gasoline business in Los Angeles. He wanted to curry favor and establish a working relationship with the Los Angeles mob. The stamps were transported to California by Clyde Smaldone's wife Mildred and son Gene, who made several trips over the course of the war. They would deliver the stamps to a gas station, a gathering place for celebrities, movie stars, and politicians. Mildred said she met Frank Sinatra there.

In another book about the period, *Celebrity Gangster: The incredible life and times of Mickey Cohen*, Brad Lewis writes, "Mickey [Cohen] had invested in several lawful businesses, prompting the FBI to list his occupation in 1940 as a "gas station owner."

There is no doubt in my mind that Mildred Smaldone was delivering black market gasoline stamps to a Mickey Cohen establishment. Garages are prominent in my dreams. Here is one of them:

DREAM: "The Bad Guys in the Garage"
April 20, 2003. 13 years and 7 months after my memory returned.

I am in a car with a woman and a young boy and a man I don't remember. The car pulls into a garage and is taken on an elevator down four floors to a place where they work on cars. When we get to the bottom a bad guy arrives. He looks at our jewelry, makes snide remarks, and then takes what he wants.

The Mafia dealt in stolen jewelry and furs, and in this dream, it appears we are delivering stolen goods. I am with a young boy who shows up in many of my dreams.

DREAM: "Am I Going too Fast?"
May 3, 1991. 1 year and 8 months after my memory returned.

I am driving down the street. A man in a green old-fashioned car is following me. It is getting darker . . .

A 1941 green Studebacker Skyway Land cruiser.

This dream caught my attention. According to Kreck, Clyde Smaldone owned a green Studebacker.

■ ■ ■

Checkers married in 1931 and had one child, "Young Eugene," born on February 5, 1936. The name Eugene is a prevalent Smaldone family name, so to distinguish Checker's son from other family members, he was always referred to as "Young Eugene." In 1948, he would have been twelve years old, and a twelve-year-old boy is present in several of my dreams.

Young Eugene followed his father's footsteps into the criminal world and had a troubled life. According to Kreck, he was involved in bookmaking, loansharking, burglary, gambling, conspiracy, and racketeering. He also dealt in narcotics, becoming an addict, and in one of several prison terms, served ten years for importing cocaine from Peru. He died in a nursing home in 2014.

The Smaldone's owned many houses around the Denver Area used for clandestine gambling games. These houses were connected by telephone. Because the house I was kidnapped from was not lived in and basically empty of furniture, I believe I was abducted from one of these homes located near Evan's School.

Now, I was open to believing my kidnappers had been deeply involved in organized crime. The connections made sense, and the puzzle was coming together.

■ ■ ■

How did all these criminals connect with Sherrie's mother, who helped with my abduction?

According to Kreck, Clyde and Checkers once worked for Ova Elijah "Smiling Charlie" Stephens, who owned and operated gambling houses complete with restaurants and shows featuring dancing girls. In addition, Stephens owned Blakeland, a place south of Denver that was open from 1933–1936. The Smaldone boys worked there for a time, and were friends with some of the dancers. Kreck's book also introduced me to James Spinelli who owned in 1948 an establishment called The Circus Bar—another location where beautiful women entertained patrons. Sherrie's mother was a beautiful woman. What if the Smaldones and Spinelli were told by their mafia connections they needed a young girl for their sex businesses? Why would Sherrie's mother have been involved in this endeavor? Is it possible these unsavory characters were threatening to take her little girl? Or was she ordered to find a child and threatened if she refused?

■ ■ ■

The Smaldones had connections with many major criminals, some of which I write about in the coming pages. For example, Tony Accardo the powerful boss of the Chicago Outfit; Joseph Sica and "Checkers" Smaldone attended the wedding of Accardo's daughter. Accardo sent Virginia Hill and Johnny Rosselli to oversee business interests in Los Angeles, where Jack Dragna was La Cosa Nostra boss.

Carlo Marcello, a member of La Cosa Nostra and boss of the Louisiana territory, was a friend of Clyde Smaldone and a business partner of Mickey Cohen. I believe I was put to work for Brenda Allen who, in association with Mickey Cohen's porn and prostitution businesses, ran a network of sex workers.

I have made a Mafia association chart to help clarify the relationships among the different mobsters relevant to my story and to show the Smaldones' connections to the underworld which, I believe, finally fully explains why I ended up in Los Angeles.

SMALDONE/MAFIA ASSOCIATION CHART

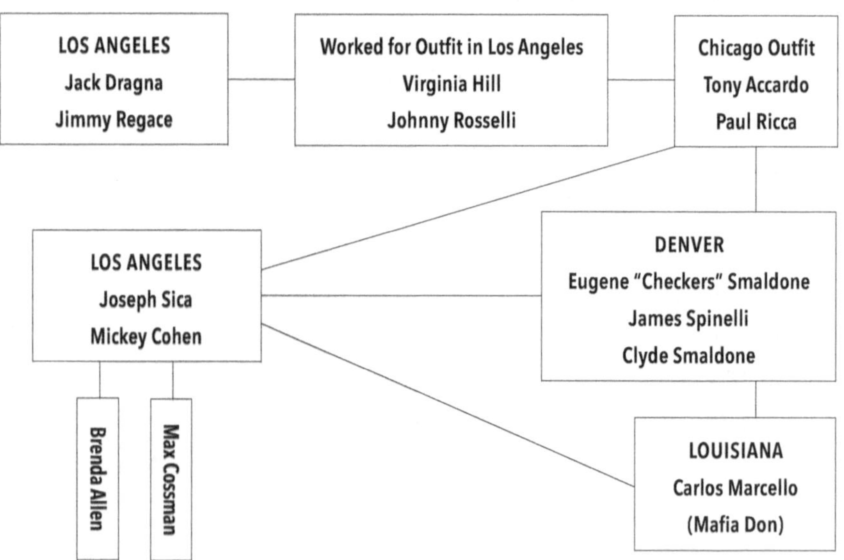

CHAPTER SEVENTEEN

THE UNDERWORLD

During my abduction I met a number of criminal members of organized crime. These include Mickey Cohen, Joseph Sica, Brenda Allen, Virginia Hill, Johnny Rosselli, Jack Dragna, and Max Cossman. I also suspect I met Jimmy Regace who ran the porn business at the time I was in Los Angeles.

MICKEY COHEN

In 1948, the criminal underworld was dominated by organized crime figure Mickey Cohen and La Cosa Nostra boss Jack Dragna. Mickey, who had worked for Benjamin Bugsy Siegel, became prominent following the murder of Siegel on June 20, 1947.

Cohen's criminal activities covered control of gambling, loan-sharking, prostitution, pornography, extortion, and narcotics. He was a larger-than-life character hounded by paparazzi who enjoyed the excitement of covering his extensive social life, as he hobnobbed with beautiful women and movie stars.

In his book, *Celebrity Gangster*, Brad Lewis writes that Cohen "spared no expense when it came to his personal pleasures. He never dined at home without monogrammed linen and imported silver.

Dandy Mickey's $20,000 wardrobe included 1,500 pairs of socks, fifty pairs of $50 silk pajamas, Chinese, Japanese, and Persian silk robes, silk underwear embroidered with his initials, never less than thirty pairs of sparkling shoes, hundreds of ties." Mickey was especially famous for his collection of ties. Lewis's mention of Mickey's ties caught my eye because I identify a man by his "ties" in several of my dreams and I believe him to be Mickey Cohen.

In 1944, Mickey purchased a mansion on Hazen Street, located in the hills of Cold Water Canyon. Lewis writes, "Soon completed, the fancy joint was a spectacular party house where a special list of Mickey's friends could spend the night in wild all-night orgies, and party-girl bouts." Mickey hosted what Lewis calls "commercial sex parties" attended by the rich and famous. He surreptitiously recorded sexual activities at these parties and used them to extort huge sums of money from his victims.

In 2016, nearly three decades after I recovered my memory, a dream disclosed the identity of the person behind my abduction.

DREAM: "The Boogie Man"

November 30, 2016. 27 years and 2 months after my memory returned.

I wake up just as I exit a room and begin to walk down a hall. I perceive there is someone there who has stepped back into an indent in the wall, attempting to hide. I turn and look. It is my kidnapper. He is short and olive skinned. I wake up, bouncing up from my bed, shaking, engulfed in fear.

I tell myself that he is dead and I don't need to be afraid. I go back to sleep.

DREAM: "Uncle William"

December 14, 2017. 27 years and 3 months after my memory returned.

I wake up thinking about going someplace with Uncle William.

Mickey's best friend, and the man who was best man at his wedding, was named William.

Here's another dream correlation with Mickey's life that is too specific to have been a coincidence:

DREAM: "Snow White and the Seven Dwarfs"
October 4, 1989. 1 month after my memory returned.

I wake up thinking the words, Snow White and the Seven Dwarfs.

Note that this dream occurred very soon after my memory returned—just one month.

In 1949, after I had been returned home, Mickey Cohen hit the headlines once again, this time for ordering seven of his henchmen to beat up Alfred Marsden Pearson, the owner of Pilot Radio. Pearson was disliked by a myriad of customers because of his overcharging and shoddy service. The public reacted when Elsie Phillips, a sixty-three-year-old widow caring for a grandchild, was forced out of her home because Pearson sued her for refusing to pay him $8.91 for work on her radio. He won an $81 judgment against her, and Elsie was forced to sell her home, which Pearson promptly bought for $26.50 and offered to rent it back to her.

A group of Los Angeles Police officers from the Wilshire station, organized by Captain Lorenson, were outraged and decided to pay Elsie's rent. They then hired a lawyer to help her recover her home. Pearson promptly sued Police Captain Lorenson for $45,000, accusing the captain of attempting to ruin his business. That's when Mickey Cohen entered the picture. Captain Lorenson was on his payroll.

In *Mickey Cohen: The Life and Crimes of L.A.'s Notorious Mobster*, Tere Tereba writes that Mickey said years later, "'I had the police commission in Los Angeles going for me. A lot of the commissioners didn't have any choice. Either they would go along with the program, or they would be pushed out of sight . . . I had . . . what you could call the main events. It was all the way to the top of the box at different police stations.'"

Apparently, Mickey took matters into his own hands and met with Lorenson. Rather than killing Pearson, they agreed to a severe beating. With Mickey watching, seven of his thugs pummeled Pearson nearly to death. To Mickey's surprise, his henchmen were arrested. When the newspapers got hold of the story a cartoon was published portraying Mickey and his henchmen as Snow White and the Seven Dwarfs. All seven mobsters, as well as three members of the LAPD and Captain Lorenson, were charged with conspiracy: assault, robbery, and obstruction of justice.

Meanwhile, Mickey bought Elsie Phillips's house and presented her with the lease.

Why would I have dreamed about Snow White and the Seven Dwarfs just one month after my memory returned if I wasn't aware of this story? It took place around the time I was back in Los Angeles for the trial against the pedophile and pornographer with whom I was found.

BRENDA ALLEN

Prostitutes and gamblers do not operate with unlimited scope unless they have help from law enforcement agents, officials and politicians.
—Sgt. Charles Stoker, Ex-LAPD Vice-Squad Officer,
author of *Thicker'n Thieves*

I remember Brenda Allen, and my research into the Mafia showed me that she was the most well-known and written about madame in 1940s Los Angeles. Her prostitution business focused on servicing high profile clients, businessmen, public officials, police, and movie stars.

In 1948, Brenda had approximately 114 girls working for her. Her operation was under the protection of the Los Angeles police department through her relationship with Sergeant Elmer Jackson, who received weekly payoffs and sexual favors. Brenda was also connected to Mickey Cohen, who used her "girls" at his "party house" and in his elaborate extortion racket.

Instead of running her business out of houses of prostitutions where men just showed up, Allen relied on a call girl service to vet prospective customers. She kept a card catalogue with information about each client, including his or her preferences.

Brenda was a redhead, always perfectly dressed and manicured. Nearly all pictures of Brenda on the internet (there are many) show her wearing her signature dark sunglasses.

In 2017, when reading through my dream journal, I came across a dream in which I describe a woman wearing sunglasses. I immediately became excited. Here are several dreams I believe indicate I knew her.

DREAM: "The Woman with Sunglasses"
June 1, 1991. 1 year and 9 months after my memory returned.

I walk past a cabin. I hear my "mother" talking in a loud voice on the telephone. I circle around behind the cabin to hide. I peak around the corner and see a woman standing by a car. She is a friend of my "mother," and she has on sunglasses. She is looking in my direction. I don't want her to see me.

Brenda Allen in her signature sunglasses.

This dream records that fact that Brenda is coming to visit my "mother" to make arrangements for me to work for her.

DREAM: "The Hidden Room"

December 8, 1992. 3 years and 3 months after my memory returned.

I go into a room with a woman. There is a senator who has come in from town. He gets paid a check. He is having an affair with the woman.

There is a bedroom at the top of the building and over at the side is a hidden room. The woman goes in there where someone is hiding.

A politician is in many of my dreams. The one in this dream is receiving payoff money. I am taken to a bedroom at the top of a building where I am going to be photographed having sex with someone as part of Brenda's and Mickey Cohen's extortion operation. A photographer is hiding in the secret room. In another dream, a politician comes to my home and buys pornographic photos of me.

I also have dreams that include someone named Max, but I had no clue who Max was until I got deeper into my research of Mickey Cohen and Brenda Allen.

DREAM: "I Make My Selection Very Quickly"
January 29, 1990. 4 months after my memory returned.

I am at a table in a restaurant. There are two small tables pushed together so four people can eat with each other. I am sitting across from a woman, next to me is another woman, and across from her is Max.

I make my food selection very quickly but everyone else takes a long time. Max studies and studies and studies his menu and hasn't even ordered by the time I wake up from this dream. The woman across the table from me also takes a long time, but not as long as Max.

Max Solomon was a lawyer for Brenda Allen and Mickey Cohen, who I believe was the man warned me not to tell the police about my relationship with her.

DREAM: "Be University"
October 12, 1990. 1 year and 1 month after my memory returned.

I am in a house preparing for a party and a man arrives in a car. He comes in and I am leery of him but say, "Can I help you?" He says,

"Yes," and reaches out his hand to shake mine. He tells me his name and asks if I remember he had been to visit me before regarding "Be University." It felt like he meant "be" as in "To be," representing life and all the things that have to do with living. I say something about getting the gist of it. I wake up and my heart is pounding.

In this instance, I am asked if I want to live (to be) or die (not to be). In other words, keep my mouth shut if I want "to be."

Brenda Allen figures largely in my experience. I believe it was she who threatened to cut off my toes in the scene at the opening of this book. She must have had clients who wanted sadomasochistic services and she would have been proficient at providing it. That chilling memory, not a dream, was a technique designed to mold a child into becoming one hundred percent compliant. By the time they finished with me, I no longer knew who I was and had become a product of their making. I complied, without question, to everything they demanded of me.

In my dreams. I also have a recurring image of a woman described as a "dragon lady" or "witch." For example, in "The Jail/Bouncing John," dream, I am smacked by a woman guard, causing a scar. At some point, my role changed from a new "recruit" to an official call girl. In one of my dreams, a woman called the "dragon lady" says to me, "We've decided to trust you. We believe you have put your past behind you." After that, I was trusted to be out on my own. My dreams record taxi rides where I was delivered to downtown hotels to meet a john.

Other dream memories report late night drives where I am transferred from one car to another to meet a man for a secret rendezvous or for an assignation at a rest stop. Sometimes I was even flown in a small aircraft to meet someone at a ranch in a remote location.

In *Thicker'n Thieves,* Sgt. Charles Stoker of the Los Angeles police chronicles his extensive interactions with Brenda Allen as he attempts to arrest and incarcerate her. He was successful a few times through wiretapping, legal in those days, but she never spent a night in jail after she contacted her police connections or lawyer and made bail.

In *Celebrity Gangster*, I came across a reference to a French sex teacher named Claude Marsan. Marsan, known as the "love guru," worked for Brenda Allen, and many of her girls were his disciples, to whom he taught special techniques in how to please a man. Because a Frenchman is mentioned in several of my dreams, I looked Marsan up on Newspapers.com and found many articles discussing his nationwide lecture tour in which he produced a sex manual and demonstrated his methods using a young model. Numerous newspapers throughout the United States are peppered with amusing headlines describing Marsan's public performances.

Marsan was instructed to give me lessons.

DREAM: "The Frenchman Makes Love to Me"
July 12, 1990. 10 months after my memory returned.

I meet a man who is French. He suggests we go home. He is not happy with me. His penis is stiff. I squeeze it and he says he doesn't want to make love. I encourage him even though I know he doesn't want to and he is not particularly interested in me. We have sex, and I start to have an orgasm, but I can tell by the look on his face that even though he is doing it, and he is having me, he doesn't like me.

He looks down and says, "Don't worry, I'll take you home. Would you like to go for a drink or something?"

I'm sure you can imagine that a man known as "The Love Guru," accustomed to teaching sex techniques to beautiful, mature call girls, would not enjoy showing an eight-year-old child how to please a man. And yes, children can have orgasms.

On the morning of May 5, 1948, as chronicled in *The Los Angeles Times,* Brenda Allen's prostitution business came crashing down when an elaborate police raid took place. Police stormed her house of pleasure on Harold Way, located above the Sunset Strip. Police confiscated a box of index cards containing the names of approximately 250 names of members of the film industry, politicians, law enforcement, and other prominent members of the Los Angeles community. The box listed information about each man, including contact information and sexual preferences.

When the public heard about the raid, men listed on index cards in her box began scrambling. Lawyers, studio executives, and agents began behind the scenes negotiations with police and court officials to squelch negative publicity. Money changed hands . . . . Regarding the infamous "box," Judge Call announced his decision: "In the box are names of dignitaries of the screen and radio and executives of responsible positions in many great industries. Publication of their names would be ruinous to their careers and cause them great public disgrace. I order the exhibit sealed." The box remained sealed until William H. Parker became Los Angeles Chief of Police from 1950 to 1966 and ordered it destroyed. I was not with Brenda Allen during the raid—I believe I was with Virginia Hill.

On August 26, 1948, according to the *Los Angeles Evening Citizen News,* Judge Call sentenced Allen to 180 days in jail for operating a house of prostitution. Obviously, I did not talk or she would have spent many years in prison.

In 1989, the year my memory returned, I heard on the radio that Brenda Allen had died. I now wonder if that was the main reason my memory returned. Her death made it okay to remember and to speak. I was safe.

VIRGINIA HILL

Memory: Saturday, July 7, 1951

My mother: Do you remember Virginia Hill, that woman you used to know?

Me: Yes.

My mother: She was detained at the Denver airport.

Mafia bag woman, Virginia Hill.
I spent time with her to help disguise her identity.

Virginia Hill was a larger-than-life Mafia bag woman. Well known for her beauty and abilities in bed, she had been the mistress of Bugsy Siegel and New York mob boss, Joe Adonis, and offered favors to numerous other underworld figures. After Bugsy was assassinated in June 1947, Virginia continued to be of use. The Chicago Outfit supplied her with vast amounts of money to help her enter into high society where she made important connections to help mob businesses. As a bag woman, she hosted extravagant parties, travelled extensively, passed messages, transported money, jewelry, fur coats, and facilitated introductions between underworld figures.

Rocky Mountain News article, July 7, 1951, about Virginia Hills detaiment at the Denver airport. The headline states, "Virginia Hill Questioned In Denver by U.S. Agents." My friend, Gena Burson travelled to Denver to retrieve this newspaper article for me.

Virginia moved to Chicago at seventeen where she met Joe Epstein, an accountant and money launderer for the Chicago Outfit, where Tony Accardo was the boss. Under Epstein's tutelage and because she had a good head for figures, she went into money laundering, bookmaking, and learned the ins and outs of horse racing. Through this relationship, Virginia began working for the powerful Chicago Outfit, who supplied her with vast amounts of money and encouraged her entry into society. Thus, she was able to use her connections, wealth, and beauty to further the projects and businesses of organized crime.

Virginia enjoyed visiting Mexico and moved there for a time where she socialized with the wealthy and powerful. She held elaborate parties, making connections with influential members of the government. Thus, she was instrumental in helping the Mafia's Mexican drug trafficking business, using her sexual prowess and contacts with important people. Among her Mexican lovers were Chato Suarez, son of the past Secretary of the Treasury, and Luis Amezcua Torrea, a military man with the Mexican Air Force and the main contact between Mexican federal officials and American drug traffickers. He was eventually promoted to captain and became part of the presidential staff of Miguel Aleman (1946 to 1952). Many believe he was also one of Virginia's lovers.

As my memory slowly returned, I began to sense I had met Virginia during my abduction experience. I read in Ed Reid's book *The Mistress and the Mafia* that Virginia, who sometimes travelled under a number of different pseudonyms, had been seen disembarking from a ship in Genoa with two children—a girl aged nine, and a boy aged twelve. This reportage by gossip columnist Lee Mortimer of *The New York Mirror*, a nemesis of Virginia's, turned out to be a case of mistaken identity (which ruined the vacation of the misidentified woman). But the story alerted me to the fact that authorities knew Virginia traveled with children to disguise her identity. I'd had several dreams in which

I am with a twelve-year-old boy, and I had turned age nine during my abduction. I went back and read all my dreams and found many I previously had not understood suggested I had spent time with her.

According to these dreams, and the memories they triggered, I met Virginia Hill at a "family gathering"—"family" referring to the Mafia. She often appeared at "family" Mafia parties where I was in attendance with my kidnappers. The paparazzi were hounding her, and she looked for opportunities to be anonymous.

DREAM: "The Country Club"
March 13, 1994. 4 years and 6 months after my memory returned.

I am at a place like a country club. A woman is there and there are people who want to interview her. She hides because she does not want to be seen.

DREAM: "I Am Going to Make a Movie"
June 5, 1991. 1 year and 9 months after my memory returned.

I am with a group of people and an older woman. She is wealthy. She announces she wants to go to the races and asks who wants to go. People run after her and I decide I want to go, too. I run to get my shoes and pass a man who is going with us.

Later, we are all sitting together on bales of hay at the horse races and the man joins us. He talks about me being in a movie with him.

He says, "I like what I see. Don't worry about yourself physically. I am happy with you. There is one thing I am wondering though. Do you think you can learn the lines? Do you think you can do it?"

"You bet I can!" I reply enthusiastically.

I'm happy because I am going to make a movie with him. I'm going to be his girl. I imagine myself nude being photographed with him.

The man stands up and shows me his gun. He puts the gun away and there is a metal thing in his hand and a callus on his thumb. It is like one of those things people put in their hand when they are going to hit someone.

"Do you know why I have this callus here?"

"Yes, so people will be afraid of you," I giggle.

I believe the first dream is of Virginia at a mafia family party, and the second recounts a trip with her to the racetrack. She and her deceased lover, Bugsy Siegel, owned a box at Del Mar Racetrack and she was savvy to the ins and outs of horse racing.

DREAM: "Two Women Fight"

January 14, 1990. 4 months after my memory returned.

People begin to arrive for a family gathering. A woman and my mother have been shuffled out the door and on to the porch. I know that something has happened. I turn to one of the Black men and ask if he knows what happened.

"Yes", he says. "The two women had a fight and attacked each other."

I think this is peculiar and go to find out what happened. I find my mother sitting on the porch with my dad and another person. No one is talking about what has happened.

I had two dreams about a fight between two women, and I now believe they were between Virginia Hill and a woman who is taking care of me.

In this brawl, I believe Virginia was informing the woman that kidnapped me that the Mafia had decided I was to be used to help Virginia disguise her identity. She had begun to travel under pseudonyms to hide from paparazzi and law enforcement, especially when travelling outside the United States conducting business for the Mafia. A child posing as her daughter would help hide her identity.

Virginia had the backing of the Chicago Outfit—Joseph "Joe Batters" Accardo, Paul Ricca, Johnny Rosselli and Jack Dragna—who were using her to connect with drug dealers and potential users. If the Smaldones, and or Spinelli, were the people I lived with while there, they would have had to comply; they had no power over these formidable gangsters. After I was placed with Virginia, the Smaldones, Spinelli, or other caretakers, would have ceased profiting from my work in pornography and prostitution, and returned to Denver.

My life improved while I was with Virginia. She stayed in fabulous homes and luxurious hotels. She dressed me in beautiful clothes and took me to restaurants and parties where I met Mafia family members.

Virginia Hill was short tempered and impatient, but overall treated me well. Her maid, Mrs. Della Gordon, who testified at the Kefauver Commission Hearings, accompanied us, and took care of me when Virginia was occupied with Mafia business.

I had a dream I'd named "The Banquet Room." Tere Tereba's book, *Mickey Cohen, The Life and Crimes of L.A.'s Notorious Mobster*, mentions that according to Cohen, in 1950 he sponsored a fundraising dinner for Richard Nixon, held in the "banquet room" at the Knickerbocker Hotel. When I read this, I remembered the dream and realized it suggests I had been in the Knickerbocker Hotel with Virginia.

DREAM: "The Banquet Room"
December 24, 2017. 27 years and 3 months after my memory returned.

I am in a huge hotel. I go down to eat in the Banquet Room. It is a large area with many round tables. A low partition separates the buffet from the rest of the room. I am sitting with a woman and am waiting for my mother to arrive. When she enters, I go to meet her thinking she will not be able to see where we are sitting. She has on a fox stole and is dressed in a forties' outfit. She is tall and slender.

Why would I have named this dream "The Banquet Room," if I had not known it was the name of the room? The physical description of the woman I'm with is Virginia Hill. I am with her maid, Della Gordan, who is taking care of me.

TRAVELING WITH VIRGINIA

We traveled to Miami in summer 1948 where she planned to sell a house she owned. From there we went to Cuba where I believe she met with Mayer Lansky to discuss the Mexican drug cartel business and his interest in developing gambling casinos in Acapulco. Virginia's Mexican connections could help facilitate introductions to prominent politicians, and she could transport messages.

DREAM: "Am I Going to Crash?"
September 16, 1989. 7 days after my memory returned.

I am in a commercial airplane, sitting in the front row, and we are flying over the ocean headed to an island. The water is a brilliant aqua marine color. Down below I can see groups of people treading water. It is unclear if they are male or female or if they are nude or are in bathing suits.

I have the impression the people think the airplane is going to crash. The plane begins to lose control and it becomes turbulent. I put my feet on the manifest to brace myself.

I wake up with a pounding heart.

The airport in Cuba is next to the ocean, and a plane needs to approach the runway just above the ocean, making it easy to see people swimming.

DREAM: "The Restaurant above the Sea"
*May 23, 2018. 28 years and 8 months after my memory
returned.*

I am with a couple of women. We are in a town and decide to have dinner at an Italian Restaurant. There are men with us, and we travel in two cars. The restaurant is located across the road from the sea. There is a cement barrier along the ocean across from the restaurant.

In this dream, I am aware that I am actually in a moving car. As I look out of my face, I see and feel the car move in slow motion as we drive down the road beside the sea and the cement barrier and turn left beside the Italian Restaurant, drive to the back, pull in, back up and move around to the side of the restaurant and parked beside other cars.

Havana Nocturne, by T. J. English, is an excellent book about Mafia's activities in Cuba in the 1940s and 1950s. In the introduction, English writes,

> On stormy days and nights in Havana, Cuba, the ocean batters the sea wall that rims the northern edge of the city. Waves crash against the rocks and splash upward, spraying the sidewalk avenue, and cars driving along the famous waterfront promenade known as the Malecon.

I have a memory of being dressed up and walking by myself beside a swimming pool next to a park. The scenery is tropical. We could also have been in Mexico, but the dream gave me the feeling that I spent a weekend in Cuba with Virginia.

I was definitely in tropical areas, as evidenced by this peculiar dream:

DREAM: "The Watermelon Fruit"
May 15, 1989. 4 months before my memory returned.

There is something about trying to climb a banana tree. There is a long fruit–the skin looks like a watermelon except it is quite elongated. "What kind of fruit is it?" I ask.

I believe this dream references my first encounter with a papaya, which only grows in subtropical climates. At age eight, living in Colorado, I would not have known about papayas.

From Cuba, we returned to Miami, packed up Virginia's house, and travelled through Louisiana on the way to Mexico. I have wondered if Virginia then had contact with Carlos Marcello, the Cosa Nostra Don of the area and business partner of Mickey Cohen. Several of my dreams and memories suggest scenery from the area, such as low hanging trees covered with moss, sugar cane fields, swamp-like areas, and some buildings that sound like places that Marcello owned as described in John H. Davis's book, *Mafia Kingfish*.

I have a memory of seeing a mansion down a country road and behind a gated entrance, with nearby dwellings where servants lived. I stayed in one of those houses for a day or so. I have gone over this memory in my mind hundreds of times, trying to remember where I was.

Dreams about border crossings were at first puzzling, but describe attempts to cross the U.S. border into Mexico—or the other way around.

DREAM: "Stopped at the Border"
April 12, 2017. 27 years and 7 months after my memory returned.

I am a spy and am stopped at the border. I must show the guards my papers. I am worried because it is a fake and they might discover I am a spy. I make up a story to tell them that I dropped my papers in the water and that is why they look funny. They take the papers. I ask for them back. They say, "Go to the local office."

DREAM: "Get Your Papers Ready"
April 27, 1989. 5 months before my memory returned.

I am driving somewhere with a woman. Suddenly, she says, "He's coming around to your side. Get your papers ready."

Several other dreams suggest that Virginia and I were invited to a military base to watch a review:

DREAM: "I Am on a Military Base"
February 28, 1994. 4 years and 5 months after my memory returned.

I am on some sort of military base. Service men are serving us tea. There is a white rug, the military sergeant is sitting at the front, and I am up there with him.

Virginia had a connection with the Mexican military through her relationship with Luis Amezuca Torrea. Because of their association and his being an officer in the Mexican Air Force, it's probable she was invited to a military review.

DREAM: "Storm Troopers"
November 23, 1993. 3 years and 2 months after my memory returned.

There are some people with me and one is a woman who is beautifully made up. We turn around. Storm troopers, dressed in army uniforms, are coming across the field. They have landed by parachute.

I also had a dream about a rodeo that must have been somewhere in Mexico:

DREAM: "Rodeo"

October 20, 2017. 28 years and 1 month after my memory returned.

I am on a hill overlooking a rodeo where helicopters are landing.

Rodeos were (and still are) popular in Mexico, where cowboys sometimes arrive for events in helicopters.

Well into finishing the writing of this book, I had the following dream. (Trigger warning: human body parts.)

DREAM: "The Bloody Head"

November 25, 2022. 33 years and 2 months after my memory returned.

I am looking out of the kitchen window and see a severed head lying on the patio. There is blood everywhere. A Chihuahua is

licking the head. The house is located on a hill and the scenery suggests Mexico. There are no trees, just scrub brush. Virginia Hill comes out of the house, and we discuss what to do as I wake up.

This dream felt like an actual event. Despite its gory nature, it did not feel like a nightmare. What should be a horrible memory comes off as "matter of fact." I am looking at a bloody severed head. *No big deal. It is just something that happens.* It is likely that I was dissociated at the time of seeing the head and recorded the memory in my dissociated state; that would make the dream emerge from my memory as dissociated. It's also possible that my unconscious is still protecting me from the feelings that would have occurred while experiencing such a thing.

In any case, the Spanish language book *La Cosa Nostra en Mexico,* 1938–1950, recounts the activities of the Mafia's and Virginia Hill's involvement in drug trafficking of marijuana, opium, and heroin during the time of my abduction. The practice of beheading, or guillotining, is mentioned. This reminded me of one of my one-word dream.

DREAM: "Guillotines"
July 15, 1989. 2 months before my memory returned.

I wake up thinking the word guillotines. I don't know why.

After Virginia completed this "business travel," we returned to Los Angeles. According to the chapter "Time Line for Virginia Hill" in Kevin John's book *Bugsy and His Flamingo: The Testimony of Virginia Hill,* on June 28, 1948, Virginia was called back to Chicago. I remember accompanying her to the airport with another woman, and that we said goodbye.

DREAM: "Goodbye"

May 19, 1994. 4 years and 8 months after my memory returned.

I am at an airport and am telling a woman goodbye. She shakes my hand and thanks me for everything and tells me she appreciates everything I have done. She tells me that the thing she likes about me most is my beautiful music.

I believe the word "music" in this dream is a metaphor for my performances in porn.

Virginia died in 1966 from a drug overdose, in Switzerland, under suspicious circumstances. Reportedly, Virginia had threatened to turn over her diary to authorities.

Today, I find myself full of empathy for Virginia. Things improved for me after the horror of my life before I was with her. She became involved with the Mafia when she was seventeen, and once that happens, there is no turning back. No one who has knowledge of the Mafia's activities can leave. Throughout her life she made numerous attempts to kill herself.

The empathy I feel for her exists even though she never tried to save me from my circumstances, but rather used me for her own purposes. She kept me in bondage when she could have at least tried to save me, and then she abandoned me.

When Virginia left me at the airport, I was still of use to the Mafia. There was no one who would, or could, take care of me. My abductors had returned home and Brenda Allen was being watched closely by the authorities. I believe that is how I ended up living with the pedophile and pornographer with whom I was found during the police raid.

MAX COSSMAN

At some point, Virginia connected with Max Cossman (aka Max Webber), a major drug trafficker known as the "King of Opium" who had worked with Bugsy Siegel, Mickey Cohen, and Joseph Sica.

I mention Cossman here because the dates of his freedom from a Mexican prison dovetail with the dates of my abduction, and the time I was with Virginia. I believe I met him and his three children—two boys and a girl.

Here is a dream that recounts a conversation with his three children. The dream begins with a dinner party where he and his children are in attendance. I believe we are at Mickey Cohen's house.

DREAM: "Sex Has Been Perpetrated"
October 4, 1990. 1 month after my memory returned.

The scene changes to a house where there is a man wearing a tie. He has produced a movie and wants to show it. A couple of the ladies in the movie are at the party. It is a porn movie. On the couch is a man and two young girls of the promiscuous type. The man who made the movie and the two girls are rowdy and I think this is going to turn into an orgy. After a brief announcement the movie begins. There is a fountain of bubbly water that is kind of gooey. This is how the movie begins. It is about a girl losing her virginity.

The wife, who is the hostess, is bored by the whole thing and is sleeping in the bedroom. She comes in and is upset. She doesn't want this going on while there are children present. She gets up to leave with the three children. There is a girl who is older and then two boys. I make conversation.

"Where do you live?" I ask.

"We live just south of the border," they reply.

"You mean Mexico?"

"Yes, in Mexico."

"Where do you go to school?"

"We go to school there."

"Do you speak Spanish?'

The young boy is embarrassed and says, "No."

He feels I am criticizing him.

I say, "What I mean is, isn't it great that you live down there and go to school where you get to speak Spanish."

"No, they speak English in the school. They don't speak Spanish."

I want to make sure he understands I am not criticizing him. I say, "I assumed you know Spanish because you are in school in Mexico."

I have a strong emotional reaction when I think about my conversation with Max Cossman's children. In the dream I am concerned about offending his children; I was in an inferior position and had no power. They probably knew that I was being used in porn movies and as a prostitute and looked down on me. I was trying hard to be accepted.

The dream mentions a man in a tie, and of course I have wondered if he is Mickey Cohen, who also did business with Cossman and was heavily into the pornography and prostitution business. He may have financed some of the movie productions.

DR. MARGARET "MOM" JESSIE CHUNG

I believe that during my time with Virginia, I met Dr. "Mom" Chung, Virginia's good friend who was involved in drug trafficking on behalf of, at the time, our Chinese allies, helping to raise money for Chiang Kai-shek in his fight against Mao Tze-Tung and the Communist rebels. A couple of my dreams mention "a Chinese lady."

"HANDSOME" JOHNNY ROSSELLI

Johnny Rosselli is famous in the annals of organized crime for his influence as a member of La Cosa Nostra. He was sent to Los Angeles to infiltrate the movie business and work with then Mafia boss Jack Dragna.

Johnny was known to like children. Charles Rappleye and Ed Becker write in their book, *All American Mafioso:*

> Children are sometimes considered a true test of character, whose affections cannot be bought by flattery or false attention, and Rosselli always made a deep impression on them. "All my children fell in love with him," said Bob Maheu, a private investigator and CIA operative who met Rosselli in the middle 1950s. "He had that ability to make children feel important." "He was always wonderful with the kids," added Joaun Cantillon. "It wasn't that he sat and played with them on his lap, but he listened to them, he paid attention."

Lee Server reports in his book, *Handsome Johnny,* that Rosselli "had great sympathy for children in poor and neglected situations. Children without fathers, without hope." Johnny built a swimming pool for an orphanage and paid dowries for girls who wanted to become nuns.

I have no proof I met Johnny Rosselli, only a feeling, but I have had one dream that made me think of him:

DREAM: "Pat Garfield Stimulates a Lucid Dream"
March 12, 1981. 7 years and 6 months before my memory returned.

All of a sudden, a window scene zooms at me and becomes very sharp in focus. It is a lucid dream. I realize a man and two women are coming to visit me. The man walks from behind a big redwood tree and approaches the window. He looks right at me. He is handsome, open faced, and very friendly in appearance. His eyes are blue.

I became acquainted with Patricia Garfield, PhD, at a social function in San Francisco in 1981. She is the author of ten books about dreams and was one of the founders of the International Association for the Study of Dreams (IASD). She inspired me to read about lucid dreams, and I shortly began to realize I was experiencing them during my nighttime adventures. The above dream is an excerpt of a much longer lucid dream.

This dream makes me think of Johnny Rosselli and his blue eyes. In 1948, he was producing movies for Bryan Foy through Eagle Lion Films. One movie, *Canon City*, was released on June 30, 1948. I have watched this movie, about a real-life prison escape, on You Tube.

One of my earliest memories was that I had just made a movie and had started a second when the police raid took place. I have wondered if I was introduced to Rosselli to see if he could use me in some capacity. I also might have met him at "family gatherings," where he was serving as consigliere to Jack Dragna.

I believe Rosselli had something to do with the fact that I was not murdered. He would have been one of the people who had to approve my death. Did he, someone who cared about children, make an agreement with the FBI to leave me alone on the condition they return the favor?

I found myself upset when I read that Rosselli was murdered, at age seventy-one. As with Virginia Hill, I have fond feelings for him. Why? He too left me to the wolves. Perhaps it is because they were the only ones among these monsters who treated me kindly in some way. Or perhaps the Stockholm Syndrome is causing me to identify with them because I had become a member of the group.

JACK DRAGNA

Dragna, also called the "Los Angeles Don," was a member of La Cosa Nostra but worked directly with the Chicago Outfit—Tony "Batters" Accardo and Paul Ricca—through his relationship with Johnny Rosselli and Virginia Hill.

Six of my dreams record my attendance at "family gatherings," which I believe to be Dragna's "family." Virginia Hill and Joseph Sica had a working relationship with Dragna and as such would have been invited to "family gatherings." Due to his association with the Smaldones/Spinelli, I was most likely included.

DREAM: "The Movie at the Swimming Pool"
November 27, 1989. 2½ months after my memory returned.

My dream last night was based on characters from the Francis Ford Coppola movie, The Godfather.

Tom walks into the swimming pool room where the Don is meeting with the family. There is going to be a party and they want to show a movie. The best place to hang the screen seems to be from the ceiling in the middle of the pool. Tom jumps into the pool, with all of his clothes on and mounts the screen on something hanging from the ceiling. The Don doesn't like what is going on and tells Tom to shape up.

I believe this dream, using the Francis Ford Coppola *Godfather* movie as a metaphor is a memory of a Dragna family gathering I attended in 1948. Jack Dragna was known as the LA Don and his brother was named Tom, as was Robert DuDuvall's character Tom Hagen, consigliere for the Godfather, Marlon Brando's character. Why, I ask myself, only two months after my memory returned, would I dream about a Mafia boss presiding over a family gathering?

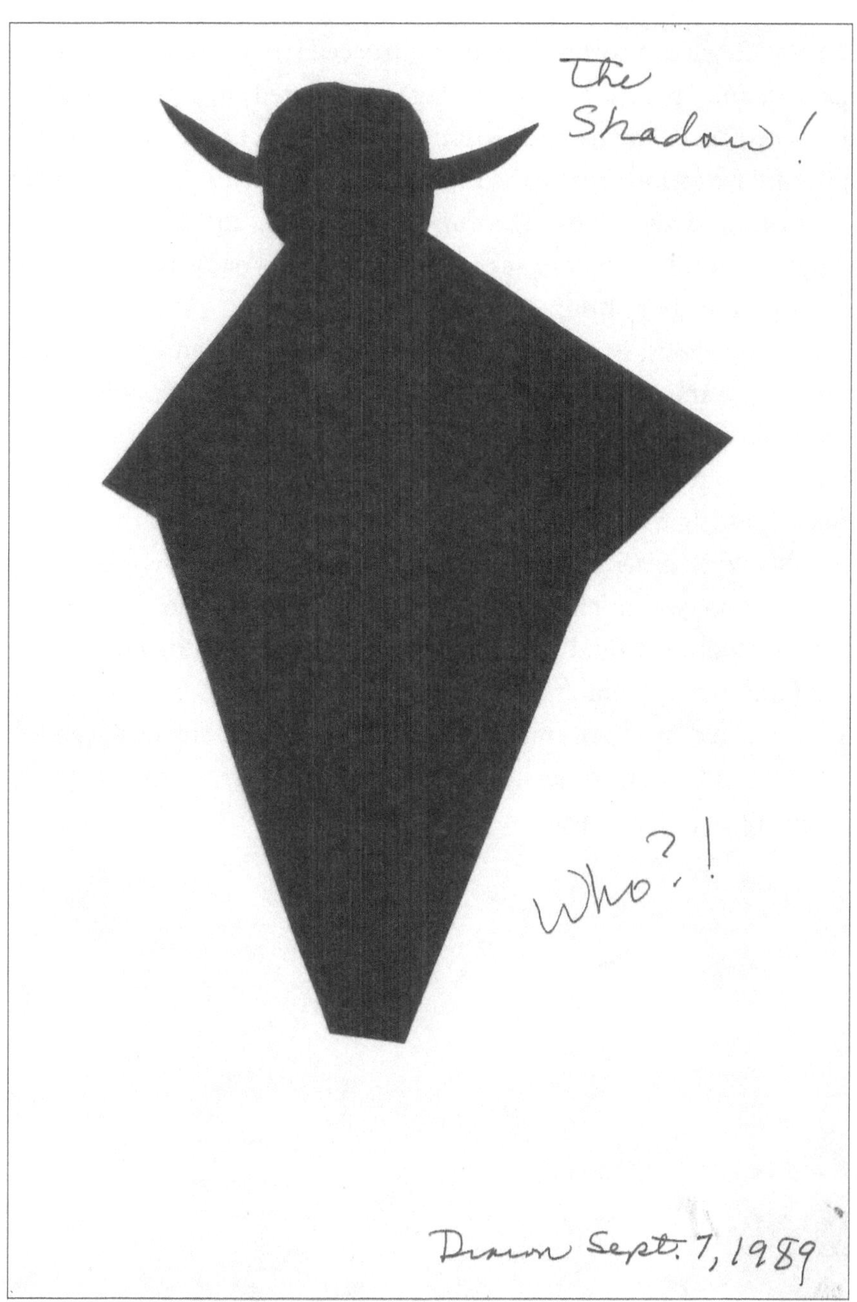

The
Shadow!
Who?!
Drawn Sept. 7, 1989

JIMMY REGACE

Jimmy Regace, (born Domenico Brucceleri) worked for Mickey Cohen, and later, Jack Dragna. Regace attracted my attention when I learned that Dragna and Rosselli put him in charge of pornography and extortion during the time I was there. In 1974, Regace, who later changed his name to Dominic Brooklier, became boss of the Los Angeles "family." I had to search all three of his names to find good information about him.

In the 1980s, Brooklier was convicted of extortion in a pornography case and imprisoned in 1983 at the Federal Metropolitan Correctional Center in Arizona. He died there in 1984. I have a visceral reaction to photographs of him. I have an image of him and another man dragging a black man to his death, memorialized in the dream, *The Bloody Murder*, talked about in the next chapter. He was a thug who had no qualms about murder, and his interest in porn suggested a perverted individual who had no qualms about using children in revolting ways to enhance the income of the mob. I believe Regace was involved in the pornography racket that led to my enslavement and that of so many others. I think he is the murderous monster who often appears in my dreams.

CHAPTER EIGHTEEN

STORY OF MY ABDUCTION

MY MEMORIES DID NOT COME IN CHRONOLOGICAL ORDER. In fact, sometimes years passed before gaps in the story were filled in by another dream or memory. More than thirty-three years have passed and I still have dreams that help fill in elements that were missing. This will likely continue to well after this book is in print.

In this chapter, I tell the story through memories I recorded as soon as they came to me, all arranged chronologically—not in the timeline of when they came to me, but in that which I lived during those few months. At the end of each section, I provide the list of dreams that helped me regain my memories of those experiences, and the pages on which those dreams appear in the Appendix. Keep in mind that both my memories and my dreams are explicit and can be triggering to the reader.

Over many years, I remembered the methods my kidnappers used to break and control me. Before the terrifying moments in a basement (recounted in the prologue), my captors imposed a programmed series of procedures designed to intimidate captives and make them submissive. These methods are still employed by human traffickers today. Tactics included both physical and verbal abuse that reached the level of torture. They deprived me of water, called me a dog, and injected me with drugs, threatening to kill me if I did not comply.

I believe my captors also confined me for long periods of time in a space so small I could barely move, which to me was the worst form of torture I endured, and thus have still repressed the details even all these years later.

My abductors knew what they were doing. I don't know how long it took, but in the end, I obeyed their every command without hesitation, and eventually completely forgot my identity. This became apparent when, after my rescue, I did not remember my real name.

So, here is my story.

TORTURE

My abusers started with insects. This recall surfaced the day after my memory returned:

Memory: "Bugs"

I am nude on a table in the center of a kitchen.

A three-burner stove sits next to the wall.

A man stands over me.

A boy watches.

The man douses a centipede in a wet white powder and drops it on my chest.

I scream as the bug squirms.

"This is fun," he says as he drops more bugs from a vial.

The bugs scurry frantically.

Something slimy is on my legs.

I tremble and kick.

I plead and cry.

"Sorry," he says. "It has to be done. You won't cooperate."

Another torture technique was simulated drowning. I had three dreams about a man drowning me, the first one in 1963. The following memory returned two months after I remembered my abduction:

Memory: "Drowning"

I am in a rowboat with a boy and a man.

We are on a small lake in a park.

It is spring and the weather is warm.

We are alone.

The man grabs me and throws me into the water, holding me under.

I can't get away from him.

I struggle.

He holds me tight.

I can't breathe. I gasp for air.

I'm going to die.

I let my arms and legs founder, loose in the water.

He pulls me out.

I sit shivering and gasping for air.

"Why did you do that?" I whine.

"I don't know, I just thought I would," he says smirking.

I had not yet learned to swim.

The one thing I learned from this abuse was that if I gave up, the torment would stop. Unfortunately, that became a mantra for my life.

My abductor and his accomplices continued to mistreat me as they worked to control me. I never knew when someone was going to grab me and torment me some new way. They poured the fishy juice from cans of tuna down my nose, tricked me into eating human excrement, and threatened to burn me if I did not comply.

The word "burlap" appeared in several of my dreams—the first time one month after my memory returned. My regular experience of awakening with a particular word in my mind had taught me that seeking the meaning of it would help me restore my memories; once I learned the importance of the word "burlap," I never had another dream about it.

Memory: "Burlap Bag"

I am in a garage.

"Get in this bag," the man orders.

I step in.

"Lie down," he says as he pulls the cord.

The bag smells musty.

"Stay there until we get back."

I hear him leave.

I lie there, anxious.

I itch.

Should I get out and run away?

What if they are watching?

I can't risk it.

They will hurt me again.

Better stay here.

Frank returns and knows that I am his.

Curiously, after I moved to New York and began buying books, I wrapped each one in different colors of burlap and placed them on a shelf in my tiny apartment. Was this an unconscious homage to my trauma?

Dreams associated with torture: (page 274) *Bugs Are on Me, The Polka Dot Footprints, I Am Being Drowned, I Am the Dog; The Tortured Dog, Eating Shit, Burlap.*

LOS ANGELES

As my memory slowly returned, I realized I was taken to Los Angeles where my abductors had connections with the criminal underworld. There, my kidnappers became my family. I had a new "mother," "father," and twelve-year-old "brother." I forgot my name, and was drugged and forced into prostitution and pornography. I lost myself and all sense of reality.

I have chosen to call the twelve-year old boy of my dream, "John." I don't know if he was a kidnapped victim or if he was the son of my kidnappers, but he became my friend. From here on I will put quotation marks around "mother," "father," and "John," to denote that these people were not my real family.

Life in Los Angeles was chaotic. There was always something intense happening. Many of my dreams recount orgies and sex parties. In one dream I am walking around a large house with an actor. He says he wants to show me something. He gets ether so we can get high.

Memory: "Over Time"

I spend time in rooms with lots of people.

Everyone smokes, drinks, and takes drugs.

The rooms are dirty and messy.

Each day I go to huge warehouses where there are directors, technicians, production assistants, scenery, moving flats, lights, and cameras.

I wait around until they need me.

I play hide and seek with other children.

I take care of babies for porn stars while they are working.

I want to be liked.

I do what I am told.

I am in a dangerous business.
I am drugged when it is time to perform.
I put my arm out to receive the needle.
Gone.

During my research, I learned that some major movie studios during hard times rented out production space to pornography companies to keep their studios afloat, which would explain my memories of walking around on vast movie lots and being in enormous warehouses with stagehands working and scenery being moved around.

DRUGGED

Many of my dreams record the use of drugs to control me. The sex acts I was required to perform would have been too difficult for me if I hadn't been in an altered state. As I learned in a 1986 report commissioned by the U.S. Department of Justice: "Narcotics are often distributed to performers who appear in pornographic materials to lower their inhibitions and to create a dependency." By the time I was found, I was a drug addict and required hospitalization.

Memory: "Dressing Room"

I am in a dressing room primping in a mirror.
A blond curly wig is on my head.
A production assistant arrives.
She looks at me.
Frustrated, she leaves.
I'm not ready.
We wait.
A garden appears.
I feel good. A pear-apple tree appears.
Huge colorful flowers surround me.

I am serene.
I'm ready.
I walk to a bare platform stage with nothing but a bed.
Flood lights bear down on me.
I walk into a garden of beautiful cosmos flowers.

I had dreams in which I experienced a wonderful feeling of floating in waves, flying around, seeing things that weren't there, and talking to myself. In a dream called "The Snake Bite Pills," a man brings pills to a party to sell and gives me one, telling me that it is for snake bite.

Everyone surrounding me used drugs and some were traffickers. In one memory involving drugs, I'm getting ready for a film shoot before walking out onto an enormous, lighted sound stage where a director and producer are sitting behind a table.

Dreams associated with drugs: (page 279) *The Beautiful Yellow Flowers, Floating in The Waves, The Snake Bite Pills, You Think I'm Loaded with Money?, Ether.*

PORNOGRAPHY AND PROSTITUTION

One of the techniques pornographers use with children was to show them activities they want them to participate in, thus normalizing the behavior.

Brenda Allen's establishment was considered "high class." I had several dreams that suggest I also worked in bordellos set up along country roads in the mountains.

Memory: "Cabin"

I am in a car with the "man", the "boy," and the "woman."
I am in the trunk in a cage.
We are traveling in the mountains.

We stop at a motel.

"Be quiet or there will be consequences," warns the woman.

The man plays craps with a group of men.

He loses and is livid.

"You must go to work now," he says to me.

I am taken to a cabin. It is small with one twin bed and a window in the door.

"A man will come and visit you. Do exactly what he says" warns the man.

I wait. *Anxious.*

An ugly old man appears at the window.

He enters.

"Hello lovely," he says. "What are you called?" His voice is caressing.

I reply with my new name, "Baby Candy."

"I like your name," he says as he pulls me toward him. "You're so sweet. Come here."

He hugs me.

He smells bad.

He pushes my head down.

He groans.

He is happy.

He calls me darling.

He kisses me goodbye, tenderly.

Memory: "Whore House"

We are in our car outside a house in the mountains. The house sits alone.

The woman takes me out of the car and walks me into the house.

An obese old woman is behind a desk.

There are chairs around the room.

Men and women watch.

"This is Baby Candy," says the woman, addressing the old lady. "Might you have work for her?"

"Absolutely, I have no one on the roster like her." She points. "Have a seat, Baby."

The women talk business.

I sit, waiting.

A man comes and points to a woman. They walk through a door.

There is a boy sweeping the front steps.

Soon the boy is requested. He smiles. He wants to work.

A man enters.

Spying me, he asks who I am.

He selects me.

We go into a room in the back.

I perform my duties.

He is happy. I have done my job.

I work two days. My pay is collected.

We continue our journey.

Dreams associated with pornography and prostitution: (page 281) *The Porn Class, The Circular Staircase Down into the Porn Theater, The Love Me Fish, I Work in a Whorehous, The Sex Lesson.*

AGENT

My dreams relate that I have a female agent who I describe as being between forty-five and fifty-five years of age, is "dumpy," and wears a cotton dress. She tells a man that I will not be able to work on Friday. He tells her that they are open seven days a week and I can come when I can, they will be glad to use me—all while a pregnant woman is about to be filmed using a vibrator.

Memory: "The Pregnant Woman"

I am on a balcony overlooking a large room.

    Below is a bed surrounded by theatrical flats.

    Lights are radiating.

    They are getting ready to film.

    A nude pregnant woman is lying on the bed.

    Filming is stalled.

    There is a discussion going on.

    A man is trying to make a determination.

    Would it be harmful to the woman's baby if she uses a dildo?

    The answer is "no."

    Filming begins.

One of my first recollections was that I had made one movie and started on a second one when the police raid occurred, and I was found. I remembered my regret over the fact that my "movie career" was over. I thought that acting was fun.

In the 1940s, many B-movies were made, which I was reminded of while reading *Baby I Don't Care,* Robert Mitchem's biography, which describes his period making B-westerns. B-movies were filmed in about a week and their run-time was about an hour.

Dreams associated with agent: (page 284) *I Go Undercover as a Porn Star.*

AUDITIONING

Several of my dreams relate to auditioning. In one, a director says, "What's so special about you?" I go into an act, do a majorette bow, point my toes, put my hands on my hips and thrust them forward, look back over my shoulder at him. I am adorable. In another, an actress shows me what they want me to do. She runs around the stage acting crazy. I get on stage and repeat what she did, yelling, "Que

Bizzaro," and knock scenery around. In the dream, I know I've done a good job.

Two dreams recount an interaction with a Japanese director. He grabs me and drags me around on the floor. I yell and scream, and he decides to use me for the film. I work in his disaster movie as an extra, as described in the dream *The Script is Already Written*. In the dream, I am a passenger in a car outside a Japanese village located on a hill. A dam is beginning to break while I am a passenget in the car driving down into the danger area to pick up some stranded people. I am required to scream and yell.

The dream "The Compatibility Interviews" recounts people being interviewed to see if they are compatible with me. A young boy comes in and gets in bed with me. We move around. The same boy is in another dream. He tells me that because he has metal in his head from a brain injury, he has trouble talking in a coherent manner.

Memory: "I am in a Pinafore Dress"

I am beautifully dressed in a pinafore.

I have on black patent leather shoes with short white cotton socks.

A blond curly wig is on my head.

I am standing in a small hotel lobby surrounded by movie flats.

A taxi pulls up.

A doorman opens the door.

I run out and jump into the cab.

The cab races away.

I am standing in the back of a restaurant.

A car comes crashing through the window.

Dreams associated with auditioning: (page 285) *The Japanese Director, The Script is Already Written, The Compatibility Interviews.*

MAKING PORNOGRAPHIC MOVIES

In 2012, statistics on child pornography gathered by the National Center for Missing and Exploited Children show the breakdown by percentages of the most frequently submitted photographs of identifiable victims.

- 84% of the series contained images depicting oral copulation;
- 76% of the series contained images depicting anal and/vaginal penetration;
- 52% of the series contained images depicting the use of foreign objects or sexual devices;
- 44% of the series contained images depicting bondage and/or sadomasochism;
- 20% of the series contained images depicting urination and/or defecation, and;
- 4% of the series contained images depicting bestiality.
  —Testimony of Michelle Collins, National Center
  for Missing and Exploited Children, February 15, 2012

Some of my dreams tell of specific sexual activity. For example, in one I have sex with a man with one leg, in another with a transexual woman with a penis, and in still another I'm used to depict bestiality with dogs.

In 1974, *New York Magazine* undercover reporter Ken Sproat worked as a recruiter in a child porn "factory" and wrote about the experience. In his article entitled, *The Working Day in a Porn Factory*, he was told to emphasize the innocence of the children, and the lechery of adults. Boys were to be from six to thirteen, and girls, six to fifteen. He was to emphasize hairlessness, tiny privates, and lack of tits, etc.

Dreams associated with making movies: (page 288) *A Woman Makes Love to Me, Would I Help the Man with His Leg Cut Off?*;

A Woman Has Been Kidnapped, I Am in a Porn Theater Again;
I Go Back to the Zen Center, I Need to Refresh My Memory.

ACTION

Early in my quest for answers, I realized many of my dreams suggested I was in a movie and undertaking actions that are unlikely for an eight-year-old. In June 2019, I contacted a therapist in Denver, Colorado, who had worked with sex offenders, and asked if it was possible the porn industry would make movies or vignettes for pedophiles in which children played adult roles. The answer was "yes."

In many of my dreams, I am involved in what appears to be an action movie, with fighting, guns, and the Mafia. Two of these movie dreams feature a Mafia character called Vandici; these dreams appeared thirteen years apart. Other movie dreams involve Asian people, along with some white men, and we are all fighting the Japanese, as in World War II. In addition, in some of these dreams, lines of what could only be called "dialogue" suggest movie scripts. Here are some:

> "There is only one left."
> "Help, the Zulu man has Joannie. What can you do to help?"
> "Call Vandici."
> "Get the police."
> "Let's go, guys."
> "Stop that car, stop that car!"
> "That won't be a problem."

Dreams associated with action: (page 291) *I Am fighting the Japanese with a Needle Gun,* two dreams with the name *"Vandici:" The Zulu Man, Vandici and Gregory Bates, I Pull Out a Gun and Shoot Him, Get the Police, Danger in the Warehouse, I Try to Defend Myself with A Gun, I am Being Pursued by an Assassin.*

VIOLENCE

Dreams containing cruel and extreme violence have suggested that I observed this kind of behavior. In one, I watch a man being dragged to a room where he is murdered, and in another, a man is secured to the ground and run over by two men in a car. (Artwork I made depicting these scenes appears in the appendix.) Other dreams recount flogging.

Memory: "They Kill a Black Man"

I am in a room with some women.
 Two men enter, dragging a sobbing black man.
 They take him into a bedroom.
 I imagine something bad is happening.
 I am terrified.
 One of the men comes out of the room.
 He sees me.
 He comes at me.
 The women jump up.
 "She didn't see anything," they say nervously.
 The man relaxes.
 She saved me.

Memory: "A Car Runs Over a Man"

I am in a mountain parking lot.
 It is late at night.
 A hiking trail is nearby.
 A man is secured to the ground.
 People are standing around, drinking, and laughing.
 I watch as a car drives over the man.

Dreams associated with violence: (page 296) *Three Men are Being Tortured, The Bloody Murder Without Any Sound, They Decide Not to Kill Me, I Knew It Was Violent, Whipping the Black Man.*

ANIMALS

It took me a long time to understand my dreams about animals and to admit what they were about. It is very difficult to recount them. I could leave them out, but want you to know what trafficked children are subjected to.

In *The Murder Machine: The True Story of Madness and The Mafia,* authors Gene Mustain and Jerry Capeci write:

> Roy [DeMeo] directed Dominick to a Bensonhurst bar, where a man came out and transferred several cartons of film from his car to the trunk of Roy's Cadillac. Roy showed Dominick the titles. "It's eleven-year-old kids and people with dogs," he said . . . .
>
> "Dominick knew that through a loan Roy had become a partner in a combination peep show and whorehouse in Brockton, New Jersey, where the child pornography and the films depicting bestiality were made. Roy cheerfully said he was buying the "sick shit" for the sex emporium in Brockton as well as "asshole" customers in Rhode Island, where he had a good connection."

Dreams associated with animals: (page 300) *Are You Up Late, The Excited Dog, The Horse.*

THE POLICE

Police are prominent in my dreams, and in many cases I recount them leaving from a scene where I am being "robbed," a metaphor for being raped. In the 1940s, corruption in the Los Angeles Police Department was rampant. Mobsters routinely paid off police, politicians, and other public officials to protect their criminal enterprises. During my time in Los Angeles, I had several encounters with police. I was afraid to tell them what was happening to me. What if they didn't believe me, or didn't care? The mobsters would not have hesitated to punish or even kill me.

Dreams associated with the police: (page 301) *The Police Find my Stolen Car, I Keep Getting Robbed, Ghost Dog.*

MY ORDEAL ENDS ... SORT OF

My abducted time came to an end when I was accidently rescued by a surprise police raid, perhaps in August 1948—I cannot be certain of the time. My dreams indicate the pornography ring knew that the police were on their trail, but the particulars as to how the police found us is unclear.

My kidnapping saga ends with a raid, my hospitalization, my work with the FBI, and finally, my return home.

RAID

I was kept by different people during my abduction. The abductor who took me to Los Angeles did so for monetary gain. When Virginia Hill came into my life, she was able to take me away from these abductors due to the power of the Mafia's Chicago Outfit. She had become so well known to the authorities that she was unable to carry out business as she travelled. While I was no longer with them, my "family" returned home. Then, when the Chicago Outfit recalled Virginia Hill to carry out new business, I was left with no one to take care of me, which led to my being deposited with the pedophile and pornographer I was with when the FBI raid occurred. I am uncertain of his actual name, but call him "Frank," in my dreams. He became both my caretaker and molester/rapist. I slept in his bed every night and satisfied his needs. "Frank" appears to have been the head of the porn ring I ended up with.

While living with Frank my care was poor. We lived in dirty places, had little money, and my health was neglected. Due to Brenda Allen's arrest and the legal troubles of Mickey Cohen, the Mafia had backed off from some of its activities. Because the porn ring still had to pay tribute to the criminal underground for money made through its activities, money was tight. One dream recounts the fact that there is no money to pay for a new production.

The pedophile ring somehow knew the police were aware of their activities. This was made clear when I had the dream "It's Hot Over There." A guard at a private club advised us not to go someplace because the police were looking for us. I had been taught that police were bad men and that I shouldn't trust them. I shared this dream with friends who believed "too hot" was referring to the weather, which reminded me of how innocent most people are. At this point in my abduction, I understood "too hot" to mean that the police were after us and that we had to be careful.

The raid occurred in the middle of the night while I was asleep with "Frank" in a house where members of the ring were also sleeping. I believe the house was located somewhere in the San Bernardino Mountain around Big Bear Lake or Lake Arrowhead.

Memory: "Raid"

I am in bed with a man.

We are asleep.

A loud noise, a bang, startles us awake.

There is running in the hallway and up the stairs.

The bedroom door is kicked open.

Huge, muscular men enter.

I bounce off the bed next to the wall, terrified.
The man in my bed tries to pull a gun.
The men grab and secure him.
I try to take the man's hand.
He pushes me away.
"That is over," he says.
Everyone is arrested.
I huddle in a truck-like vehicle.
It is dark and I am frightened.
Families are organized together.
I am left alone.
A big man comes.
He picks me up and says, "You don't belong here."
He separates me from the group.
I am in a kitchen.
"What is your name?" he asks.
"Baby Candy," I reply.
"No, your real name."
"Baby Candy."
"Don't you know your real name?"
I shrug.
He leaves and returns later.
"Fine group of people you have been hanging around.
No one will tell me who you are."

My dreams told me the porn ring ended up in someplace like a school gym. The police took individuals into another room and questioned them, smacking some of them around. I also learned I was holding a pamphlet about devil worship, which a policeman took away from me.

The appearance of the pamphlet about devil worship is interesting. In 2010, although I had dreams that suggested a satanic cult,

I had not come to the realization it might be true. And all the way back in 1989, I had told Barbara Cook at our first meeting after my memory returned that I thought I was involved with a satanic cult.

It took the police some time to find out who I was. In 1948, police records were not readily available across state lines. They learned from a pedophile, who said he loved me, where I had come from.

Dreams associated with the raid: (page 304) *It's Hot Over There, Knock at the Door, I Don't Know Who I Am, The Man Everyone is Afraid Of, One Man Takes Me Away from the Group.*

HOSPITALIZED

Following the raid, I was hospitalized. One dream suggests it was a Catholic Hospital, and another suggests there was a bridge walkway over the street from one section of the hospital to another. This could indicate two different hospitals in two different cities: Los Angeles and Denver. In any case, I was put with adults, as was done in 1948. I believe I was in a psych ward to detox from the drugs.

I have had more dreams about my hospitalization than just about any other dream topic.

My dreams reveal I had cloudy urine, smelled, had sperm in me, and was infected with chlamydia. It was necessary for me to see a gynecologist. These dreams remind me of the shame I felt. Everybody—doctors, nurses, police, FBI, lawyers, judges, family and friends, and government officials—knew what had been done to me. Everything was out in the open and the humiliation was overwhelming.

According to MedlinePlus, "Women can get chlamydia in the cervix, rectum, or throat. It usually doesn't have symptoms, but if it does, it can have a strong smell, cause a burning sensation, and be painful." I find myself wondering what would have happened to me if I hadn't been found and hospitalized.

In one dream, the word cancer is mentioned. I believe this is a metaphor for drug addiction as suggested in the dream by the white powder on my nose. This dream came to me three months *before* my memory returned and, at the time, its meaning was a complete mystery. Over the course of my life, I have never taken drugs, not even marijuana, though offered. I believe a hypnotist cautioned me to stay away from them.

One dream suggests I became catatonic as I withdrew from drugs. I'm not sure what kind of drugs were given to me, but my dreams recount the use of a needle, sniffing white power, and taking pills.

MEMORY: "I Am Catatonic"

I am sitting in a chair, in a large empty room.
I am alone, can't move, and am frozen.

Another dream memory tells that a cheerful and friendly black woman is taking care of me and is checking my hair for lice. I smile when thinking of this woman.

Two men are guarding me in "I join a group," which could be either a lucid or a flashback dream based on the way people are moving in slow motion. It appears I am hypnotized. A black man appears, and he is the man they murdered. I can clearly see his face. The dream feels like I am recreating a real happening.

Finally, a dream reports that I was "vaccinated" and suggests that chemicals were used to help me remember some of the particulars of my abduction. Memory enhancement experimental drugs were known to be used in the forties, and perhaps these drugs were used by the doctors at the hospital where I was placed, or later when I was working with the FBI.

In *Trauma and Memory,* Peter Levine writes, "By the time of World War II, hypnosis and phenobarbital (narco-abreaction) were utilized to elicit intense emotional catharsis. However, these methods were eventually abandoned because the results were often deleterious or, at the least, only short-lived."

Dreams associated with my hospitalization: (page 306) *I Am Being Monitored, Tuna Fish, I Have Sperm in Me, I Am Helping a Sick Child, I'm Going to Be Checked, Cancer, I Am in a Catatonic State, The Nurse; My Brain, I Am in a Study,* I Am in a Group.

THE KEFAUVER COMMISSION

In 1950, the Senate Select Committee on Organized Crime in Interstate Commerce, known as the Kefauver Commission, began its investigation into organized crime. Brad Lewis quotes Kefauver in his book, *Celebrity Gangster:*

> The Mafia is a shadowy international organization that lurks behind much of America's organized criminal activity. . . . It is an organization about which none of its members, on fear of death, will talk . . . . The Mafia, however, is no fairy tale . . . it has scarred the face of America with almost every conceivable type of criminal violence, including murder, traffic in narcotics, smuggling, extortion, white slavery, kidnapping, and labor racketeering.

I was called to Washington to testify in secret for the Kefauver Commission in their enquiry into organized crime in Los Angeles.

WORKING WITH THE FBI

In the books, *Man Against the Mob* and *The Enforcer,* by William F. Roemer, Jr., I learned that investigating the mob was a complicated matter in the mid-20th century, even for the FBI. Roemer writes that one thing he didn't study during his FBI training was organized crime, which J. Edger Hover didn't believe existed until 1957 when a large group of underworld bosses were discovered meeting at the private home of mobster, Joseph Barbara in upstate New York.

THE MAFIA KEEPS TRACK OF ME

Now, after decades of making sense of my dreams and memories, and years of research into the background of my experiences, I believe the FBI made an agreement with the Mafia to ensure my safety. These agreements were not atypical. In fact, based on FBI agent Willam F. Roemer, Jr.'s books, they were more common that you would think.

My dreams indicate I was flanked by two FBI agents who guarded me after I was found. I was interviewed extensively by the FBI and asked to identify criminals, pornographers, politicians, and police-man. I eventually participated in a secret meeting in Washington D.C. in connection with the Kefauver Commission. Thus, they had knowledge of the Mafia's connection to me and the activities of orga-nized crime in 1948. In order to save my life, I believe records of these interviews are sealed in the files of the FBI. The deal in my case was likely, "You leave Alice alone, and we will leave you alone."

The Mafia had a reputation for murdering witnesses to their criminal behavior, and I certainly could have done them great harm. In those days, there was no such thing as a witness protection pro-gram, and if there was, my entire family would have to be uprooted.

However, this did not keep these criminals from worrying about me. I have had several dreams which indicate they checked in with me from time to time during the 1950s.

Dream: "The Man on Alameda Street"

September 4, 2017. Nearly 28 years after my memory returned.

I am riding my bicycle on Alameda Street near where my fam-ily lives. A man dressed like a businessman is standing near his expensive car. He is well dressed and in his late forties. The lid of the car engine is raised.

"What's the matter?" I ask.

"My car has broken down," he replies.

I tell him where a garage is located. I get into the car so I can show him.

I knew not to refuse him. The car was obviously not broken down. I can only conclude that the man wanted to remind me I was to keep my mouth shut.

Dream and Memory: "My Father Is Not Doing a Good Job of Protecting Me"

April 9, 1990. 7 months after my memory returned.

I am thirteen years old. My father is mowing the front lawn of our house on East Stanford Street, in Cherry Hills. Along the street in front of the house is a row of tall bushes. A gate there gives access to the mailbox. I am sitting on the front porch watching my dad. A car pulls up on Stanford Street. My father goes out to talk with whoever is in the car. He then returns and tells me to go talk to the two men. I do not remember the conversation, but think it is something like a warning.

An entry from my journal written on Labor Day, September 7, 1992 reads:

Mom told me today that she wasn't able to sleep last night and that she was awake for a couple of hours. She said she had a pain in her heart, but thought it was a dream. I asked her to describe it and she pointed to both sides of her breasts and pushed them in and said, "It was a piercing pain in my heart. I was worried and thought it might be a real heart attack, but pretty soon realized it was a dream.

Dream: "I'm Running Away"

January 23, 2019. 30 years and 4 months after my memory returned.

I'm running across a field trying to get away. I get on a tractor, but it sinks in the mud. I think,"I've waited five years after my case to come out of hiding so everyone would forget about me. It seems they haven't forgotten."

Five years after my kidnapping would make me thirteen years old, the age at which my father told me to go talk to the men in the car. This kind of odd corroboration of time and place, in dream and memory, is far from an isolated occurrence in my experience.

Four months after my memory returned, my dreams began to inform me of my work with the FBI. In them, I describe huge buildings in Washington, D.C., and even the entrance to the Department of Justice building in 1948 that housed the Federal Bureau of Investigation.

According to FBI agent, William F. Roemer, Jr., the FBI was located in the Justice Department Building at Ninth and Pennsylvania NW in Washington D.C., where it was headquartered from 1908 until 1975. A picture of the building is on page 312. This dream occurred two months *before* my memory returned.

I tell of wandering around with Uncle CB, my father's older brother, as we tried to find where we were supposed to go. My uncle worked for NASA and lived in the area. I believe he helped my parents. As I write about him here, I find my eyes tearing up. I have a special feeling for him. Unfortunately, he died well before my memory returned. I'm certain he would have corroborated my memory.

One dream tells of attending a showing of a pornographic film on a small screen in a marble building, attended by a small audience. I am with my father. My mother does not want to attend and stays in our hotel.

In my original dream journal, I state that this trip to Washington D.C. might have taken place around 1951. I have no idea what I was thinking at the time or why I would come up with this date, but I now know the Kefauver hearings were taking place at that time.

I contacted Roger Young to ask if a child would be asked to watch a pornographic movie in order to identify perpetrators in the film. He said, "Yes." It would be necessary as evidence to convict the criminal.

In one dream I am given pictures of policemen to see if I can identify any who might be involved in organized crime. I am afraid to "finger" anyone for fear of repercussions, but I do eventually point out a policeman. In another dream I am asked to identify a criminal I might have had contact with, and in several other dreams I mention "family members" and gatherings. I believe this is in reference to the Mafia. I would have been unsure if I should "finger" them out of fear, and because I had identified as part of the group.

I also learned that I took part in a secret taping late at night in a huge warehouse, attended a movie with two FBI agents who are protecting me, and finally that the FBI made a deal with the Mafia to save my life and the lives of my family.

Additional dreams associated with the FBI: (page 310) *I Am in a Huge Building, The Elegant Woman at the Top of the Stairs, I Identify a Policeman, I Go to the Movies with Two Men, The Secret Taping, Section Four, Undercover Agent, The FBI Makes a Deal.*

CARTOONS

Discovery of the meaning of the word "Cartoon" in my dreams was huge in helping me know my memory was correct. Although this word appears in several dreams spread over twenty-eight years, I first came to understand it as important when I had the dream, "*The Cat Cartoon,*" two months *before* my memory returned. I made an artwork for the dream, and it is included in the appendix.

This dream describes working with the FBI. They are handing me objects of a sexual nature and a strip of film to find out if I know what they are. When writing down the dream, I call a strip of film, "A Cat Cartoon." A cat, in some dreams, is a metaphor for men. Men are cats, and cats "cat around."

It wasn't until 2019 that I discovered its meaning. When I saw the 2012 movie *The Iceman,* I understood why "Cartoon" was in my nightmares. The movie is about Richard Kuklinski, a real life hit man for the Mafia, thought to have killed more than a hundred people. Michael Shannon plays the title role and Winona Ryder plays his wife. At the beginning of the movie, Kuklinski works in a store where he sells pornographic pictures and vignettes. Over the course of the movie, I learned the industry called porn films and photographs "cartoons." This word first appeared in my dreams in 1989, before my memory returned. In a document entitled *Final Report of the Attorney General's Commission on Pornography,* published by Rutledge Hill Press, I read:

> At times the child abuser will merely keep the photograph [he has taken] as a memento, or as a way of recreating for himself the past experience. Frequently, however, the photograph will be given to another child abuser, and there is substantial evidence that a great deal of "trading" of pictures takes place in this manner.

Dreams associated with cartoons: (page 314) *The Cat Cartoon, He Develops Film, The Movie in the Marble Building.*

TRIALS

It has taken me a long time to sort out the "what, when, where, and how" of the two trials in which I testified. I don't know for sure when the trials took place. They could have been scheduled a year or more after my return home. Unfortunately, my mother destroyed all of my school records from this time, and I had asked my parents to get rid of the box of court reports.

I do know there were two trials: A grand jury trial in Denver and a jury trial in Los Angeles. I do not remember the name of the pedophile I was with when found. However, I have memories of the trials, and my dreams record events around the trials. I do have dream names of men I do not remember and have been unable to find in my research. Criminals often use aliases, and I may never have known the birth names of some of the people who abused me.

In the grand jury trial in Denver, my lawyer, Charles S. Vigil, a Hispanic deputy district attorney for the third judicial district, and who is memorialized in my dream "The Vial," states that a Latino lawyer asks me, as I sit in the witness box, what the "vial" represents. I tell the jury that the vial was used to sprinkle bugs on me. Vigil's name is not used in the dream, but in the year 1948 a Latino district attorney was so unusual that there can be no doubt that he was my lawyer. He was extremely competent, and President Harry Truman named him U.S. District Attorney in October 1951 for the State of Colorado.

MEMORY: "Trial"
November 11, 1989. 2 months after my memory returned.

I am in the witness stand.
>The courtroom is empty
>There is a jury to my left
>A woman sits below me.
>Two males sit next to their lawyer.
>They smirk.
>My lawyer approaches.

"What is this?" he ask, holding up a glass vial.

"They used it to put bugs on me," I reply.

The woman below winces and sucks in her breath.

I look at her.

I don't feel anything.

"What did they call you?" my lawyer asks.

"Baby Candy," I answer, seductively.

Their lawyer approaches.

"You're lying," he says.

"No, I'm not!'

"Yes you are."

"No, I'm not," I reply, frightened.

■ ■ ■

I am standing next to my mother as she talks to Mr. Vigil (pronounced V-Hill), and he says, "I'm disgusted, but I can't do anything about it. I can't prove it."

I remember my distress over not being able to bring the men I now believe were Checkers and Clyde Smaldone, and/or James Spinelli, to justice. Charles S. Vigil and Max Melville were, however, instrumental in successfully prosecuting the Smaldones in another case in which Checkers attempted to bribe the jury.

I mentioned earlier a memory about a conversation between a Latino district attorney and my mother. In June 2022, a friend of mine, Gena Burson, on my behalf, called the Denver office of the Justice Department and asked if the public has access to Grand Jury court reports. She found that the public can have access, but only if the case is sent to trial.

I have less recollection of the Los Angeles trial, except for the aftermath.

Memory: "Empty Halls"

I am sitting on a marble bench with my mother.

We are in a hallway in a courthouse building.

The halls are empty.

A woman approaches.

She sits down beside me and says,

"You don't need to be afraid anymore.

 He is going away for life."

Later . . .

I am standing next to my mother.

She is talking to court officials. I tug on her skirt.

She is talking and pays no attention.

I tug again, harder.

She finally looks at me.

"What is going to happen to John?" I ask.

"Oh, he'll be alright," she answers and turns back to her
conversation.

I hurt.

I want to know.

They don't tell me.

This memory caused me pain. I had forged a friendship with this
boy I called John and adults around me were insensitive to my feelings. I never found out what happened to him.

Dreams associated with the trials: (page 316) *The Two Men in
Church, The Vial.*

MEMORY: "I'm Returned Home"

I am in a long narrow conference room in a police department.

A door opens and my parents enter.

My memory switches around here. Was I brought into the room where my parents were waiting, or was I already in the room when they arrived? I recall no emotion or physical contact. Nothing. My eyes well up with tears as I write about it. The only explanation I can offer is that the reunion was so painful I don't want to remember it.

I can only imagine what was going on with my mother. The word numbness comes to mind. From my father, stoicism. The reunion with my brothers is also in a void. It seems that life simply . . . went on.

From looking at family photographs, I can recall my crazy behavior after returning—flapping my arms around with my tongue hanging out, speaking too loudly, and generally presenting myself as a nervous and ugly child. Yet, as my memoir chronicles, I went on to lead a productive and interesting life and am alive today to tell the story.

CHAPTER NINETEEN

MY LIFE TODAY

ORE THAN THIRTY-FOUR YEARS HAVE PASSED SINCE I began the journey that led me to write *Abducted*. I am now eighty-four. Money is tight, but not at this point a huge issue, and friends and activities keep me busy. I exercise every day by riding my recumbent bike at least three miles. I can honestly say that there are days when I feel happy, and the weight of my past has lifted somewhat.

However, I continue to experience occasional nightmares and, though it is not obvious to my friends, symptoms of PTSD continue to surface. When I moved to Arkansas and lived in my woodland home, I joined Crime Watch. I drove the roads in my area and memorized places where I could hide from imaginary pursuers. I explored back roads and looked for various escape routes in anticipation of bad men out to get me. I concocted elaborate scenarios of where I could hide. One spot, in a cul-de-sac hidden in the woods, became one of my secure locations. I imagined bad men driving by without seeing me.

Yet, there is a dichotomy. Although I busily plotted finding my safety locations, I was also comfortable leaving the sliding glass door to my backyard open so that my dogs could come and go in my fenced-in backyard. To this day, I am not strict about locking my doors. It appears that I am simultaneously afraid and not afraid.

Through my dreams, memories of my abduction continue to surface.

Dream: "The Padded Room"
August 17, 2021. 32 years after my memory returned.

I am in a house. There is a rectangular section at the back where two bedrooms are located. A driveway to the side leads to a garage which is accessed through a door at the back. This extra section of the house is entered down a few stairs.

I am in one of the bedrooms. It is completely carpeted—floor, walls, and ceiling—and there is a toilet sitting out in the room. A small kitchen area with a sink, and a large bed are there. I say to a woman, "I could have lived here."

I am unable to remember where this house is located, but feel I was held in this room for a time.

I have wondered what I would have done with my life if I had not been abducted. Would I have matured faster and continued to pursue my singing career? Would I have married and had children? Would I have become a history teacher, or pursued a career as a journalist, like Christiane Amanpour, whom I admire? Would I have learned to fly an airplane?

On September 28, 2020, I had a dream in which I am talking to a reporter who is going to interview the man I put in prison.

She asks me what I would like her to tell him.

"Tell him I forgive him," I say.

Did this really happen? I think so.

Some say that forgiveness is part of healing. But I would need to forgive the entire menagerie of people who were complicit in what happened to me.

Many professional persons assist organized crime families and their associates in the pornography business: Realtors (sell property to pornographers); Landlords (rent property); Bankers (process revenue): Printers and film processors (develop images); Transportation companies (ship obscene materials); Academics (paid experts); Public figures (Prosecutors, Judges, City, County and State officials); Zoning board members and health department officials (subject to monetary and political influences).
> —Testimony of Michelle Collins, National Center for
> Missing and Exploited Children, February 15, 2012

Does one ever recover from a trauma like mine? Today, I find myself feeling that what happened to me is not important. I am thinking of the millions of people around the world who are traumatized by the upheaval of their lives as they flee from climate disasters, war zones, poverty, and crime-infested homelands. What will be the long-term consequences of these horrific events?

I have wondered why others who experienced trauma end up in jail or become addicts. What was it about me that kept that from happening? I returned home to a structured household, lived in a clean house, had three nourishing meals a day sitting around the table with my family. I was active in our church, held down summer jobs, and had school activities. I believe my singing, photography hobby, expressing myself emotionally, and being outside enjoying nature, had an enormous influence on my life. These activities helped bring balance and made it possible for me to survive.

Dr. Bessel van der Kolk writes:

We now know that there is another possible response to threat which our scans aren't yet capable to measure. Some people simply go into denial: Their bodies register threat, but the conscious mind goes on as if nothing has happened . . . . It is so much easier for them to talk about what has been done to them—to tell a story of victimization and revenge—than to notice, feel, and put into words the reality of their internal experience.

Perhaps I fall into this category. I remember, but don't feel.

Art and Stephen continue to say they don't remember my abduction. That has been hard for me to accept. I have longed for their validation of my memory. I didn't remember what happened to me for forty-two years, so why should they? I wanted to. They don't, and I must accept that.

I see my life as one long battle. I have boxed my way through adversity and disappointments, and somehow have managed to end up standing.

Dream: "My Dream"
June 15, 1992. 2 years and 9 months after my memory returned.

I ask my dreams if I was kidnapped, and my dream answers
    "Yes."

I wake up.

My brothers Arthur, Stephen, and I are getting ready
to board a United Airlines flight to visit
our grandparents (Momo and Paba) in Selleck, Washington.

APPENDIX

DREAMS

Chapter eighteen tells the story of what happened to me during my abduction, and events are written in chronological order. This appendix is a partner to that chapter; it contains the dream narratives that supported me in reconstituting my memories of those experiences, and the months in which I lived as a sex-trafficked young girl.

Some of these dream narratives are very difficult to read. However, if they help one other sexually abused person remember so that they may begin their own healing process, then I have achieved something important by recording and including them here. They have of course been at the center of my own profound journey.

HYPNOSIS

DREAM: "Would You Mind Getting Rid of The Cigarette?"
August 22, 1993. 3 years and 11 months after my memory returned.

I go to another therapist in Dr. Yapko's office. At the moment I can't remember the reason, but I am in an office with an older man. There is a window on the left. I am sitting across the desk from him. It is a small office, and my back is to the wall. The door to the office is behind him on the right. I am talking to him about why I have come to see him, and he is listening to me.

He says, "Would you mind getting rid of that cigarette?"

I am puzzled but he points, and I look around and there is a little row of cigarette ashes on the back of my chair. It is as if a cigarette had just burned itself out. I see it.

"Please hand it to me," he says.

"No, I'll push it into the waste basket," I say. I brush the cigarette ashes off.

"Your hands are restless."

"I am always nervous."

I put my hands quietly in my lap and notice I can no longer see him. I realize he is trying to hypnotize me. Just as I make this realization, I enter into a trance. I have a surge of energy . . . a shift. I have several of these shifts and it turns into a sexual dream. Each time I surge it is like a sexual charge.

I wake up.

DREAM: "Who Are You?"

March 29, 2010. 10 years and 6 months after my memory returned.

I am in a room with my therapist. I am telling him a dream. I am breathing very heavily. There is some phlegm caught in my throat.

Suddenly a man appears, and he is grinning at me. I look at him and say, "Who are you? What are you doing here?"

The therapist is writing this down and I turn to him and say, "Is this a figment of my imagination? Am I hypnotized, or is this a real person and not a figment of my imagination.

The man I am seeing looks rather nice, and I say to him, "You look familiar, but I can't remember who you are." He is waiting for me to remember. I repeat, "Who are you? What are you doing here?"

I realize that I am in a lucid dream and in a trance. I ask my therapist why I am breathing heavily. "There is something in my throat and it is making me wheeze." He reaches over and puts his two fingers on my nose. I stop wheezing.

This dream appears to be of a hypnotic session in which the therapist is attempting to find out information. The wheezing developed as part of the exercise. He put his fingers on my nose to enable me to stop.

SATANIC CULT

DREAM: "The Girl in the Black Robe"
December 7, 1987. 2 year and 3 months before my memory returned.

I walk into a room and glimpse a girl in a black robe with a gun. I gasp in fright and wake up.

Women priests walked around in black robes at the Zen Center, but certainly no one carried a gun, and I was never in fear of them. The women in robes likely nudged my unconscious regarding my experiences in 1948.

DREAM: "I Light the Candles"
June 15, 1990. 1 year and 9 months after my memory returned.

I am in a huge church and a man is playing the organ. I am practicing lighting candles. A priest in a black robe sees me and is angry because I have spilled some wax. Frightened, I wake up.

I wonder if the church in this dream is in the Rialto Theater where the Ordo Templi Orientis had ritual ceremonies—the theater had a Wurlitzer organ.

DREAM: "Cartagena"
December 28, 1990. 2 years and 3 months after my memory returned.

I am in a church and hold a cross with the side bent up and it looks like a fork. I describe the room. There is a man and a woman who calls him "Art." He says, "If you really loved me, you would call me by my real name, Cartagena. If you loved me, you would know my name."

I searched thoroughly for names used to symbolize the devil, but none suggest the name "Cartagena." But, I found *Between the Devil and the Inquisition: African Slaves and the Witchcraft Trials in Cartagena de Indies,* by Heather Rachelle White. The city of Cartagena is in Colombia, South America. I recently learned there is a Cartagena Street in Juarez, Mexico, a place known for drug trafficking. It's hard to say why that name appeared in my dream, but I do have memories of traveling in Mexico, and it could be another one of those incidences when disparate information is processed together in one dream.

DREAM: "The Man with the Black Cape Massages My Bottom"
November 17, 1992. 4 years and 2 months after my memory returned.

There is a man. He is wearing a black cape and is massaging my bottom. It feels good.

It wasn't until I put all of these dreams together that I realized the porn ring might have been involved in Satanism.

TORTURE

DREAM: "Bugs Are on Me"
September 9, 1989. 1 day after my memory returned.

There is something on the upper right side of my chest. It's coming into focus. It's a long bug with legs. Ugh! I can feel it. It is awful. I wake up in fright, gasping.

DREAM: "The Polkadot Footprints"
October 25, 1989. 1 month after my memory returned.

The image of a car with black and white polka dot footprints covering it is placed before me. I am itchy and imaginary bugs are biting me.

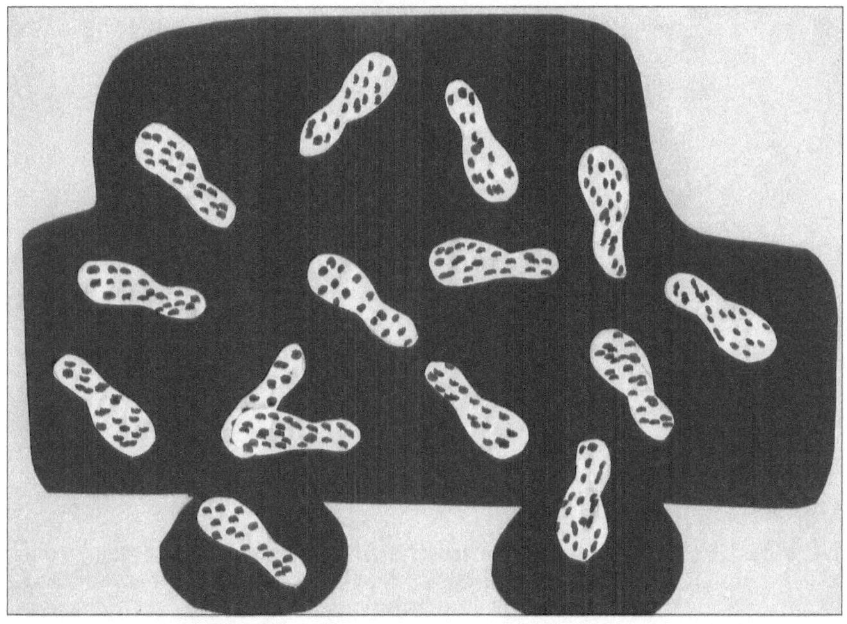

DREAM: "I Am Being Drowned"
May 22, 1963. 26 years and 8 months before my memory returned.

I am with a man and a boy in a rowboat in the middle of a lake. The man grabs me and throws me into the water, holding me under. I cannot swim. At first, I fight and try to save myself. Then, I understand and accept the fact that I can't do anything about it.

This is one of three dreams about being drowned.

DREAM: "I Am the Dog"

May 5, 1991. 1 year and 8 months after my memory returned.

I come home and the dog is very happy to see me. He jumps up and I realize he is hungry. There is no food in the house. I go to the store and ask the man at the counter if he has dog food. He says that he doesn't but that he has a can of tuna fish. He opens the can and pours the tuna fish juice down the dog's nose. The dog gags, coughs, and sputters. He then turns his face toward me. The dog is me. I wake up in fright.

DREAM: "The Tortured Dog"
November 26, 1992. 3 years and 1 month after memory returned.

I am in a house somewhere. It is an older house, and it is not kept up very well . . . the bathroom is a mess. It is old and there are breaks in the floor. I look down and see a basement below. A dog is trying to get out of there.

"There is a dog down there," I say to a man and woman.

She says, "He is going to burn him and then kill him."

I say, "What do you mean he is going to burn him and then kill him?"

He says, "I like to torture him."

This is the most disturbing dream I have ever experienced. I believe the dog is me, and the dream is a replay of one of the things that happened in the basement following my abduction. The woman is threatening me with the possibility my "father" is going to burn me if I don't do what they want. They often called me a dog. Even today, after over thirty years, I have a visceral reaction to this nightmare. My body tingles and I become light-headed.

DREAM: "Eating Shit"
September 9, 1989. 1 day after my memory returns.

I am facing sideways next to a man and a woman. The woman opens a baby diaper and peels out something that is square and brown. It looks like a candy bar. She starts eating it. The man next to her does the same. I feel they are trying to trick me. I then realize I am eating human infant excrement because I can taste it. It is horrible.

This dream provides an example of a sensory experience, as it resulted in my having a taste memory—I could taste the baby's excrement all over again. This dream, I believe, shows one way my kidnappers tested me. If I will eat shit at their behest, then I will comply to any commands. Eating excrement is a fetish called coprophilia.

DREAM: "Burlap"

Monday, October 9, 1989. One month after my memory returned.

I wake up. The word burlap comes to mind. I am unable to go back to sleep.

I often wake up with a single word in my mind and have learned it is a good idea to write these curious thoughts down. Many have proved to have important meaning. This is one of four dreams about burlap. I mention this here to show how I believe my psyche was trying to help me recover my memory. Once I realized the importance of burlap, I never had another dream about it.

DRUGGED

DREAM: "The Beautiful Yellow Flowers"
July 29, 1989. 1 month before my memory returned.

I go home to sleep. My house has no walls, windows, or doors. It is entirely open and is only a wooden platform.

I am in bed but decide I need to go to the bathroom. I walk out into the courtyard. It is bursting with beautiful giant bright yellow cosmos flowers growing wild out of the brown dirt. The flowers make me feel good because they are beautiful. I have a complete sensation of being surrounded by brilliant yellow. The weather is balmy and I marvel at the wonderful scene.

This dream records my drugging as I am about to perform in a porn vignette.

DREAM: "Floating in the Waves"
August 25, 1992. 2 years and 11 months after my memory returned.

I have gone someplace to be interviewed to be in a movie. I go upstairs and I am alone in a room. There is a pile of black clothing, t-shirt types of things with black pants. I put them on, and while I am in this room some men arrive whom I am supposed to meet. I open the door to let them know that I am there and will be out in a minute.

They say something like, "Don't worry, we are not going to rape you."

I walk out and find myself mesmerized by an enormous room. It is a huge sound stage with high ceilings. I am drawn to the place where movies are made. Four men are sitting around doing various things. There is a worktable with a light on it. I walk past one man who is the producer. I am overwhelmed and I stand there and start to float. There are lights on me. I have this buoyant feeling and then I am lying in the ocean. There is no ocean, but I am feeling a surge of water on me. The invisible water comes in gently. I wake up, and I am afraid.

DREAM: "The Snake Bite Pills"
December 16, 1990. 1 year and 3 months after my memory returned.

Les comes. He says he has something to show me. They are snake bite pills. He opens a box. In the box are little plastic packages. In the packages there are three kinds of round white pills. Six or seven M and M's, and something else. He opens a package and tells me to eat a white snake bite pill. I eat a couple. They taste okay so I give them to mom. I eat the M and M's too and then there is a third thing you are supposed to take. It was the snake bite serum which you are supposed to mix with the other pills. I don't take that because I don't have a snake bite and it might be harmful. I go to mom and tell her what Les said. He has put them on the counter so he can sell them to everybody standing around getting ready for the pot luck.

DREAM: "You Think I Am Loaded with Money?"
August 22, 2019. 20 years and 11 months after my memory returned.

I am in bed with Frank, who is speaking in Spanish on the telephone. He is trying to make some sort of deal. Even though there is lots of laughing and carrying on, the conversation is on the dangerous side.

"You think I am loaded with money?" Frank yells into the phone, as he suddenly gets out of bed and walks out the door to get a shotgun.

There is reason to be afraid.

I wake up and my heart is pounding.

This dream appears to be about a drug deal.

DREAM: "Ether"
May 2, 1989. 4 months before my memory returned.

I am with a [movie star] who is going to show me things. We are walking around in a house, and he has his arm around me. The house is big, and there are so many people it is hard to find a place to be alone. He takes me upstairs and we go into a bedrrom. He is thinking about how he is going to teach me.

He says, "First let me get some ether."

I say, "What do you mean, ether?"

He goes down the hall into the next room. I can't see him, but imagine what he is doing. He is filling up a bottle with ether so he can give it to me. We are going to do it together as foreplay. While he is in the next room, a girl comes and starts talking to him. I can see that he wants to get rid of her. I wonder where he sleeps in the house and whether he has ever slept with her. She sings and they laugh and have a good time. He comes back and we get into bed together. He has cream and he is working on my toes. Someone else is watching us. Some people arrive. I'm embarrassed because he is doing my toes in front of them. A woman says, "Oh my God, it's [a famous movie star.]

"Sing," in this dream is a metaphor for an orgasm.

PORNOGRAPHY AND PROSTITUTION

DREAM: "The Porn Class"
January 15, 1994. 5½ years after my memory returned.

I am in a room full of people who are taking an acting class on how to become porn stars. They are teaching techniques and ways to do sex acts. I walk in and sit down. The room is full of men, but there are some women. Some have their clothes on, and some are naked. There are two instructors. A male and a female are discussing how to masturbate someone. There are three or four couples and they are practicing in front of the class.

The instructors talk about the schedule over the next few days. They hand out vouchers for drinks and dinner for the duration of the class.

DREAM: "The Circular Staircase Down into the Porn Theater"
March 12, 1990. 6 months after my memory returned.

I am with a friend. We go down a carpeted circular staircase into a theater where pornography is being shown. It is also a place where actors perform live sex shows.

There is an old lady with gray hair. She is selling tickets for the performance. There is a line of people waiting to go into the theater. The seats are all taken for the first show, so we must wait for the next performance. I wake up, am sweating, and my heart is pounding.

In this dream I am taken to see a live sex show so I can learn what I am expected to do, and to normalize the behavior. A circular staircase is described in several dreams. Many theaters have such a staircase leading down to the stage from dressing rooms.

DREAM: "The Love Me Fish"
May 5, 1989. 4 months before my memory returned.

Two men are with me. There is a storm. Everything is gray.

There are many fish, and I am trying to identify the difference species. The two men are helping me with the identification.

There is a fish swimming upside down. Its fins are fluttering. Two other fish are interacting with it, and their fins are also fluttering.

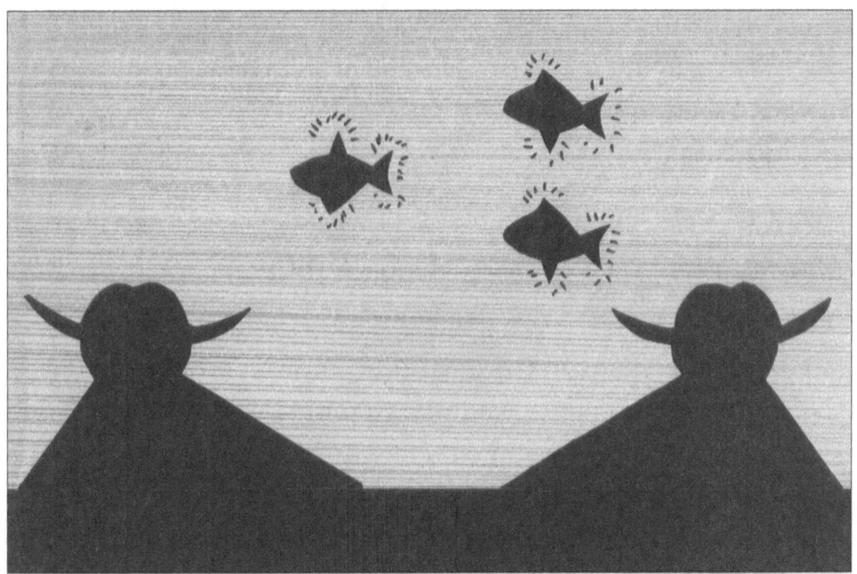

I ask, "What kind of fish are they?"
"They are love-me fish," the men reply. I wake up.

I believe the fish are metaphors for performers being filmed in a three-way porn scene. The quivering fins exemplify the response of the actors to what they are doing.

The two men pictured here often appear in my dreams. One of the techniques pornographers use with children is to show them activities they want them to participate in, thus normalizing the behavior. By telling me the porn actors are "love-me fish," they are describing the behavior as loving and are teaching me the activity is okay.

DREAM: "I Work in a Whorehouse"
June 1, 1991. 1 year and 9 months after my memory returned.

I am going someplace to a room. It is in a building behind a church. In the back of the room are two bedroom. It is a place where one goes to have sex and that is why I am there. There is a desk where a woman is sitting and there are women and a teenage boy sitting there. You fill out a form and the woman puts you with the next available man. I sign up and she puts me with a man. We go in the back room and have sex. I have no impression of what that is like.

I go back the next week.

DREAM: "The Sex Lesson"
May 12, 1990, San Francisco. 8 months after my memory returned.

I am with a woman, and she is taking me to find her boyfriend, Ernie. I go into a building with large rooms. The hall is crowded with people. It is messy and dirty. We go into a movie theater and squeeze past some people and look over a wall where there is a side theater. A teacher is standing there. She is giving a sex lesson. At one point three boys stand up. They are showing their penises to the teacher.

In several of my dreams I am attending classes where sexual techniques are taught. The classes cost money and are held over several days. Drinks and lunch are provided.

AGENT

DREAM: "I Go Undercover as a Porn Star"
November 5, 1993. 4 years and 1 month after my memory returned.

I have hired a woman agent to help me get work as a porn performer... The woman is between 45 and 55 years of age. She is chubby, dumpy, and she is wearing a cotton dress.

She takes me to a building where there is a gym and a balcony. I peek over the balcony and I see there is a woman in a bed who is quite good looking and is pregnant. She is waiting for something to happen.

Old-fashioned hospital screens on metal frames with cloth curtains gathered from top to bottom surround her.

I hear a man talking in a room near the balcony....My agent is telling him that I will not be able to work on Friday. He says, "That is okay. We are open 24 hours a day, seven days a week, and she can come whenever she wants, and we will be glad to have her." My impression is I will sit and wait, and if he can use me, he will.

I see a man....He is talking like a news commentator and has a mike in his hand. He is saying that the Commission that regulates the porn industry is having a controversy as to whether it is safe to masturbate with an electric dildo, as opposed to a regular dildo, if one is pregnant. They are concerned it might not be good for the baby.

AUDITIONING

DREAM: "The Japanese Director"
December 30, 1989. 3 months after my memory returned.

A Japanese director is looking for a child to be in a show. It seems like a nice thing for a child to do. The director comes over, grabs me and drags me around on the floor. I yell and scream and do a good job. The director decides to use me.

Through my research I have learned there was a large Asian market for pornography. Many of my dreams have Asian actors and it seems reasonable to believe that a Japanese director would be hired to provide porn content that would appeal to some Eastern proclivities.

DREAM: "The Script Is Already Written"
March 2, 1994. 4 years and 6 months after my memory returned.

This is a disaster movie. It takes place in a Japanese town. There is a dam and the dam breaks and floods the town, drowning everyone including some of the characters who are trying to get away from the disaster. In the script, I am an actor. All the actors have seen the preview and know that the dam is going to break and that we are going to have a difficult time getting out and escaping the flood. The movie is going on and all the actors act like they don't know what is going to happen. Even though I am caught up in the story I know there is nothing I can do about it. It is part of the plot and inevitable.

I spend the entire dream trying to help everybody get out as if there is something I can do about it. This is a frustration dream in that sense. We have a warning that the dam is going to break, and we are trying to evacuate. But everyone must go to the bathroom or do something else. We even get clear to the top of the mountain (the town is in a valley) and we hike up and out and we get into a house where we are going to be safe. A famous actor is driving the car. He gets us back in the car and takes us back into the danger area.

I yell, "Why are you taking us back into the danger area? You know we were all safe. You know the dam is going to break. You know we are all in danger. Why are you driving us back?"

He says, "I have to get Joannie."

I say, "Why can't you leave us at the top and then go get her?"

But it is in the script. It is the plot of the movie. We are all supposed to deny that the dam is going to break. We must play out the story as if it won't or might not happen. I am trying to change fate. I am trying to change the outcome.

I am getting more and more hysterical. If I play my part right, I think the dam might break, but am not sure. I hope and deny it is going to break. Instead, even though I know it is going to play out.

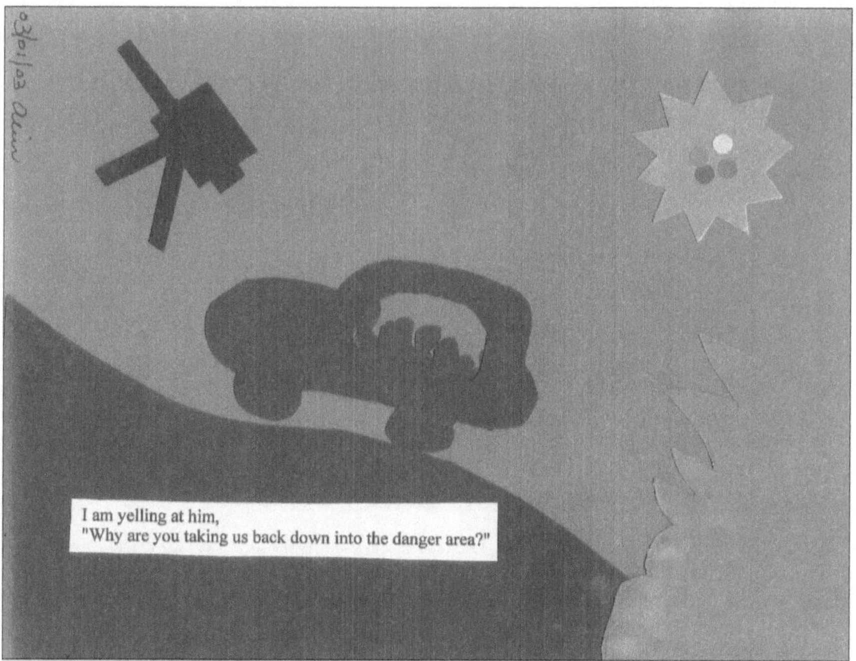

I tried to find a Japanese disaster film produced in 1948 without success.

DREAM: "The Compatibility Interviews"

June 9, 1992. 2 years and 9 months after my memory returned.

I am in a hotel room. A man and a woman with a young boy are with me. People are coming in to be interviewed to see if they are sexually compatible with me. A woman who is conducting the interviews is aggressive and she kisses me. A young boy enters and gets in bed with me. I wait to see what will happen. We move around on the bed and talk. He tells me his problems. He mumbles at first and I ask him to repeat what he said.

He replies, "When I was a boy, I had a brain injury and have metal in my head."

This young man appears in another dream. He had trouble speaking because of his brain injury. He is working in the porn industry because he cannot find work elsewhere.

MAKING MOVIES

As my time in Los Angeles continued, I began to make movies. I was good at memorizing lines, photogenic, and skinny. This set of dreams seems to suggest scenes from movies.

DREAM: "A Woman Makes Love to Me"
August 25, 1989. 2 weeks before my memory returned.

Naomi is making love to me. She gets on top of me, and I can feel her penis between my thighs. The sensation is pleasant, but it is all very matter of fact.

"Did you enjoy it?" she asks.

She has makeup and false eyelashes on, along with bikini pants. She is high above me and is leering at me. I am very small. I ask her, "Who are you?"

I slowly reach my hand toward her vagina so I can feel her and see if I can tell anything about her. There is a penis where her vagina should be. It fits right into my hand. It is not a penis in full erection. It is small and narrow and then I realize there is also a man there. He is holding my feet down. I start screaming and kicking and flailing my arms, but it feels like they are stuck in mud and everything is in slow motion.

I wake up and my heart is pounding.

This dream has the feeling of a vignette being filmed of me with a transexual man. As this dream takes place before my memory began returning, I believe my unconscious, through this lucid dream, is attempting to help me recover specifics of what happened to me.

DREAM: "Would I Help the Man with His Leg Cut Off?"
November 25, 1991. 2 years and 2 months after my memory returned.

I am in an airplane, and we are flying to a ranch. The movie is about retaliation, and a man who has done something bad gets his leg cut off. I then imagine the man crawling down the road trying to get help. I visualize him at my house and knocking on my door.

I think about the situation. Would I try to help the man, and if I did, how would I? Would I tie a tourniquet around his leg so he wouldn't bleed to death? I become fearful and think, "Should I open the door and let him come in, or should I call the police and leave him outside? The situation might be a trick."

I wake up feeling uneasy and my heart is pounding.

This dream suggests that the director of the movie is helping me with my acting by giving me ideas for a range of emotions to portray while the action is going on. A wounded man knocks on my door. What might be going in my mind? Should I try to help him, let him in, use a tourniquet, call the police? Maybe it is a trick. Maybe he is trying to get into my house so he can rape me. This would be a scenario that a pedophile might appreciate.

DREAM: "A Woman Has Been Kidnapped"
December 9, 1991. 2 years and 3 months after my memory returned.

I am in a western movie with Native Americans, cowboys, and out-laws. I am on a movie set, and there are bright lights. I am hiding behind a wall so the bad men can't see me. A woman has been kidnapped by the "Indians" and I am afraid I am going to be kid-napped, too.

DREAM: "I Am in the Porn Theater Again"
December 4, 1992. 3 years and 3 months after my memory returned.

I am visiting a porn theater. I am with some men who come in at different times. I think a couple of the men like me. At this point, a porn movie comes on, but I don't recall what happens in the movie.

For some reason I am backstage now in a costume and am getting dressed.

There is a belly dancer, or stripper who is sexy looking but a little plump. She is not pretty, but sexy. She gets on the stage and starts doing her bumps and grinds.

The belly dancer comes to me. She is crying because she has been fired. The people who run the theater are not happy with her. I hug and comfort her.

She asks me if there is any chance that I am a lesbian because she would like to get acquainted. I tell her I am not.

This belly dancer appears in another dream. I must have had a connection to her as I remembered her in my dreams, fifty-four years after I met her in 1948.

DREAM: "I Go Back to the Zen Center"
November 14, 1993. 4 years and 2 months after my memory returned.

I go back to the Zen Center and find they are moving the floors around. For example, what was in the basement has been moved to the first floor and something has been moved to the third floor. Now that they have moved the floors, one whole side of the building is no longer there.

This dream suggests a scenery change.

DREAM: "I Need to Refresh My Memory"
July 7, 2003. 13 years and 10 months after my memory returned.

I am making a movie. It is the night before shooting is to begin and I realize I have not gone over my lines to refresh my memory. There is a tricky entrance. I decide to get a copy of the script so I can remember my lines. A female stage manager gives me a copy. There is a production meeting, and we are all sitting around. The head guy tells us that we won't have any money so no one is going to get paid. This is very upsetting to the directors.

ACTION

DREAM: "I Am Fighting the Japanese with a Needle Gun"
May 21, 1963. 25 years and 8 months before my memory returned.

A war is going on. There are four of us. Two American men, a Japanese man who is on our side, and me. We are fighting against the "Japs."

I have a tiny gun that looks like a needle, but it shoots pretty well. When the fighting begins, the Japanese man on our side is wounded. One of the American men takes my needle gun and kills some of the enemy. The enemy Japanese get mad and start shooting at us with a machine gun. I give my needle gun to one of the American men and he shoots it very well. It turns into a machine gun. The enemy Japanese kill him.

A second American man appears and shouts at the wounded Japanese man on our side. The enemy Japanese turn on a water hose. The American doesn't care about this because it is only water, however, when it hits him, he floats up into the air screaming, and then disintegrates.

The enemy Japanese shout, "There is only one left," meaning me. Frightened, I run around the outside the house and break a bathroom window and climb in. I hear a noise but have no weapon. It is my wounded Japanese friend. He gives me his gun. It is rather crude, and I wonder if it will work. We try to fix the window but can't. He stays with me and acts like he is the one who has broken the window so when the enemies arrive, they will not know I am there. They shoot him. I wake up.

This dream suggests I am drugged. The needle gun is a syringe. Asians are present in many of my dreams in a variety of occupations: restaurant owners, production assistants, and gangsters.

The following dream is the third dream I ever recorded.

TWO DREAMS WITH THE NAME VANDICE IN THEM

DREAM: "The Zulu Man"

November 9, 1980. 9 years and 1 month before my memory returned.

There has been an election and a crooked Mafia bad man has won.

I am in Zululand and a Zulu man is chasing me. I am running along a dock and decide to jump into the water and hide under a boat in one of the air pockets.

The scene changes and my friend Joannie is put in my place under the boat as I fly above, observing. I decide to get help from my uncle and run into a room where he is being filmed having sex with a woman.

I yell, "Help, the Zulu man has Joannie. What can you do to help?"

My uncle finds a telephone book and looks up the number of the bad man and hands it to the woman and says, "Call Vandice."

We all run and find Joannie who has been dragged out of the water and is sitting on the dock. By then, Vandice has arrived with his men. We look for the Zulu man and find him. I wonder how we should punish him and ask what the customs of the land are. They say, "public spanking!"

I was probably told the Black man in this movie was a Zulu. In this dream I think "public spanking" probably means flogging. The dream suggest that I dissociated because I fly up above and observe.

DREAM: "Vandice and Gregory Bates"

October 22, 1993. 13 years after the above dream and 4 years and 1 month after my memory returned.

A senator is in this dream. I am reading a document and the name Vandice is written on it . . . V- A- N- D- I- C- E. Excited, I say to myself, "Why did that name appear?

This is the second time Vandice has appeared in a dream. The dream takes place in Washington D.C., which may have some meaning, as I was there to speak with officials after I was found. The name Gregory Bates comes to mind, but I have no idea who Gregory Bates is or why his name appeared in the dream. Perhaps he had something do with my case.

I believe Vandice is the name of a Mafia movie character. What is interesting about this dream is that this name appears nine years before my memory returned, and then again one month after my memory returned, a thirteen-year gap between the two dreams.

DREAM: "Two Action-Packed Dreams"
September 4, 1990. 1 year after my memory returned.

I am out on the street and realize I am about to be attacked by a group of men. I face them and charge, furiously kicking one in the balls.

There is a battle going on with lots of shooting between two black armies. I am a journalist and am reporting on the battle.

There is a piano bench, and the two forces are shooting at each other under the piano. An explosion occurs when the gunshots hit a gas tank.

When I transcribed this dream in June 1991, I had a flashback: The director of this movie is telling the male actors to be careful not to hurt me.

DREAM: "I Pull Out a Gun and Shoot Him"
December 12, 1990. 1 year and 3 months after my memory returned.

This is a scene from a movie. It is winding down and the villain has me in the bathroom. He puts me into the toilet. The toilet has urine in it and he attempts to drown me. Somehow, I get away and grab him around the neck and stick his head under the water. He struggles and gets away, but I pull out a gun and shoot him. My heart is pounding when I wake up.

This dream is similar to the dream "I am fighting the Japanese with a needle gun," which I had twenty-seven years before this dream on May 21, 1963.

DREAM: "Get the Police"
March 19, 1991. 1 year and 6 months after my memory returned.

I am on a narrow circular stairway by an elevator. Frightened, I move down the stairwell and notice a pair of shoes. I yell, "Who is that over there?" It is a man with a gun, and he runs down the stairs. I yell, "Stop!" Then I run after him. Outside a big car is waiting. He throws the gun on the front seat and says to several men standing there, "Let's go guys."

I grab a chair and use it to defend myself against the guy who is now thinking of shooting me. I straddle him with it, and holding him down, scream, "Get the police, get the police." The car starts to drive away. As the traffic clears, I notice a police car and yell, "Stop that car, stop that car!" I continue to hold the guy down until the police arrive. The van has escaped. I wake up and my heart is pounding.

DREAM: "Danger in the Warehouse"
May 5, 1991. 1 year and 8 months after my memory returned.

Two women and a boy are being pursued by the Mafia. The scene is a dock area with a small beach next to it. The Mafia comes after them in a speedboat. The women and the boy hide underneath the dock.

I look down at them through the boardwalk planks. There is a hole and I decide to help. I reach down and pull the little boy through. He is the only one small enough.

I put the boy under my arms and run through the warehouse passing isles of stock. The bad guys see us and chase us. There is a shootout. The police arrive and help us. We run through the warehouse and hide.

My alarm goes off as the police and the Mafia are about to confront each other.

DREAM: "I Try to Defend Myself with a Gun"
January 23, 1994. 4 years and 4 months after my memory returned.

Bad guys are after me. I have a gun and I try to defend myself, but I don't know how to use it very well. I hold the gun up to my eye to aim it. My finger is in the way. I can't focus. I try to shoot from the hip, or straight ahead without aiming and hope I can hit them.

It is more like water coming out of the gun. Kind of like a "splat." It didn't really have too much effect.

DREAM: "I Am Being Pursued by an Assassin"
March 3, 2003. 3 years and 6 months after my memory returned.

An assassin has been sent to kill me. I have observed him assassinate other people. I try to figure out how to kill him first. He is a big bruiser. He appears at my back door. I secure the door with three locks. He laughs and says, "That won't be a problem." He grabs the door and lifts it off the hinge. I am frustrated because when I try to reach into my closet to find something to kill him, I can't do that and hold the door closed at the same time. Because he has another job, he leaves me alone for the moment.

I had a gun, in the earlier part of the dream, but the police take it away. They think I am one of the bad guys.

The last line of this dream makes me think of the police raid when I was found. It suggests I might have had a gun, making the police think I was part of the porn group. When no one would claim me, they discovered I was a kidnap victim.

VIOLENCE

DREAM: "Three Men Are Being Tortured"
January 28, 1994. 4 years and 4 months after my memory returned.

This dream is set in Biblical times in a city like Damascus. A baby has been kidnapped by infidels. One of the characters walks by three kneeling men and cuts them with a knife. The men are screaming. The guards are trying to make them tell what they did with the baby.

This dream has the feeling of a movie. There is a kind of a sweep across the scene as if a camera on rollers is passing by.

DREAM: "The Bloody Murder without Any Sound"
September 15, 1990. 1 year after my memory returned.

There is a group of men and they are in the Mafia. In the early part of the dream, they do something ghastly to one of their members who didn't follow orders. They take the unsuspecting victim into a bedroom. I am uncertain what is happening. Everyone in the dream runs and pretends they are on the telephone so they won't be suspected of being involved with the murder.

I go into the room. There is a terrible scene. It is dark with blood everywhere. They have murdered him by slicing him through with a knife. He didn't scream. I wonder how they could have done all they did to him without his making any sound. The entire room is dripping with blood. It is gruesome. I wake up with my heart pounding.

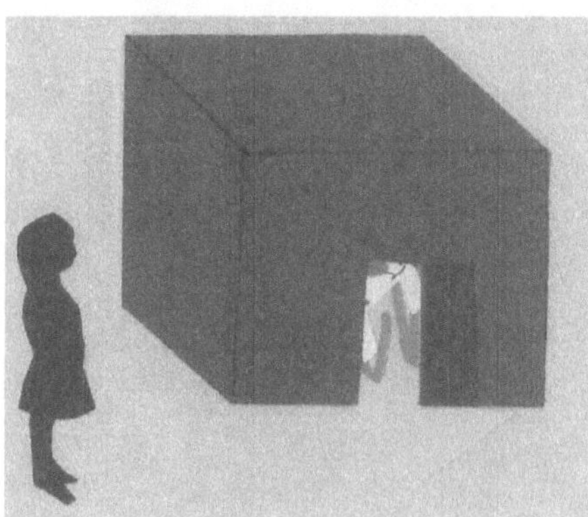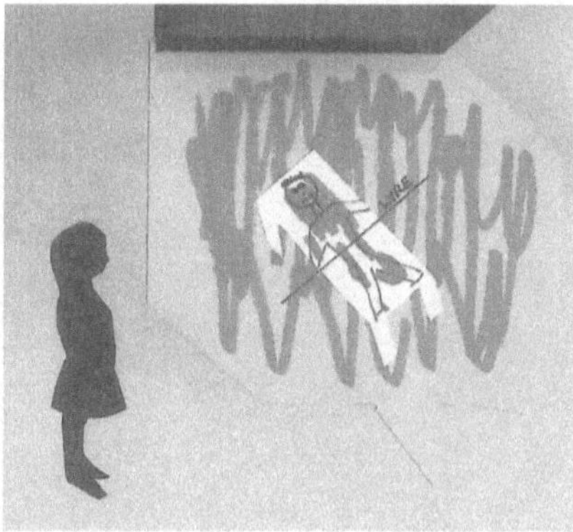

This dream that mentions the Mafia occurred years before I had any idea there was Mafia involvement in my kidnapping.

DREAM: "They Decide Not to Kill Me"
June 7, 1990. 9 months after my memory returned.

It is very dark. I see two men and think they are going to kill me. They decide not to because I didn't see them do it. They thought I was someone else.

Later, I am with two girls. One says she is sure another woman's boyfriend did the murder. Now I am on guard because every time I see her boyfriend, I know he is the murderer. I play act with him. I pretend I don't know he did it.

One of my first memories of my kidnapping was of this murder. I think the man they killed was part of the porn ring and he did something they didn't like. Everyone was upset about the murder and discussing it. One woman said, "He brought it on himself by sticking his nose in where it did not belong." I believe it had something to do with me. He was objecting to what they were doing to me. He went to the police. "Rats" are murdered.

DREAM: "I Knew It Was Violent"
April 30, 1991. 1 year and 7 months after my memory returned.

Two friends and I are watching a movie. The two male main characters are torturing another man. They have tied him spread eagled to the ground and are running him over with a car. Blood squirts out of him. They enjoy what they are doing. I hide my eyes.

I say to my friends, "I knew it was violent, but I didn't know it was that violent." The man they murdered is a policeman. I wake up with my heart pounding.

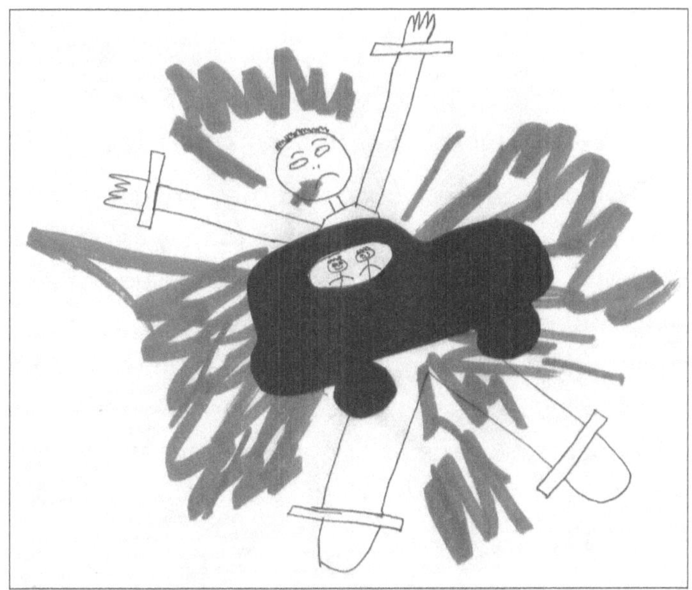

DREAM: "Whipping the Black Man"

November 3, 1991. 2 years and 2 months after my memory returned.

I am in a Victorian house with high ceilings and beautiful wood floors. There is very little furniture. I am there to be a prostitute. People are watching. I am standing and watching as they bring a black man into the room.

They tie him down on a table and whip him. A man tells them when to stop.

I see a shadow move past the door, and I am terrified and hide my eyes. I don't know what it was.

Houses were often rented to use for filming. A Victorian house is in several of my dreams and is on an estate with a sweeping lawn.

Black men and women are prevalent in my dreams, as are Mafia and "family" gatherings.

ANIMALS

DREAM: "Are You up Late, or Are You up Early?"
August 10, 1989. 1 month before my memory returned.

There are children in the house and they are preparing for an entertainment. There are two poodles, and they are in the hallway practicing tricks to perform. At one point the male poodle comes up behind me, sticks his nose under my behind and between my legs and lifts me up and down several times. I can feel his nose between my legs and the ride up and down makes me feel uncomfortable. However, this is quite an accomplishment. I am compelled to tell him how wonderful the trick is, pat his head and say, "Nice dog."

DREAM: "The Excited Dog"
October 29, 1989. 1 month after my memory returned.

A dog falls out of an icebox. He falls into my arms. He is a small dog with short brown curly hair. He is on his back and my head is on his stomach. He is very excited. I can hear him barking and yapping in my ear. It is a real bark.

I wake up. I can hear the blood pumping into my heart.

DREAM: "The Horse"
April 18, 2017. 27 years and 7 months after my memory returned.

I am lying on a bed looking up at the ceiling. A horse is brought in and he is upside down on the ceiling. A prostitute comes in and is hoisted up under the horse.

Pornographers often show children examples of how things are done so they will think certain activities are okay. I don't know if I was forced to have sex with a pony, but from this dream I can surmise I was at least shown the activity.

POLICE

In the 1940s, corruption in the LAPD was rampant. Mobsters routinely paid off police, politicians, and other public officials to keep their criminal enterprises operating. During my time in Los Angeles, I had several encounters with the police. I was afraid to tell them what was happening to me. What if they were corrupt or didn't believe me? The mobsters would not have hesitated to punish me and or even kill me. Several of my dreams mention murder.

Dream: "The Police Find My Stolen Car"
October 15, 1989. 1 month after my memory returned.

The police have found my stolen car. I am in the driver's seat. They ask me if my car is okay. I tell them yes. They drive away.

I realize my car is not okay. It has been vandalized. I scream at the top of my voice. I am very angry.

I learned early on that a car symbolizes me moving through life. I believe that in this dream the stolen car is me and "stolen" is a metaphor for being raped.

DREAM: "I Keep Getting Robbed"
October 26, 1989. 1 month after my memory returned.

My phone is not working. The cord is broken and keeps coming out of the plug in the wall. People keep coming into my house to rob me. I get more and more upset because I can't get a phone call through to the police so they can rescue me. A famous movie actor is one of the robbers. He knows my phone is not working and he comes back to rob me a second time. I grab the phone and hit him on the head. He crumples down beside me under the coffee table. I call the police but can't think of the address. I scream at everyone, "What is the address here?" I am so excited and upset that I can't think straight, and no one is helping me.

The police are trying to get the address. I can't think of it. I am screaming and yelling and am angry and agitated. Finally, I get control enough to look in my address book. I try to get someone to give me my purse, which I can't reach. I don't want to get too far away from the movie actor in case he wakes up and I have to hit him again. I then remember I am on Cold Water Canyon Road. I yell at the police so they can start on their way while I am finding the exact address.

There is another thief. He enters my house but claims he has not robbed me. I am confused about this. He has entered my house, but has not taken anything. Therefore, did he rob me or not? I feel like he did, but he wants me to tell the police that he did not.

The police who are now with me start to leave before I am rescued and I yell, "Where are you going?" A policewoman gets into the car and drives away. I can't believe that she is leaving before I am okay. I wake up agitated, nervous, frustrated and exhausted.

This is a very disturbing dream. Entering my house and robbing me are metaphors for rape.

DREAM: "Ghost Dog"
March 6, 2010. 20 years and 6 months after my memory returned.

I walk down a narrow alley which leads to an abandoned lot surrounded by buildings. Suddenly a train comes around the corner and heads toward me. Frightened, I stand against the wall of the alley and because the train turns the corner, I am saved.

A mad dog comes racing down the alley at me. The dog's fur is gray and his face is funny looking. He has no eyebrows or eyelashes and he looks like a ghost. I shield myself with my right arm and the dog bites me. Blood begins to come out of my arm. The dog turns around and comes at me again. I start running down the alley screaming, "Mad dog, mad dog."

Policemen drive into the alley. They get out of their van. I scream, "Mad dog, mad dog!" They argue about who should come and help me. I continue to scream and the dog comes at me again and again. Blood is spattering on his head and there is blood on his teeth and on my arm. I see a rock on the ground. I pick it up to defend myself. I hit the dog on the head. I hit him again and again. Blood is everywhere. I hurt the dog, but he keeps coming at me.

The policemen get into the van and drive away. They are not going to help me.

Terrified, I wake up.

RAID

DREAM: "It's Hot over There"
February 21, 1989. 7 months before my memory returned.

We are at a big ranch or party place. We get to a gate and the man at the gate says, "You better stay here tonight because it's 'too hot' over there."

The next day as we drive out of the park the old man says, "It is still too hot to go over to the other place, so you better go home."

DREAM: "The Knock at the Door"

February 21, 1989. 6 months after my memory returned.

There are three men built like wrestlers and they are looking for someone. They run up a flight of stairs and are out of breath, huffing and puffing. They have guns drawn. There is a noise at the door. I wake up frightened and my heart is pounding.

DREAM: "I Don't Know Who I Am"

October 3, 1989. 1 month after my memory returned.

There is a list of names. Information is written about each person. My name is on the list and it says, "doesn't know who she is." Under a man's name it says he is in love with her.

DREAM: "The Man Everyone Is Afraid Of"

August 18, 2010. 20 years and 11 months after my memory returned.

I am with a group of people, men and women, and I am young. We are in a big room with wood floors. Everyone is afraid of a man who is there. They are worried he is going to take them into another room where he is going to be mad at them.

A man from my group is taken away. Later, I am sitting next to a wall and look down the row of people and see that this man is back. I ask him if he is okay and if the bad man hurt him and he says, "no, he just hit me."

The bad man comes back into the big room and walks around lecturing and yelling at everyone. I am reading a pamphlet. It is one piece of paper folded over twice about devil worship. The bad man comes over to where I am and grabs the pamphlet from me. He looks it over and that is when I gradually wake up and realize I am dreaming.

DREAM: "One Guy Takes Me Away from the Group"
August 5, 2016. 26 years and 11 months after my memory returned.

I am in a car with two guys. One of the men has taken me away from the group. He introduces me to the other man, who goes to get food.

In this dream I believe I am with two policeman who are taking me to the hospital. This dream memory returned to me 68 years after my abduction.

HOSPITALIZED

DREAM: "I Am Being Monitored"
August 25, 2018. 28 years and 11 months after my memory returned.

My health is being monitored. I have cloudy urine.

DREAM: "Tuna Fish"
September 16, 2018. 28 years and 11 months after my memory returned.

My vagina hurts. I put tuna fish on it, thinking it might help.

DREAM: "I Have Sperm in Me"
October 16, 1989. 1 month after my memory returned.

I am in a hospital. A woman doctor tells me I must go downstairs for a female examination. I don't want to because there is semen in me, and I don't want her to find out.

DREAM: "I Am Helping the Sick Child"
April 22, 2003. 3 years and 4 months after my memory returned.

We run into Dr. Anderson in the hospital lobby.

He says, "Oh yes, this is the little girl that has such-and-such disease."

It is a disease I don't understand. Dr. Anderson gets out his chart and says, "She has this other disease too. Take her upstairs and I will be right up."

I don't know who Dr. Anderson was, but could this be his or her real name? On the other hand, it could be the name of another doctor from my past, used as a substitute here because I don't remember the real name.

DREAM: "I'm Going to Be Checked"

December 16, 2017. 28 years and 3 months after my memory returned.

I am going to be checked to see if I am pure. I know that I am not and try to think how I can fool the court officials.

DREAM: "Cancer"

June 18, 1989. 3 months before my memory returned.

I am standing at the mirror in the bathroom and there are white crystals around my left nostril.

Two doctors are talking about me. They say the white crystals mean I have cancer.

I say, "Oh my goodness, really?"

I look closer and the white crystals are like white snowflakes. I get a pair of tweezers and pull the crystals off. They fall onto a glass mirror. The crystals now have legs and are running around the mirror like little white spiders. I realize I do have cancer and that and I am going to need a doctor's care.

The word "cancer" in this dream, I believe, is a metaphor for drug addiction as suggested by the white power on my nose. At the time I had the dream, three months before my memory returned, its meaning was a complete mystery.

DREAM: "I Am in a Catatonic State"
September 13, 1990. 1 year after my memory returned.

I have become catatonic. I am blocked behind my face. It is a strange sensation because I have disappeared within myself. I can see out of my face and observe my surrounding, but there is no connection with the outside world. My body is totally closed off. The feeling is vivid.

I believe this dream is about detoxing from drugs.

DREAM: "The Nurse"
August 19, 2018. 28 years and 11 months after my memory returned.

I am in a large building. A pleasant Black woman appears. I can see her clearly. Her face is round, and she is friendly, smiling, and energetic. We walk across the room as she inspects the back of my head.

This dream relates to my memories of a Black nurse taking care of me in the hospital. I wonder if he was checking my head to see if I had lice.

DREAM: "My Brain"
September 26, 2018. 29 years after my memory returned.

I am somewhere where my brain is being tested by doctors. When they finish the test, I can tell by the way they are acting that something is wrong. I ask them to explain.

"We are not supposed to tell you," they say.

"I want to know so I can fix the problem," I say.

"We can't tell you."

I become angry. "What's the point of testing if you are not going to tell me the results?"

One doctor says, "I agree, but I still can't tell you."

In this dream I have had a blood test and the doctors are not allowed to tell me the results.

DREAM: "I Am in a Study"

April 15, 2003. 13 years and 7 months after my memory returned.

I am in a study to learn about dreams. In the study they shoot a chemical into my leg, and it comes out in my head in the form of a dream.

This dream suggests that chemicals were used to help me remember some of the particulars of my abduction. Memory enhancement experimental drugs were known to be used in the 1940s.

In the documentary movie *Let There Be Light* directed by John Huston, he shows a doctor helping a shell-shocked veteran through hypnosis and the injection of a "truth serum" in their leg. This term was commonly used for barbiturates like sodium amytal and sodium pentothal. This dream suggests a barbiturate was used on me.

DREAM: "I Am in a Group"

March 23, 2003. 13 years and 6 months after my memory returned.

I am in a dream group in a meeting room. People are beginning to sit down in a circle. A doctor is the leader. Two men sit down beside me. Their movements are in slow motion. It feels like my mind is recreating a real happening.

I move and stand near the doctor. A Black man slowly walks into the room. He looks at me and I can see his face. I recognize him. He is the man they murdered, whom I dreamed about in "The Bloody Murder without Any Sound."

I slowly wake up and feel rested and calm. I feel like I have had a catharsis and have been released after a struggle.

On some level, this dream felt like a lucid dream, although I was not aware of shifting into one like in my other experiences of lucid dreaming. On another level, it feels like a flashback to a real event. I'm basing this idea on the way people are moving and the fact that I can clearly see the Black man's face. I know I could recognize him if I saw a picture.

Another thought is that a doctor is hypnotizing me and I am recalling the memory of a Black man. In this dream I believe I am in the hospital, but the two men I am sitting between appear to be protecting me. I have several dreams where two men are protecting me.

FBI

DREAM: "I Am in a Huge Building"
May 14, 1989. 4 months before my memory returned.

I am now in Washington D.C. taking part in some sort of a seminar both as a speaker and as a participant. I'm with a man. We arrive and don't know where anything is. It is a huge building and takes up several blocks. We don't know where we are going. The man is in a hurry. He has some things to do before the meeting. He rushes ahead and stops to talk with someone to ask where we have to go. They give him a book which has all the instructions. It takes him a while to get oriented and to figure out where we are and where we are going.

I wake up and am uneasy.

I believe the man in this dream is either my father, or my dad's brother, Uncle C.B., a scientist working with NASA in the Washington D. C. area.

DREAM: "The Elegant Woman at the Top of the Stairs"
July 20, 1989. 2 months before my memory returned.

I walk up the stairs of a courthouse and move around a fountain before approaching a woman standing at the top. I am accompanied by three tall, handsome men. The woman is poised and slim and looks to be in full command of herself. She has on a uniform that comes in at the waist like a tailored suit and there are insignias on her shoulder and on her left breast pocket. The weather is balmy and there is a slight breeze. We approach her.

I realize I want to say hello to her. I move around the circular fountain and walk up to her.

She is leaning over talking in a whisper to a short man dressed in a black cape and hat. He is in silhouette. She eventually looks up at me and we have eye contact for a moment.

At the same moment, we both say, "I don't have your address!"

I dash over to her, but don't have a piece of paper to write down her telephone number. Several people are standing around and they want to help. They give me a piece of paper and a pencil.

I run down the stairs and shout back, "Call me when you get your act together!"

I wake up feeling very good.

This dream, and the one before, came to me before my memory returned and was during the time I was serving on the jury. I believe

The Justice Department Building at Ninth and Pennsylvania NW in
Washington D.C., where it was headquartered from 1908 until 1975.

this dream is about three FBI men escorting me into the Justice
Department, which has stairs leading up to the entrance of the building. You must walk around a fountain, as described in the dream. The
woman may be a court official who is there to chaperone us into the
building. I looked on the internet at pictures of uniforms worn by
officers of the court in 1948. My dream description is similar. As to
the "short man in silhouette wearing a black cape," he appears every
now and then in my dreams. I believe this dream is indicating that
I am at the Justice Department to be questioned about this man. As
I leave the court house we realize that we need to have each other's
local contact information.

DREAM: "I Identify a Policeman"
*September 9, 2018. 28 years and 12 months after my memory
returned.*

Pictures of policemen are placed before me. One of them I recognize as a family member. I am unsure as to whether I should identify him.

DREAM: "I Go to the Movies with Two Men"
December 17, 2019. 29 years and 3 years after my memory returned.

I walk into a movie theater with two men. We sit in the back row, and I am in the middle. Something unusual is happening on the stage. I can't quite see what it is, but a man is doing it.

In this dream I believe I am being protected by two FBI men. We are watching a pornographic movie and they are hoping I can help them identify the man in the film.

DREAM: "The Secret Taping"
April 10, 2018. 29 years and 7 months after my memory returned.

It is the middle of the night. I am taken to a secret meeting in a warehouse. I sit at a table. There is a microphone. Men question me and tape what I am saying.

DREAM: "Section Four"
April 11, 2018. 29 years and 7 months after my memory returned.

I wake up thinking the words "Section Four."

At first, I thought this dream might indicate an area of a large building, or perhaps a section of a movie studio, but when I searched online for the words "Section Four of the FBI," up came Criminal Justice Information Services (CJIS). It took hours, but I eventually learned that Section Four is part of the Freedom of Information Act code that lays out rules for disseminating FBI information.

DREAM: "Undercover Agents"
August 6, 1989. 1 month before my memory returned.

I am driving around with a man in a station wagon. We are undercover agents picking up something, maybe mail. There are people lurking in the dark. We have a flashlight. We catch a man and decide to convert him into an informer who can go undercover with us.

A photographer is sneaking around trying to get pictures for the newspapers and she takes a photograph of our informer. We don't want any pictures of him floating around because it might blow his cover. We try to get the picture from the photographer, but she gets away.

My partner is doing most of the work. I am the one who sees the photographer escape because my partner is occupied with our prisoner.

In this dream I seem to be working with the FBI. I have several dreams in which newspaper photographers are hanging around. I would have been able to identify criminals the FBI would be interested in. If I helped find a witness, we would not want his picture in the newspapers.

DREAM: "The FBI Makes a Deal"
February 12, 2019. 29 years and 5 months after my memory returned.

The FBI is talking to a Mafia guy, and he says, "If you leave Alice alone, we will leave you alone. Do we have a deal?"

The Mafia guy replies, "Yes."

CARTOONS

DREAM: "THE CAT CARTOON"
July 2, 1989. 2 months after my memory returned.

I am a partner with a man, and we are with a firm that is helping the police investigate a crime. I am opening a box in which each item in the box is wrapped in newspapers. I unwrap each object to see what it can mean to the investigation and give it to the policeman. I unwrap two "cat cartoons." The cartoons are shaped like bookmarks or comic strips.

This is when I notice that because one of the cartoons is so faded that I can't really see it. The cartoons have some clue or key to the case.

In this dream an investigator is showing me sex toys and a strip of film to see if I know what they are. The word "cartoon" appears in several of my dreams as a reference to porn films; the word first appeared in my dreams in 1989 prior to the return of my memory.

DREAM: "He Develops Film"
November 9, 1989. 2 months after my memory returned.

Now I am in a house with a man. He is developing film. On the floor are pieces of paper that look like artwork. He is collecting cartoons. He shows me one. Two friends arrive. They are working on collections of cartoons and copying them.

This dream suggests that the man I am with is selling, or trading, pornographic photos he has taken of me and is developing in his house.

DREAM: "The Movie in the Marble Building"
April 13, 2017. 27 years and 7 months after my memory returned.

I am someplace with my mother. The building is made of marble. It is huge and there are people walking around. A circular center room has a few doors around the periphery. We take an elevator and exit on a floor where there is a theater. A movie is to be shown. There is no marquee, and the front entrance is flat where you would usually buy tickets. It is not time for the movie to begin so we go back to our hotel.

A man arrives. He is tense. I tell him we are going to the movies and ask if he wants to come. He says yes. We realize we need to hurry. The man and I leave but my mom does not want to go. We arrive at the movie and take seats in the first row on the side.

The movie starts. It is being shown on a small screen, and the theater is not like a regular movie theater, though there are people there. The movie is not what we expected. It seems to be a science fiction cartoon of some sort. I wake up.

TRIALS

Several dreams recount two trials in which I was a participant. The dreams compress the two events into one. I believe a grand jury was called to discern if there was enough evidence to convict my abductors, and a second trial was held to convict the pedophile I was with when found. They were held in Denver and Los Angeles. The pedophile, whose name I have not remembered but whom I call Frank in my dreams, was convicted in yet another trial in Los Angeles.

DREAM: "The Two Men in Church"
May 17, 1989. 4 months before my memory returned.

I'm in church in the back pew. On the left are two men and on the right is a little girl with her family. She sees the two men and is very upset because she recognizes they have done something bad to her. The little girl is terribly afraid because she thinks they are going to hurt her. She writes this down on a piece of paper and gives it to a lawyer.

I get angry and am going to defend her. At this point I can't see anymore—I'm lopsided and can't see.

I'm floundering. My eyes are blank. I am frustrated because I can't see the two bad men although I know where they are. I stand in front of them and denounce them in front of the church.

I say, "You are going to leave her alone and you are not going to hurt her, or I am going to kill you."

This dream took place before my memory returned and has the feeling that recurs in my dreams of being lopsided. At the time I had no idea what it meant, probably because of where the dream took place, and I did not recognize "church" as a metaphor for "court." I think this dream is recounting a pretrial courtroom meeting with my abductors.

DREAM: "The Vial"
October 5, 1989. 1 month after my memory returned.

I am in a courtroom, testifying. A Hispanic lawyer is questioning me. He holds up a vial and asks me to tell the court what it is.

I wake up and I am scratching myself. I feel like bugs are all over me—in my hair and on my legs, chest, and arms.

BIBLIOGRAPHY

Alexander, Shana. *The Pizza Connection: Lawyers, Drugs, and the Mafia.* United States: Weidenfeld and Nicolson, 1988.

Applegate, Debby. *Madame: The Biography of Polly Adler, Icon of the Jazz Age.* New York: Doubleday, 2021.

Barrett, Deirdre, PhD. *The Pregnant Man: And other cases from a Hypnotherapist's Couch.* United States: Times Books, 1998.

Barrett, Deirdre. *Trauma and Dreams*, edited by. Cambridge, Massachusetts: Harvard University Press, 1996.

Bharara, Preet. *Doing Justice: A Prosecutor's thoughts on Crime, Punishment, and the Rule of Law.* New York: Alfred A. Knopf, 2019.

Binder, John J. *The Chicago Outfit: Images of America.* United States: Arcadia Publishing, 2003.

Bonelli, William G. *Billion Dollar Blackjack: The story of Corruption and the Los Angeles Times.* California: Civic Research Press, 1954.

Buntin, John. *L.A. Noir: The Struggle for The Soul of America's Most Seductive City.* United States: Harmony Book, 2009.

Capeci, Jerry. *The Complete Idiot's Guide to The Mafia.* New York: Alpha Books, 2002.

Carposi, George Jr., *Bugsy: The High-rolling, Bullet-riddled Story of Benjamin "Bugsy" Siegel, of Murder, Inc.* New York: Pinnacle Books, Inc.,1973.

Cedillo, Juan Alberto, *La Cosa Nostro En Mexico 1938–1950* (Spanish Edition). Mexico: Grijalbo, 2011.

Cohen, Mickey. *In My Own Words: As told to John Peer Nugent.* United States: Prentice-Hall, Inc. 1975.

Corso-Steinmeyer, Bambi. *DreamTracking.* Florida: , 2021.

Crawford, Phillip, Jr. *The Mafia and the Gays*, 2015.

Dark, Tony. *Mob Boss: Chicago Mob Bosses, Paul Ricca & Tony Accardo.* United States: Hosehead Productions, 2016.

Davis, John H. *Mafia Kingfish: Carlos Marcello and the Assassination of John F. Kennedy.* New York: McGraw Hill 1989.

DeMaris, Ovid. *The Last Mafioso: The Treacherous World of Jimmy ("the Weasel") Fratianno.* Bronx, New York: Ishi Press International, 1981.

Edmonds, Andy. *Bugsy's Baby: The Secret Life of Mob Queen Virginia Hill.* New York: Carol Publishing Group, 1993.

Edwards, Bradley J. *Relentless Pursuit: My Fight for The Victims of Jeffrey Epstein.* New York: Gallery Books, 2020.

English, T. J. *Havana Nocturne: How the Mob Owned Cuba . . . and Then Lost It to the Revolution.* United States: William Morrow, an imprint of HarperCollins Publishers, 2008.

Final Report of the Attorney General's Commission on Pornography. Tennessee: Rutledge Hill Press, 1986.

Foo, Stephanie. *What My Bones Know: A Memoir of Healing from Complex Trauma.* New York: Ballantine Books, 2022.

Freud, Sigmund. *On Dreams: The James Strachey Translation.* United States: W. W. Norton and Company, 1952.

Friedrich, Otto. *City of Nets: A Portrait of Hollywood in the 1940's.* United States Treasury Department Bureau of Narcotics. Mafia: The Government's Secret File on Organized Crime. United States: HarperCollins, 2007.

Giancana, Sam and Chuck. *Double Cross: The Explosive, Inside Story of the Mobster Who Controlled America.* New York: Warner Books, 1992.

Gladstone, B. James. *The Man Who Seduced Hollywood: The Life and Loves of Greg Bautzer, Tinseltown's Most Powerful Lawyer.* Illinois: Chicago Review Press, 2013.

Gordon, Neil. *Tony Accardo is Joe Batters: Mob Boss Murderer*. No Place of Publishing or Publisher name is mentioned, 2018.

Hanna, David. *Virginia Hill: Queen of the Underworld*. United States: Belmont Tower Books, 1975.

Hartmann, Ernest, M.D., *Dreams and Nightmares*. New York: Perseus Publishing, 1998.

Herman, Judith L., MD. *Truth and Repair, How Trauma Survivors Envision Justice*. New York: Basic Books, 2023.

Hoss, Robert J, Gongloff, Robert P. Editors. *Dreams that Chance Lives*. Ashville, North Carolina: Chiron Publications, 2017.

Jennings, Dean. *We Only Kill Each Other: The True Story of Mobster Bugsy Siegel, The Man Who Invented Las Vegas*. New York: Pocket Books, 1967.

Johnson, Lacy M. *The Other Side: A memoir*. Oregon, Tin House Books, 2014.

Johnstone, Kevin. *Bugsy & His Flamingo: The Testimony of Virginia Hill*. Google Books, 2011.

Jordheim, Alisa. *Made in the USA: The Sex trafficking of America's Children*. Florida: Higherlife Publishing, 2014.

Jung, G.G. *Memories, Dreams, Reflections*. United States: Random House, 1961.

Kelly, Robert J. *Encyclopedia of Organized Crime in the United States: From Capone's Chicago to the New Urban Underworld*. Connecticut: Greenwood Press, 2000.

Kinzer, Stephen. *Poisoner In Chief: Sidney Gottlieb and the CIA Search for Mind Control*. New York: Henry Holt and Company. 2019.

Kreck, Dick. *Smaldone: The Untold Story of an American Crime Family*. Colorado: Fulcrum Publishing, 2009.

Kruzan, Sara. *I Cried to Dream Again: Trafficking, Murder, and Deliverance*. New York: Pantheon, 2022.

Lacey, Robert. *Little Man: Meyer Lansky and the Gangster Life*. United States: Little, Brown & Company, 1991.

Langer, Lawrence L. Langer. *Holocaust Testimonies: The ruins of Memory.* Massachusetts: Yale University Press, 1991.

Levine, Peter A., PhD. *Trauma and Memory.* Berkeley: North Atlantic Books, 2015.

Levine, Peter A. PhD. *In An Unspoken Voice.* Berkeley: North Atlantic Books, 2010.

Lewis, Brad: *Hollywood's Celebrity Gangster: The Incredible Life and Times of Mickey Cohen.* United States: Brad Lewis, 2009.

Lewis, Brad. *Mickey Cohen: The Gangster Squad and the Mob: The True Story of Vice in Los Angeles 1937–1950.* United States: BBL Books, 2012.

Lewis, Brad. *Mickey Cohen: The Rat Pack Years: Elder Statesman's Life and Times 1960–1976.* United States: Brad Lewis, 2014.

Lieberman, Daniel Z., MD. *Spell Bound, Modern Science, Ancient Magic, and the Hidden Potential of the Unconscious Mind.* Dallas, Texas: BenBella Books. Inc., 2022.

Lieberman, Paul. *Gangster Squad: Covert Cops, The Mob, And the Battle for Los Angeles.* New York: Thomas Dunne Books, 2012.

Miller, Chanel. *Know My Name: A Memoir.* United States: Viking Press, 2019.

Moore, Judith. *A Bad, Bad Boy: The Most Feared Mobster in Southern California for 30 years.* United States: San Diego Reader, 2009.

Moore, William Howard. *The Kefauver Committee and the Politics of Crime 1950-1952.* Missouri: University of Missouri Press, 1974.

Mortimer, Lait. *U.S.A. Confidential.* New York: Crown Publishers, Inc., 1952.

Moulden, Stuart. *The Kefauver Organized Crime Hearings. Abridged.*

Mustain, Gene, and Jerry Capeci. *Murder Machin: A True Story of Madness and the Mafia.* New York: Onyk Books, 1993.

Nikolidakis, Lisa. *No One Crosses the Wolf, A Memoir.* New York: Little A, 2022.

Olnick, Cindy. *L.A. Landmarks: Lost and Almost Lost.* Los Angeles: Photo Friends of the Los Angeles Public Library.

Rako, Susan, M.D and Harvey Mazer, M.D., ed. *Semrad: The Heart of a Therapist*. United States: Jason Aronson, Inc., 1983.

Rappleye, Charles, and Ed Becker. *All American Mafioso: The Johnny Rosselli Story*. New York: Barricade Books, Inc.1995.

Reid, Ed. *Mafia: A Sensational Expose of the Notorious Rulers of Organized Crime*. United States: Signet, 1954.

Reid, Ed. *The Mistress and the Mafia: The Virginia Hill Story*. United States: Bantam Books, 1972.

Renner, Joan. *The First with The Latest: Aggie Underwood, The Los Angeles Herald, and the Sordid Crimes of a City*. Los Angeles: Photo Friends of the Los Angeles Public Library, 2015.

Rhodes, James. *Instrumental: A memoir of Madness, Medication, and Music*. New York: Bloomsbury Publishing, 2014.

Roemer, William F. Jr. *Man Against the Mob: The Inside Story of how the FBI Cracked the Chicago Mob by the Agent who Led the Attack*. United States: Tribune Company,1989.

Roemer, William F., Jr. *Enforcer: Spilotro—The Chicago Mob's Man Over Las Vegas*. United States: Designed by Irving Perkins Associates, 1994.

Roemer, William F., Jr. *Accardo: The Genuine Godfather*. New York: Donald I. Fine, Inc., 1995.

Rosner, Elizabeth. *Survivor Café: The Legacy of Trauma and the Labyrinth of Memory*. United States: Counterpoint, 2017.

Rothschild, Babette M.S.W., L.C.S.W. *The Body Remembers: The Psychophysiology of Trauma and Treatment*. New York: W.W. Norton and Company, 2000.

Rush, Florence. *The Best Kept Secret: Sexual Abuse of Children*. New York: McGraw-Hill, 1980.

Russo, Gus. *The Outfit: The Role of Chicago's Underworld in the Shaping of Modern America*. New York: Bloomsbury, 2001.

Sarnoff, Conchita. *TrafficKing: The Jeffrey Epstein Case*. United States: Post Hill Press, 2020.

Schiller, Linda Yael, MSW, LICSW, *PTS Dreams: Transform Your Nightmares from Trauma through Healing Dreamwork*. Woodbury Minnesota: Llewellyn, 2022.

Schwarz, Ted, and Rustam, Mardi. *Candy Barr: The Small-Town Texas Runaway Who Became a Darling of the Mob and the Queen of Los Vegas Burlesque*. Maryland: Taylor Trade Publishing, 2008.

Seal, Mark. *Leave the Gun, Take the Cannoli, The Epic Story of the Making of The Godfather*. New York: Gallery Books, 2021.

Server, Lee. *Handsome Johnny: The Criminal Life of Johnny Rosselli the Mob's Man in Hollywood*. London: Penguin Random House, 2018.

Server, Lee. *Robert Mitchum: "Baby I Don't Care."* New York: St. Martin's Press, 2001.

Siragusa, Charles. *The Trail of the Poppy: Behind the Mask of the Mafia*. United States: Prentice Hall, 1966.

Stern, Jessica. *Denial: A Memoir of Terror*. United States: HarperCollins, 2010.

Sterling, Claire. *Octopus: How the Long Reach of the Sicilian Mafia Controls the Global Narcotics Trade*. New York: Touchstone, 1990.

Stoker, Sgt. Charles. *Thicker'n Thieves: The 1950 Factual Expose of Police Pay-Offs, Graft, Political Corruption and Prostitution in Los Angeles and Hollywood*. Los Angeles: Thoughtprint Press, 2011.

Tereba, Tere. *Mickey Cohen: The Life and Crimes of L.A.'s Notorious* Mobster. Toronto Ontario, Canada: ECW Press, 2012.

Valentine, Douglas. *The Strength of the Wolf: The Secret History of America's War on Drugs*. New York: Verso, 2004.

Van der Kolk, Bessel A., M.D. *The Body Keeps the Score: Brain, Mind, and Body in the Healing of Trauma*. New York: Penguin Books, 2014.

Weinrib, Estelle L. *Images of the Self: The Sandplay Therapy Process*. California: Temenos Press, 2004.

Wilkerson, W.R. III. Billy. *Hollywood Godfather: The Life and Crimes of Billy Wilkerson*. Chicago Review Press, 2018

Yalom, Irvin D. *Becoming Myself: A Psychiatrist's Memoir*. New York: Basic Books, 2017.

ACKNOWLEDGMENTS

Writing this book has been a lengthy journey. Along the way, I have met many individuals who have mentored and encouraged me as I fought to comes to terms with my memory.

Susan Shankin, of Precocity Press, has been an important mentor in helping me through the process of bringing my book to fruition. Her artistic cover and book design have added immeasurably to the development of my book, and for this I am eternally grateful. Thank you, Susan for your guidance, understanding, and interest in my project. And, for always being there.

Victoria Brock, my London editor, who took over my project when I needed to reduce my manuscript by 20,000 words. Within a short-time she was able to tighten my story while at the same time keeping interest flowing. She has been a delight to work with via Zoom. Thank you for your honesty, knowledge, and encouragement.

Marketing Director, Darcy Hughes, and her assistant, Sarah Lizama, remained calm, and patiently explained the workings of the computer when I wanted to pull my hair out from frustration.

Dr. Dianne Bradley, LMFT, has been a major influence in my struggle to recreate my past. From our first encounter, she believed my story and put me on my writing journey by empowering me to believe in myself and my story. She was the first person to encourage me to use the internet to research my past, an option I did not know was possible. I am eternally grateful.

I was lucky to have met clinical psychologist Dr. Michael D. Yapko shortly after my memory returned, when I was trapped in traumatic memories, unable to move forward. His maxim, "Focusing on your strengths," quickly pulled me out of my depression and sent me on a path toward a brighter future. I will forever be grateful for his insight, compassion, and encouragement, which pushed me forward and sent me down a new path.

Barbara Cook, RN, MSW, my therapist at the time of my memory return, kept me from a complete psychotic breakdown. Her loving care and understanding were my rock and helped me to get through the first year as I coped with the trauma of remembering. Thank you, Barbara, for being there.

Retired FBI Special agent Roger Young responded to my "crazy lady" letter (most didn't) and agreed to meet and talk with me. He has been an invaluable source of information. He corroborated what my dreams revealed happens to children who are abducted into the world of pedophilia and pornography, criminality he worked to prevent throughout his FBI career. He gave me courage to accept what I remembered and made it possible for me to begin the healing process. His support has upheld my belief that FBI agents are fantastic human beings who care about the people they serve.

Gena Burson, my "happy friend," has supported me on my journey. We meet once a month at our hairdresser, Thurman Metcalf's Salon, where we all spent a hilarious time together laughing. Gena, who has roots in Denver and visits there frequently, conducted research for me at the Denver Library. She found the newspaper article announcing Virginia Hill's detention, thus validating my memory. She also contacted the Denver Department of Justice to find out if I could access Grand Jury court reports. Gena's friendship and positive interest have been heartening.

My friend Vicky Stallion, who rescued me over and over again when I was stuck on how to do something on the computer. Her patience and calming spirit kept me grounded and able to learn.

Joanne Hunt, my friend from San Francisco days, read my book and enthusiastically cheered me on. Joanne, who has written and published her own memoir called *Shatterproof,* about her attempts to break through the glass ceiling, advised me on the ins and outs of publication. Our telephone conversations always invigorated me and sent me back to my computer eager to get on with it.

Georgia Alderink, my neighbor, responded positively when I asked her to read my book. I am grateful for her interest. She corrected typos and took the time to write out suggestions. Georgia has also written and published a memoir called *Adaptation,* about life as the wife of a veterinarian in Montana from 1960–1980. Her knowledge of the process reassured me.

Linda Leavell, published author of the multi-award winning biography, *Holding on Upside Down, the Life and Work of Marianne Moore,* has given me invaluable advice on the publishing world and encouraged me along my path to publication. She always answered the phone when I called and spent time helping me; she also enthusiastically read my manuscript and offered much needed encouragement and positive feedback.

My good friend Susan Raymond asked to read my book and did so three times. During telephone conversations, she made suggestions on how to make my stories clearer, asked questions, and generally made me believe people might want to read my book. Her encouragement kept me going.

Thanks to Dick Kreck, retired newspaper reporter, who agreed to meet me in Denver, Colorado, and whose book *Smaldone: The Untold Story of An American Crime Family,* sent me down a path toward the validation of my memory. Dick answered my emails and was able to help me fill in some of the blanks.

Long-time friend Kathy Siegfried encouraged me to join a writing group and drove me, week after week, to meetings. Her knowledge of grammar and love for the English language has been invaluable as she helped clean up spelling errors and typos and supported me throughout my journey.

In Fayetteville, Arkansas, the Dickson Street Writers group were the first friends who nurtured my writing as I struggled to make sense of my memory. They listened to my stories, week after week, year in and year out. Their encouragement helped me improve my writing and formulate a coherent memoir as I struggled to put it all together.

Computer guru, Javier Martinez of Plaza Technologies who helped me though numerous computer crises when I had a deadline to meet and couldn't make heads nor tail of what was going on with my computer. He always supported me, calmed me down and was a patient teacher. Thank you, Javier, for being my friend.

Thanks also to long-time Bella Vista friends Nancy Brown, Melody Kunnecke, and Barbara Kempke-Becker, who stood by me as my memory and dreams continued to plague me. Your friendship and support have been invaluable.

A special thanks to Joan Kapcar, my long-time friend from New York days. She has been with me through illnesses, moves, and boyfriends, and has supported me as I struggled to finish this book. Thank you, Joannie, for always being there.

Finally, I would like to thank my brothers, Arthur and Stephen, and their wives Sharon and Maryanne, who have put up with me for over thirty years as I created this book. They have loved and protected me, while never making me feel like I was on the wrong track, despite the fact that they have been unable to support my position. In fact, they have encouraged my writing and have embraced the publication of this book.

Thank you all for helping me find joy in my journey.

ABOUT THE AUTHOR

 Alice Cunningham, born in Arkansas, was raised in the Denver, Colorado area. After attaining a liberal arts education at William Jewell College, with a major in music, she was encouraged to move to New York to study opera, which she did, for thirteen years. During that time, because of her volunteer work at two opera companies; The New York School of the Opera, and the Opera Theater of New Jersey, she changed her life goal to opera management. Hired by San Francisco Opera to run their Merola Opera Training Program as Executive Director, she spent fourteen years helping young singers in their pursuit of operatic careers.

When her father died, she moved home to help her mother, went to graduate school at National University in San Diego, California, and obtained a master's degree in counseling psychology. She then worked with foster children for the next eight years, and retired to Northwest, Arkansas in 2004. She began serious efforts to find out what happened to her, and began writing her first book, *Abducted*.

To read Alice's blog, visit alicecunninghamdreams.blogspot.com and contact her at sallierascal@cox.net.